Table of Contents

THE *InterActive* READER™

TEACHER'S GUIDE

Active Reading Strategies for All Students

McDougal Littell
A HOUGHTON MIFFLIN COMPANY
Evanston, Illinois   Boston   Dallas

ISBN 0-618-17994-1

4 5 6 7 8 9 – PBO – 06 05 04 03

What is *The InterActive Reader*™?

A book that helps all of your students develop stronger reading skills

It offers
- a consumable format that allows students to mark the text, take notes in the margins, and respond to prompts
- on-level literature selections broken into short, manageable sections
- extra reading support throughout each selection

A PURPOSE FOR READING

NOTE-TAKING

EXTRA READING SUPPORT

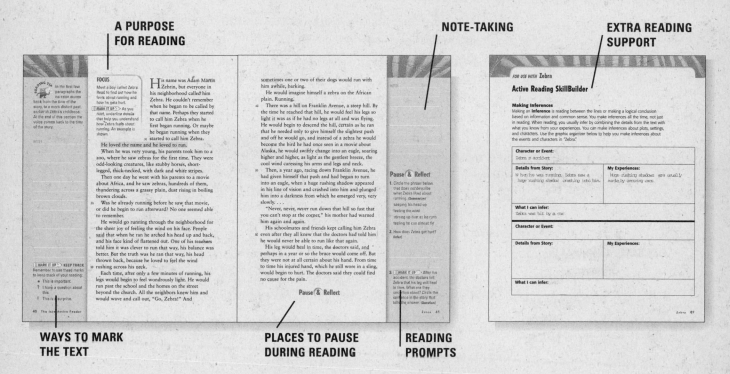

WAYS TO MARK THE TEXT

PLACES TO PAUSE DURING READING

READING PROMPTS

What does *The InterActive Reader*™ include?

- The most commonly taught literature selections from The Grade 7 anthology *The Language of Literature*
- In-book postreading activity sheets
- A special section on reading informational texts

How can you use *The Interactive Reader*™ in the classroom?

- **To develop skills in close reading.** Use *The InterActive Reader*™ in place of the anthology to help all students develop stronger reading skills.
- **For assessment preparation.** Use the Reader to help students develop the analytical reading and note-taking skills they need on most assessments.
- **To provide equal access for all students.** Use *The InterActive Reader*™ with less proficient readers in classrooms where students display a wide range of reading abilities. The Reader gives students access to the same quality literature that the rest of the class is reading in the anthology.

The InterActive Reading Process

Unlike most literature anthologies, *The InterActive Reader*™ encourages students to write in their books!

As students read a work of literature in *The InterActive Reader,*™ they record responses, opinions, and insights right beside the passages to which their notes relate. By making the dialogue between reader and text active and explicit, the process increases students' involvement with what they read.

Following are the features in which students interact with the text:

[MARK IT UP] **KEEP TRACK** Using a system of stars, question marks, and exclamation marks, students monitor their understanding as they read.

FOCUS Each literary work is divided into manageable sections. A section begins with a Focus box, which contains a purpose-setting statement.

Pause & Reflect Students read until the *Pause & Reflect* symbol occurs, signaling them to stop and answer the questions provided. These questions allow students to follow up on the purpose-setting statement and to learn and practice a variety of reading skills and strategies, including

- summarizing
- inferring
- questioning
- predicting
- visualizing
- connecting
- clarifying
- evaluating

- drawing conclusions
- stating opinions
- locating main ideas
- making judgments
- analyzing
- identifying cause-and-effect relationships
- understanding an author's purpose
- distinguishing fact from opinion

[MARK IT UP] At specific points in each selection, students are directed to underline, circle, or highlight key passages that help clarify meaning.

 Frequently, students are asked to read a particular passage aloud and focus on some particular aspect of its meaning or intent.

 Often, students are told to read a key passage again and then given a question that checks their basic comprehension.

NOTES Extra space is provided in the side columns for students' personal notes about the literary selections and the ideas that spring from them.

SkillBuilder Pages During or after reading, students are encouraged to complete the SkillBuilder pages that follow each lesson. There are three types of SkillBuilder pages, which help students practice and apply important skills:

- Active Reading SkillBuilder

- Literary Analysis SkillBuilder

- Words to Know SkillBuilder (for most selections)

Ongoing Assessment In addition to increasing students' involvement in the reading process, *The InterActive Reader*™ offers you, the teacher, a clear window on students' progress and problems. Students' notes, responses, and other markings should be looked at periodically as part of the ongoing informal assessment process.

Who Will Benefit?

Regardless of students' reading levels, _The InterActive Reader_™ works!

Any student will benefit from materials that increase his or her involvement in the reading process. Therefore, _The InterActive Reader_™ can achieve excellent results with most students, whether reading at, below, or above grade level.

Struggling Readers

The InterActive Reader™ is an excellent tool for use with the following students:

- Students who are likely to benefit from increased direct instruction in reading comprehension skills, vocabulary skills, and reading strategies

- Students who have difficulty maintaining focus and interest while working in traditional programs

- Students Acquiring English who have reached an intermediate proficiency level

How Do You Decide Who Fits This Profile?

- Administer an Informal Reading Inventory in which students read and then respond to questions (see page 16 of this Guide). Assess the fluency and accuracy of the reading and the accuracy of the responses.

- Look at students' test results, including standardized tests and records or recomendations from previous teachers.

- Administer a reading placement test, such as the one found on pages A2–A10 of McDougal Littell's _Reading Toolkit_.

Average and Above-Average Readers

The InterActive Reader™ is perfectly matched to the needs of struggling readers. However, it can be used with other student populations as well to help build solid skills in reading literature. For example, _The InterActive Reader_™ can be used with average, above-average, or pre-AP students to prepare them for future literature classes that will emphasize close analytical reading. The guided, active reading format helps make good readers even better. In addition, Challenge questions and activities in both the student book and the Teacher's Guide help these students go beyond the basics. Finally, _The InterActive Reader_™ can be used for assessment preparation, since most assessments require exactly the kind of close reading and analytical skills reinforced in the _Reader_.

Suggested Reading Options

A variety of methods can be used with *The InterActive Reader.*™

The InterActive Reader™ allows you to choose from a number of different reading options as you assign students work. Each Lesson Plan in this Guide suggests one of the following options, the suggestion being based on the nature of the selection itself. However, any reading options may be used at any time. Options marked with an asterisk (*) are especially effective with Students Acquiring English.

Independent Reading

Students can read independently, using the questions in the margins of their books for guidance and focus. Though most often this option is used with students who need little support, all students should have some opportunities to read independently. In this situation, *The InterActive Reader*™ may be used as a take-home text.

Note: If *The InterActive Reader*™ is being used in conjunction with *The Language of Literature,* you may wish to begin the prereading activities, such as Connect to Your Life and Build Background, in class; the main anthology can then be left at school while students carry home their smaller and less cumbersome readers.

Partner/Cooperative Reading*

Students can read in pairs, pausing at the indicated places to discuss the questions, write answers, and compare notations and highlighted passages. Alternately, students can read in small groups, pausing in the same manner to discuss the selection and respond to prompts. In either setting, encourage students to discuss the strategies they use as they read.

Teacher Modeling*

Read aloud the first part of a selection, discuss key events or concepts that are important for comprehension, and then have students continue reading on their own. For particularly challenging selections, reading aloud can continue farther into the selection, or there could be an alternating of silent reading and teacher read-aloud.

Oral Reading*

This option works well for plays, speeches, or selections that contain an abundance of dialogue. It can also work well with narrative passages, providing an aural dimension to the comprehension process.

Audio Library*

Recordings of almost all selections in *The InterActive Reader*™ are provided as part of *The Language of Literature* core program. You may find it useful to have students read along with these recordings.

Note: In order to familiarize students with the lesson structure and format of *The InterActive Reader,*™ you might consider reading aloud the beginning of each selection and modeling the *Focus* and *Pause & Reflect* activities provided.

Reciprocal Teaching

Reciprocal teaching is an instructional activity designed to increase students' comprehension of text. The activity consists of a dialogue between students and teacher, with each taking a turn in the role of the teacher or leader. The dialogue is structured around four basic reciprocal teaching strategies:

- **Summarizing**—Students summarize the most important information in a specific passage.
- **Question generating**—Students identify important information in the content, form questions about content, and address their questions to peers.
- **Clarifying**—Students identify problems the passage presents, such as difficulty with vocabulary or comprehension.
- **Predicting**—Students rely on prior knowledge and information already presented to predict what the author will discuss in subsequent paragraphs.

Students should first be given an overall description of the procedure, emphasizing that it takes the form of a dialogue and that everyone takes a turn assuming the role of teacher. Introduce students to the four strategies, then model for students how to use each strategy by leading the entire dialogue.

Below is an example selection followed by an example dialogue in which Student 1 has been selected to share some of the burden of asking comprehension questions, while the teacher continues to guide the dialogue.

Example Selection

More than 35,000 cowboys rode herd along the Texas cattle trails. Although folklore and picture postcards depicted the cowboy as Anglo-American, about 25 percent were African American and another 12 percent were Mexican vaqueros—cowboys who had worked in Texas since the days before Texas' independence. There were native American cowboys, too, and a few women.

Example Dialogue

Teacher: What questions do you have for the class?

Student 1: My question is: Were all cowboys Anglo-American?

Student 2: No, 25% were African American.

Student 1: What about the rest?

Student 3: 12% were Mexican.

Student 4: Some were native American and women.

Student 2: The rest were Anglo-Americans.

Teacher: What is your summary of this passage?

Student 1: My summary is: From the stories and pictures we see, many people think all cowboys were Anglo-American, but almost 40% were minorities.

Teacher: Does anything need to be clarified?

Student 1: We should clarify *vaqueros*.

Teacher: Is *vaqueros* defined here?

Student 5: Yes, *vaqueros* were Mexican cowboys who worked in Texas before it was independent.

Teacher: What do you predict the next paragraph will be about?

Student 6: I think the author will talk about native Americans and women as cowboys.

Student 7: The author might also tell us more about the *vaqueros*.

As students become increasingly familiar with participating in reciprocal teaching, they will take on more responsibility for leading the dialogue. You should continue to guide the discussion, keeping students mindful of using the four strategies as a framework for their discussion.

Strategies for Reading

These strategies can help you gain a better understanding of what you read. Whenever you find yourself having difficulty making sense of what you're reading, choose and use the strategy that seems most likely to help.

PREDICT
Try to figure out what will happen next and how the selection might end. Then read on to see how accurate your guesses are.

VISUALIZE
Visualize characters, events, and setting to help you understand what's happening. When you read nonfiction, pay attention to the images that form in your mind as you read.

CONNECT
Connect personally with what you're reading. Think of similarities between the descriptions in the selection and what you have personally experienced, heard about, or read about.

QUESTION
Question what happens while you read. Searching for reasons behind events and characters' feelings can help you feel closer to what you are reading.

CLARIFY
Stop occasionally to review your understanding of what you read. You can do this by **summarizing** what you have read, identifying the **main idea,** and **making inferences**–drawing conclusions from the information you are given. Reread passages you don't understand.

EVALUATE
Form opinions about what you read, both while you're reading and after you've finished. Develop your own ideas about characters and events.

Reaching Middle School Readers

One of the many challenges of middle school teaching is accommodating the wide range of reading abilities and interests among students. For those students who are hooked on reading, the challenge is to provide a steady diet of rich materials. But for many students, reading is a chore that requires enormous effort and yields little success.

Students who are not able to read at grade level often do not succeed in school. While much of the focus of the early grades is on learning to read, the focus shifts in the middle grades to reading to learn. Students who do not have a strong foundation in basic decoding and comprehension skills become struggling readers. Their poor reading ability denies them access to the content of the textbooks; as a result, they fall behind in almost every subject area. Below-level reading ability most often is the result of inadequate decoding skills, poor comprehension, or a combination of both.

Decoding skills provide readers with strategies for determining the pronunciation of the written word. Basic decoding skills involve matching letters and letter combinations with spoken sounds and blending those sounds into words. As students encounter longer—multisyllabic— words, they need to divide these words into manageable chunks or syllables.

Decoding is an enabling skill for comprehension. Comprehension is a process of constructing meaning from text. Readers integrate the information in the text with their prior knowledge to make sense of what they read. Specific comprehension skills and strategies, such as main idea, sequence, and visualizing can help students recognize the relationships among ideas, figure out text structures, and create pictures of what they read.

This book provides some basic tools and strategies that will help you help your students to become readers. The lessons and articles can be used as needed, or they can be organized into mini-units of instruction.

Developing Fluency in All Readers

Reading fluency is the ability to automatically recognize words so that attention can be focused on the meaning of the written material. Fluency involves both decoding and comprehension skills; fluent readers decode text with little or no effort as they construct meaning from that text. Teachers can usually spot readers who struggle with decoding the text. Other readers, however, may be able to say the words and sound as though they are reading, but they have little or no understanding of what they read. These readers often go unnoticed, especially in the content areas.

Fluency is a developmental skill that improves with practice. The more students read, the better readers they become. The reading level at which a student is fluent is called his or her *independent reading level.* However, a student's independent reading level may vary with the type of material he or she is reading. For example, reading a short story is often easier than reading a textbook.

A key part in developing reading fluency is determining a student's independent reading level and then providing a range of materials at that level. Developing Fluent Readers on pages 14–16 offers diagnostic tools for determining reading levels and tips for improving fluency.

Helping All Readers Break the Code

There are many reasons that some students struggle with reading. Often poor readers spend most of their mental energy trying to figure out, or decode, the words. With their brains focused on the letters and corresponding sounds, there is little attention left to think about what the words mean. Until readers achieve a basic level of automaticity in word recognition, they are not reading for meaning.

Although most middle school students do have a knowledge of basic phonics, some students fail to develop strategies for using the letter-sound correspondences. They often have difficulty decoding new words, and multisyllabic words are especially problematic. As students encounter longer words they need to be able to break these words into parts.

The lessons on applying multisyllabic rules in Teaching Decoding Strategies on pages 109–120 provide students with strategies for tackling longer words. These lessons also provide a basic review of phonics within a model of direct instruction. You can expand this review for students who need more intensive work in this area. You can also skip the basic phonics instruction and focus on multisyllabic word attack strategies.

Using the Most Effective Teaching Strategies

Choosing *how* to teach something is as important as deciding *what* to teach. While a variety of methods are sound, some methods are more effective in teaching specific skills and strategies than others.

Decoding skills need to be taught explicitly and systematically through direct instruction. These skills can be taught to mastery. The lessons in Teaching Decoding Strategies offer an efficient set of steps and teaching script for short but effective lessons in these skills.

Comprehension skills, however, are developmental skills that are not easily mastered. Students will continue to grow in their understanding of increasingly difficult reading materials throughout life. Comprehension skills can be modeled so that students are shown the thinking processes behind these skills. The Comprehension mini-lessons provide passages and teaching script to model basic comprehension skills.

Establishing a Reading Process

Good readers are strategic in how they approach reading. They consciously or unconsciously do certain things before, during, and after reading. Poor readers, however, often possess few or none of the strategies required for proficient reading. To help struggling readers, establish a routine for reading that involves strategies before, during, and after reading.

- **Before Reading** New ideas presented in reading materials need to be integrated with the reader's **prior knowledge** for understanding to occur. Have students preview the material to see what it is about. Discuss what they already know about the topic and have them **predict** new information they might learn about it. Talk about a **purpose** for reading and have students think about reading strategies they might use with the material.

- **During Reading** Good readers keep track of their understanding as they read. They recognize important or interesting information, know when they don't understand something, and figure out what to do to adjust their understanding. Poor readers are often unaware of these **self-monitoring strategies.** To help these readers become more involved in their reading, suggest that they read with a pencil in hand to jot down notes and questions as they read. If students own the reading materials, they can mark the text as they read. *The InterActive Readers*™ that accompany *The Language of Literature* are ideal for this type of work.

- **After Reading** Provide opportunities for readers to reflect on what they have read. These can involve group or class discussion and writing in journals and logs.

Creating Independent Readers

As you work to give students the skills they need to read for themselves, you can also incorporate some basic routines into your classroom that will help your students extend their understanding.

- **Read aloud.** People of all ages love a good story. Read aloud to your students and hook them on some authors and genres they might not have tackled themselves. For most material, students' listening comprehension is more advanced than their comprehension of written material. Listening helps them develop the thinking skills needed to understand complex text.

- **Write daily.** Writing is a powerful tool to understanding. Encourage students to use writing to work through problems, explore new ideas, or respond to the literature they read. Encourage students to keep journals and learning logs.

- **Read daily.** Allow time for sustained silent reading. Set aside classroom time for students to read self-selected materials. Students who read become better readers, and students are more likely to choose to read if they can pursue ideas they find interesting.

- **Build a Classroom Library.** If possible, provide a wide range of reading materials so that students are exposed to diverse topics and genres. Respect students' reading choices. Struggling readers need first to view themselves as readers.

- **Promote discussion.** Set ground rules for discussion so that all opinions are heard. Model good discussion behaviors by asking follow-up questions, expanding on ideas presented, and offering alternate ways of viewing topics.

When teachers allocate time to these experiences, students see literacy as possible.

Developing Fluent Readers

Good readers are fluent readers. They recognize words automatically, group individual words into meaningful phrases, and apply phonic, morphemic and contextual clues when confronted with a new word. Fluency is a combination of accuracy (number of words identified correctly) and rate (number of words per minute) of reading. Fluency can be taught directly, and it improves as a consequence of students reading a lot of materials that are within their instructional range.

Understanding Reading Levels

Every student reads at a specific level regardless of the grade in which he or she is placed. Reading level in this context is concerned with the relationship between a specific selection or book and a student's ability to read that selection. The following are common terms used to describe these levels:

- **independent level**—The student reads material in which no more than 1 in 20 words is difficult. The material can be read without teacher involvement and is likely to be material students would choose to read on their own.

- **instructional level**—The student reads material in which no more than 2 in 20 words is difficult. The material is most likely found in school and read with teacher involvement.

- **frustration level**—The student reads material in which significantly more than 2 in 20 (or 89%) of the words are difficult. Students will probably get little out of reading the material.

If students read only material that's too easy, growth in skill, vocabulary, and understanding is too slow. If students read only difficult material, they may give up in frustration much too early.

Providing Reading Materials in the Student's Instructional Range

Most states have testing programs that provide information about each student's reading ability. Once you determine a student's general reading level, you can work with the library media teacher to identify reading materials that will be within the student's instructional level. To develop fluency, students should read materials that contain a high proportion of words that they know already, or can easily decode. Work with each student to develop a list of books to read, and have students record their progress on a Reading Log.

Repeated Oral Readings

Repeated oral readings of passages is a strategy that improves fluency. Oral reading also improves prosody, which is the art of sounding natural when you read, that is reading with appropriate intonation, expression, and rhythm.

Beginning readers sound awkward when they read aloud. They pause and halt at the wrong places; they emphasize the wrong syllables; they may read in a monotone. Repeated oral readings can increase fluency and prosody as students 1) identify words faster and faster each time they read; 2) correctly identify a larger percentage of words; 3) segment text into appropriate phrases; 4) change pitch and emphasis to fit the meaning of the text.

To improve fluency and prosody, select passages that are brief, thought provoking, and at the student's current independent level of reading. You may chose narrative or expository text, or have the student choose something he or she enjoys. Performing a play, practicing to give a speech, reading to younger students, and re-reading a passage to find evidence in support of an argument are all activities that provide opportunities to re-read. For the following exercise, you may chose to pair students together and have them read to each other, or use this as a one-on-one teacher-student or tutor-student activity.

1. Select an excerpt within the student's reading level that ranges from 50-200 words in length.

2. Have the student read the passage aloud to a partner. The partner records the number of seconds it takes to read the whole passage, and notes the number of errors. Reverse roles so that each student has a chance to read to the other.

3. Read the passage aloud to the students so that students can hear it read correctly.

4. As homework, or an in-class assignment, have students practice reading the passage out loud on their own.

5. After practice, have each student read aloud again to his or her partner, who records the time and the number of errors.

6. After repeated practice and readings the student will read the passage fluently, that is with a moderate rate and near 100% accuracy.

Example Excerpt

I have a little dream
For the flying of a plane.
I have a little scheme,
I'll follow yet again.

There is a little heaven,
Just around the hill.
I haven't seen it for a long time,
But I know it's waiting still.

from Dragonwings
by Laurence Yep

Repeated Silent Readings

Having students silently read and re-read passages that are at their instructional level also improves fluency. As they practice, students will recognize words more quickly each time, will group words into meaningful phrases more quickly, and will increase their reading rate. One nice thing about repeated silent reading is that a student can do it individually. Many students enjoy timing themselves when they read, and seeing improvement over time. Have them keep a record on a piece of graph paper.

Modeling

Students benefit from repeated opportunities to hear English spoken fluently. By listening to live models or tapes, listeners can understand the rhythm of the language and the pitch and pronunciation of particular words and phrases. They can hear when to pause, when to speed up, and what words to emphasize. In addition, you can model, or ask an experienced reader to read passages

aloud. At most advanced levels, this technique is particularly useful to introduce students to various forms of dialect. As you play the tapes aloud, have students read along silently or chorally, or pause the tapes after each paragraph and have the students try reading the same passage aloud.

Phrase-Cued Text

Less proficient readers may not know when to pause in text. They may pause in the middle of a phrase, or run through a comma or period. They may not recognize verb phrases, prepositional phases, or even phrases marked by parentheses or brackets as words that "go together." This makes their reading disjointed and choppy, or gives it a monotone quality. Some poems have essentially one phrase per line, and can be used to demonstrate to students how to phrase text. Or you may take a passage and have students re-write it with one phrase per line, so that they pause at the end of each line, after each phrase. Alternately, you can show them how a passage should be read by inserting slash marks or blank spaces at appropriate places to pause. Choose words of about 50-100 words in length from fiction or non-fiction selections. For example, you can take a passage like the following:

Example Modeling

When the man entered the room, he failed to notice the trembling brown fox crouching in the corner next to the refrigerator. When the man opened the door of the refrigerator to grab a cold soda, the fox leapt between his feet and the door and scrambled for a hiding place on the shelf behind the lettuce.

And present it to students in this way:

When the man entered the room,/he failed to notice/ the trembling brown fox/ crouching in the corner/ next to the refrigerator. When the man opened the door of the refrigerator/ to grab a cold soda,/ the fox leapt between his feet and the door/ and scrambled for a hiding place/ on the shelf /behind the lettuce.

Informal Reading Inventory

Have students read, and re-read the passage, stopping to pause at each slash mark.

An informal inventory can give an initial idea of a student's reading level. Teachers often use an Informal Reading Inventory (IRI) to place students in the appropriate textbook.

To conduct an IRI, you need at least one 100-word passage from the material in question, and 10 comprehension questions about the material. If you want more than one passage, select them randomly from every 30th page or so. Have the student read the same passage twice—the first time orally to asses oral reading skills. The student should read the passage a second time silently, after which he or she answers questions for assessment of reading comprehension. Suggestions for administering an IRI.

1. Tell the student he or she will read the passage out loud, and then again silently, and then you will ask some questions.

2. Give the student a copy of the passage and keep one for yourself. Have the student read the passage. As the student reads out loud, note on your copy the number of errors he or she makes:

   Mispronunciations: Words that are mispronounced, with the exception of proper nouns.
   Omissions: Words left out that are crucial to understanding a sentence or a concept.
   Additions: Words inserted in a sentence that change the meaning of the text.
   Substitutions: Words substituted for actual words in the text that change the meaning of a sentence.

Use these criteria for assessing reading levels after oral reading:

- Fewer than 3 errors—The student is unlikely to have difficulty decoding text.
- Between 4 and 9 errors—the student is likely to have some difficulty, may need special attention.
- More than 10 errors—The student is likely to have great difficulty, may need placement in less material.

3. Have the student read the passage again, silently.

4. When the student finishes, ask the comprehension questions you have prepared ahead of time. Tell the student that he or she can look back at the passage before answering a question.

5. Note the number of correct responses. Use these criteria for assessing reading level after silent reading.

   - Eight or more—The student should be able to interpret the selections effectively.
   - Five to seven—The student is likely to have difficulty.
   - Fewer than five—The student needs individual help or alternate placement.

6. Evaluate results from oral and silent reading to decide how good a match the material is for a student's independent or instructional level.

Another approach allows you to assess the student's choice for independent reading. Have the student independently select a book he or she would like to read. The student should open to a random page in the middle of the book (that has not been read before) and begin reading silently from the top of the page. Ask the student to extend one finger on one hand for each time he or she comes across an unfamiliar word. If, by the end of that page, the student has five or more fingers extended, the book is probably too difficult for that student. You may want to suggest that the student find a book more suitable to his or her reading level.

Research/Related Readings

The following research supports the philosophy and pedagogical design of *The InterActive Reader:*™

Beck, I., et al. "Getting at the Meaning: How to Help Students Unpack Difficult Text." *American Educator: The Unique Power of Reading and How to Unleash It* 22.1–2 (1996): 66–71, 85.

California Reading Initiative and Special Education in California: Critical Ideas Focusing on Meaningful Reform. Sacramento: California Special Education Reading Task Force, California Department of Education and California State Board of Education, 1999.

Carnine, D., J. Silbert, and E. J. Kame'enui. *Direction Instruction Reading.* Columbus: Merrill, 1990.

Honig, B., L. Diamond, and L. Gutlohn. *Teaching Reading Sourcebook.* Novato, CA: Arena, 2000.

Irvin, Judith L. *Reading and the Middle School Student.* 2nd ed. Boston: Allyn & Bacon, 1998.

Langer, J. A., and A. N. Applebee. "Reading and Writing Instruction: Toward a Theory of Teaching and Learning." *Review of Research in Education.* Ed. E. Rothkopf. Washington, D.C.: American Educational Research Association, 1986.

Lapp, D., J. Flood, and N. Farnan. *Content Area Reading and Learning: Instructional Strategies.* 2nd ed. Boston: Allyn & Bacon, 1996.

Lyon, G. Reid. "Learning to Read: A Call from Research to Action." *National Center for Learning Disabilities.* 9 Nov. 1999 <http://www.ncld.org/theirworld/lyon98.html>

Palinscar, A. S. and A. L. Brown. "Interactive Teaching to Promote Independent Learning from Text." *The Reading Teacher* 39.8 (1986): 771–777.

Palinscar, A. S. and A. L. Brown. "Reciprocal Teaching of Comprehension-Fostering and Comprehension-Monitoring Activities." *Cognition and Instruction* 1.2: 117–175.

Pearson, P. D., et al. "Developing Expertise in Reading Comprehension." *What Research Says to the Teacher.* Ed. S. J. Samuels and A. E. Farstrip. Newark: International Reading Association, 1992.

Rosenshine, B., and C. Meister. "Reciprocal Teaching: A Review of the Research." *Review of Educational Research* 64.4 (1994): 479–530.

Simmons, D. C., and E. J. Kame'enui, eds. *What Reading Research Tells Us About Children with Diverse Needs: Bases and Basics.* Mahwah: Lawrence Erlbaum, 1998.

Tierney, R. J., J. E. Readence, and E. K. Dishner. *Reading Strategies and Practices: A Compendium.* 4th ed. Boston: Allyn & Bacon, 1995.

Tompkins, Gail. *50 Literacy Strategies: Step by Step.* Upper Saddle River: Merrill, 1998.

Lesson Plans

Before Reading

Have students do the Connect to Your Life and Key to the Story activities on page 2 of *The InterActive Reader.*™ Use the following suggestions to prepare students to read the story.

Connect to Your Life
Guide students in a discussion about what things they have done to get others to notice them. Ask students to also think about consequences. What might have happened to the friend who tried to juggle apples in the cafeteria? After students fill out the chart, let them share their incidents and the results.

Key to the Story
The story is about a boy who pretends to know more than he does in order to impress a girl. Ask volunteers to read their statements about the sentence from the story. Have a brief discussion about the word *bluff.* You might ask: *Are there situations when bluffing is necessary?*

BUILD BACKGROUND
Connect to Geography Explain to students that "Seventh Grade" takes place in Fresno, California, which is located in the San Joaquin Valley, southeast of San Francisco. Fresno's dry, hot summers and cool, humid winters are excellent for growing grapes, and the town is often called the "raisin-growing capital of the world." A large number of Hispanics whose families are originally from Spanish-speaking countries are employed in Fresno's vineyards and raisin-production plants. Many, like Victor in this story, are of Mexican descent.

WORDS TO KNOW

bluff

conviction

elective

ferocity

linger

portly

quiver

scowl

sheepishly

trudge

Additional Words to Know

bulletin
  page 6, line 66
squirmed
  page 6, line 73
sprint
  page 12, line 243

VOCABULARY PREVIEW: Words to Know In Context

You can help students learn the Words to Know by reading aloud the following sentences or writing them on the board. Then show students how to use context clues to help them figure out the meaning.

bluff:	Joe tried to *bluff* his way out of the situation by pretending he didn't know me.
conviction:	My brother has such strong *convictions* about the importance of sports that he is willing to get up at 5 A.M. every weekday for practice.
elective:	I signed up for two *elective* courses this semester although they are not required.
ferocity:	Both the lion's growl and its attack showed its *ferocity*.
linger:	Most students dashed from the room, but one student *lingered* behind.
portly:	The veterinarian told me to put my *portly* dog on a diet.
quiver:	The singer was so nervous her voice *quivered*.
scowl:	The coach *scowled* angrily after the player dropped the ball.
sheepishly:	The child looked down *sheepishly* when caught with his hand in the cookie jar.
trudge:	The players *trudged* sadly to the locker room after losing the game.

bulletin:	Students were given the principal's *bulletin,* or a short up-to-date report.
squirmed:	The children *squirmed* and wiggled while the teacher tried to get them to sit still.
sprint:	After jogging slowly for five miles, Edgar finishes up his run with a fast *sprint.*

VOCABULARY FOCUS: Understanding Idioms

Teacher Modeling Remind students that they can use the context of an unfamiliar idiom to figure out its meaning. Then use the following modeling suggestions for the idiom *on the sly* (page 7, line 89).

Mini-Lesson See pages 105–106 of this Guide for additional work on **Understanding Idioms.**

You could say I don't know the expression on the sly, *but in this scene, I know that Victor is waiting after class for Teresa. However, he's keeping his head down so she won't notice that he's paying attention to her. I think that* on the sly *means "secretly."*

Student Modeling Now have students follow your lead. Ask a volunteer to model using context clues to determine the meaning of *to have a crush on* (page 7, line 108).

A student might say I'm not familiar with the expression to have a crush on, *but I do know that in this story, Victor likes Teresa and thinks she's cute. I think that* to have a crush on *must mean "to like in a romantic way."*

During Reading

COMPREHENSION FOCUS

Key Points	Strategies for Success
Target Skill → Narrative Elements The school setting, the students and teachers, and Victor's actions all make this story appealing. Students must keep track of the events of the story. They should understand that the conflict is within the main character, not between characters.	**Mini-Lesson** Before students read "Seventh Grade," you may want to teach the **Narrative Elements** lesson on pages 146–149 of this Guide. • As students read, have them stop after the *Pause & Reflect* on page 6 and discuss the people, actions, and setting in the story so far. • After reading, students can complete the **Story Map** on page 147 of this Guide.
Special Language The Spanish and French words and phrases used in this story may pose problems for students. The author makes his story more realistic and the setting and characters more vivid by including language used by young Chicano people. The French words are simply part of French class.	Explain that words in Spanish and French are set in italic type and that they are translated in footnotes on the page where they appear. Encourage students to notice the tiny footnote numbers that follow each non-English word. Show them how to read the footnotes.

Suggested Reading Options

• An oral reading of "Seventh Grade" is available in *The Language of Literature* Audio Library. ♭
• Partner/Cooperative Reading (see page 8 of this Guide).
• Additional options are described on page 8 of this Guide.

RECIPROCAL TEACHING SUGGESTION → Connecting

Teacher Modeling *Pause & Reflect, page 6* Model for students how to connect what they are reading to their own experiences.

You could say *Victor's first day of seventh grade is full of meeting old friends, of trying to make an impression on a girl he likes, and of experiencing his new classes. My own memories about seeing my friends again and meeting new teachers on the first day of school help me relate to Victor's experiences.*

Student Modeling *Pause & Reflect, page 12* Have several students model connecting their own experiences with what they are reading. Offer this prompt: *What have you done to get noticed? What do you see others doing? How do you feel when you are embarrassed?*

Encourage students to use the other five reading strategies when appropriate as they proceed through the rest of the selection. (See page 10 of this Guide.)

(See page 10 of this Guide.)

ENGLISH LEARNERS

1. Make sure that students understand that Victor does not know French. He is just mixing words together and saying them with a French accent. Spanish-speaking students may recognize words similar to Spanish words in his first sentence.

2. Students might benefit from reading along with the recording of "Seventh Grade" provided in *The Language of Literature* Audio Library. ◯

After Reading

Recommended Follow-Up

- Thinking Through the Literature, page 26, *The Language of Literature*
- Choices & Challenges, page 27, *The Language of Literature*
- SkillBuilders, pages 13–15, *The InterActive Reader*™

Informal Assessment Options

Retell Have small groups of students retell the story, using the first person, from Victor's point of view and from Teresa's point of view. Each group should select a person to speak for Victor and another person to speak for Teresa. The remaining group members should coach the speakers.

Spot Check Look at the notes students made in the margins of the story. Invite them to explain their answers, and discuss any questions they still have about the story.

Formal Assessment Options in *The Language of Literature*

Selection Quiz, page 13, Unit One Resource Book

Selection Test, pages 5–6, Formal Assessment Book

For more teaching options, see pages 20–28 in *The Language of Literature* Teacher's Edition.

Additional Challenge

1. **Examine a Character**
   Ask: *Does Teresa see Victor's pretense or not?* Have students discuss how well she understands Victor and his motivation. Ask them what instances in the story support their conclusion.

2. **▐▌MARK IT UP⟩ Compare Characters**
   Ask: *How would you compare Victor with his friend Michael?* Have students mark passages in "Seventh Grade" to support their answer.

Before Reading

Direct students' attention to the Connect to Your Life and Key to the Story activities on page 16 of *The InterActive Reader.*™ Use the following suggestions to prepare students to read the story.

Connect to Your Life
Read aloud the proverb on page 16. Then discuss with students the meaning of the proverb. Ask: *What represents "an entire village" in our society? Besides parents, who might help raise a child within a community? What can people do to help raise a child? What values do these people display?* After the discussion, have students complete their webs.

Key to the Story
Ask students to think about family members and friends who have taught them important lessons. Ask: *What did you learn from these teachers? Why were these lessons important to you?* You might share an example from your own life of a friend or relative who has taught you something of value. Then have students fill in their charts.

BUILD BACKGROUND Connect to History Tell students that the action of "Thank You, M'am" takes place in the late 1950s in Harlem, a section of New York City. Explain to students that by the mid-1920s, Harlem had become the cultural center for African-American musicians, artists, and writers, including Langston Hughes. The vibrant and stimulating life of Harlem had a deep influence on the work of these creative people.

WORDS TO KNOW

barren

frail

mistrust

presentable

suede

Additional Words to Know

combined
　　page 18, line 13

contact
　　page 19, line 54

roomers
　　page 20, line 69

VOCABULARY PREVIEW: Words to Know in Context

You can help students learn the Words to Know by reading aloud the following sentences or writing them on the board. Then show students how to use context clues to help them figure out the meaning.

barren: Since no plants had grown there for years, the front yard was *barren* and dusty.

frail: The sick bird was so weak and *frail* that it could not even lift its head.

mistrust: We *mistrust* him because he has lied to us over and over again.

presentable: He made himself *presentable* by combing his hair and washing his face.

suede: She loved to touch the soft, fuzzy leather of her father's *suede* jacket.

---

combined: We sprinkled some cinnamon and sugar on the buttered toast and discovered that the *combined* flavors tasted great.

contact: After my friend moved away, we kept in *contact* by e-mailing each other every day.

roomers: Mrs. Barrett rented out a few rooms in her house because she thought that having *roomers* would help her pay the bills.

VOCABULARY FOCUS: Using Words with Multiple Meanings

Teacher Modeling Remind students that many words have more than one meaning. When they read, students can often use context clues to help them figure out which meaning of the word the writer intended. If students aren't familiar with a word's meanings, encourage them to look up the word in a dictionary. Then use the following modeling suggestions for the word *stoop* (page 22, line 158).

You could say I know that stoop *can be a verb meaning "to bend down," but this definition doesn't seem right here. When I look up the word in the dictionary, I see that* stoop *can also be a noun meaning "a small porch or staircase leading to the entrance of a building." In this sentence, the word is used as a noun. The phrase "in the door" is a clue that* stoop *must mean "a small porch" in this sentence.*

Student Modeling Now have students follow your lead. Ask a volunteer to model using the strategy to figure out the correct meaning of *dash* (page 21, line 102).

A student might say I know that dash *can mean "a small amount of an added ingredient," but that doesn't make sense here. The dictionary lists other meanings, including "a sudden movement or rush." In this passage, the boy considers running away, so "rush" must be the right meaning.*

Mini-Lesson See pages 107–108 of this Guide for additional work on **Using Words with Multiple Meanings.**

During Reading

COMPREHENSION FOCUS

Key Points	Strategies for Success
Target Skill ➡ Making Inferences The writer does not explain all of the characters' feelings and motivations. Students must be able to make inferences in order to understand the characters in this story.	**Mini-Lesson** Before students read "Thank You, M'am," you may want to teach the **Making Inferences** lesson on pages 137–139 of this guide. • Read aloud lines 46–50 on page 19. Then have students discuss what they can infer about the characters' feelings toward each other. Ask: *Why does the woman say the boy ought to be her son? What does she want to do with the boy? How does the boy react to the woman?* • As students read the story, have them add other inferences they make about the characters to the **Inference Chart** on page 138.
Dialect and Slang The author's use of dialect and slang may pose problems for some students. They may need help understanding some of the slang and unfamiliar expressions.	• Read aloud the dialogue in lines 27–29 on page 18. Then ask: *What question does the woman ask the boy? What does "aim to" mean in line 28? What does the woman accuse the boy of doing in line 29?* • Encourage students to read other passages of dialogue aloud in pairs and to paraphrase them if necessary.

Suggested Reading Options

• An oral reading of "Thank You, M'am" is available in *The Language of Literature* Audio Library. ◯
• Partner/Cooperative Reading (see page 8 of this Guide).
• Additional options are described on page 8 of this Guide.

RECIPROCAL TEACHING SUGGESTION ➡ Predicting

Teacher Modeling *Pause & Reflect, page 19* Model for students how to use clues and details from the story to predict what the boy will do next.

You could say *I wonder if the boy will try to break free. Mrs. Jones seems determined to hang on to him, but he doesn't want to go with her. He says that he just wants her to "turn me loose." I predict he will try to get away.*

Student Modeling *Pause & Reflect, page 21* Ask several volunteers to model predicting what the boy will do now. Offer this prompt: *What does the boy do when the woman finally turns him loose in her apartment? What does the woman do for the boy? How does she treat him?*

Encourage students to use the other five reading strategies when appropriate as they proceed through the rest of the story. (See page 10 of this Guide.)

ENGLISH LEARNERS

1. Help students understand the following colloquial expressions:

   kicked him right square in his blue-jeaned sitter (page 18, line 17): kicked him in his backside

   you got another thought coming (page 19, line 56): you're wrong

   cook me a bite to eat (page 20, line 86): cook something to eat

   shoes come by devilish like that would burn your feet (page 22, lines 149–150): you would feel too guilty to enjoy wearing the shoes if you did something wrong to get them

2. Students might benefit from reading along with the recording of "Thank You, M'am" provided in *The Language of Literature* Audio Library. ◯

After Reading

Recommended Follow-Up

- Thinking Through the Literature, page 34, *The Language of Literature*
- Choices & Challenges, pages 35–36, *The Language of Literature*
- SkillBuilders, pages 23–25, *The InterActive Reader*™

Informal Assessment Options

Retell Have students retell the story from the boy's point of view. Offer these prompts:

- *Why did you try to steal the woman's purse?*
- *How did you feel when she caught you?*
- *What happened when she took you to her home?*
- *How did you feel when the woman gave you money for the shoes?*

Spot Check Look at the notes students made in the margins of the story to check their understanding. Invite them to ask any questions they still have about the story.

Formal Assessment Options in *The Language of Literature*

Selection Quiz, page 20, Unit One Resource Book

Selection Test, pages 7–8, Formal Assessment Book

For more teaching options, see pages 29–36 in *The Language of Literature* Teacher's Edition.

Additional Challenge

1. **Create New Dialogue**
   Point out that the boy doesn't get a chance to say more than "thank you" to the woman. Discuss with students what else the boy might have said to her if he'd had the chance. To get students started, ask: *What does the woman do for the boy? What might she have done? What kind of treatment do you think the boy is used to? How do you think he feels when he leaves her?*

2. **⫿⫿ MARK IT UP ⟩ Explore Theme**
   Remind students that Mrs. Jones responds to a violent act with kindness. Ask: *What message is the writer trying to convey through this character?* Have students mark passages in the story that support their views.

Before Reading

Direct students' attention to the Connect to Your Life and Key to the Essay activities on page 26 of *The InterActive Reader.*™ Use the following suggestions to prepare students to read the essay.

Connect to Your Life Guide students in a discussion about what it's like to be new at a school. Ask students to think about a time when a new student joined their class. Ask: *How did other students treat him or her? How did the newcomer behave? What are some things newcomers do to try to fit in?* Then have students complete the Connect to Your Life activity.

Key to the Essay Ask volunteers to tell how they feel about their names. After students fill out their organizers, invite them to share interesting facts or stories associated with their names.

BUILD BACKGROUND Connect to Social Studies Tell students that names, like language and religion, give important clues about a person's cultural background. In many Spanish cultures, a child has two last names—the father's name and the mother's maiden name. Often, in Spanish-speaking countries, a child's full name can include four generations of family names.

Inform students that Julia Alvarez spent 10 years of her childhood in the Dominican Republic although she was born in New York City. The Dominican Republic is a country that is located on the island of Hispaniola. This island is near Puerto Rico and Cuba in the Caribbean Sea. Have students locate this Caribbean country on a map.

WORDS TO KNOW

- chaotic
- convoluted
- ethnicity
- exotic
- inevitably
- initial
- ironically
- merge
- specify
- usher

VOCABULARY PREVIEW: Words to Know in Context

You can help students learn the Words to Know by reading aloud the following sentences or writing them on the board. Then show students how to use context clues to help them figure out the meaning.

chaotic: It was quite a change to go from the calm, orderly countryside to the noisy, *chaotic* city.

convoluted: Your answer is *convoluted;* try to write something simpler, clearer, and direct next time.

ethnicity: At the school Heritage Fair, students celebrate their *ethnicity* by bringing in food and wearing costumes from their native countries.

exotic: Jason's grandmother grew up in Russia, a country that seemed strange, far-off, and *exotic* to him.

inevitably: It doesn't matter how many times we drive to Stacey's house—we *inevitably* get lost on the way.

initial: At first Vernon's strange haircut shocked me, but soon this *initial* reaction wore off.

ironically: The kitten wouldn't go near anyone but Tomas; *ironically,* he was the only one there who didn't like cats.

merge: The two baseball teams have *merged* to become one.

specify: Please *specify* whether you'd like apple juice or orange juice.

usher: In the 1980s, many people started using personal computers, and the 1990s *ushered* in the Internet.

VOCABULARY FOCUS Word Parts: Prefixes

Teacher Modeling Remind students that sometimes they can use their knowledge of prefixes to help them figure out the meaning of an unfamiliar word. Model using the word *immigration* (page 29, line 53).

You could say *I recognize the prefix* im- *and the base word* migration. *I know migration has to do with moving from one place or country to another. I also know that the prefix* im- *sometimes means "in" or "into," as in the word* import. *I think the word* immigration *must mean "moving into a new place or country."*

Student Modeling Ask a student volunteer to use this strategy to figure out the meaning of *mispronunciation* (page 30, line 81).

A student might say *I've seen the prefix* mis- *before in words like* mismatch. *I know it can mean "wrong" or "incorrect."* Pronunciation *means "a way to say a word." I think* mispronunciation *means "an incorrect way of saying a word."*

Mini-Lesson See pages 99–100 of this Guide for additional work on **Word Parts: Prefixes.**

During Reading

COMPREHENSION FOCUS

Key Points	Strategies for Success
Target Skill ➡ Compare and Contrast To understand this personal essay, students must be able to recognize the contrasts the author develops.	**Mini-Lesson** Before students read "Names/Nombres," you may want to teach or review the **Compare and Contrast** lesson on pages 134–136 of this Guide. • Read aloud the first three paragraphs of this essay on page 28. Make sure students understand the contrast between Alvarez's correct pronunciation of her first and last names and the incorrect American versions of them. • As they read, students can use the **Venn Diagram** on page 135 of this Guide to record the contrasts between Alvarez and American students.
Phonetic Respellings Students may stumble over the phonetic respellings the author uses throughout the essay.	Encourage students to read aloud each phonetic respelling. If they are unsure about their pronunciations, they can confirm them with a partner.
Foreign Language The Spanish words and phrases used in this essay may pose problems for students.	Encourage students to read the essay for pleasure and to pay attention to its overall meaning. They can use the footnotes to help them understand the meaning of Spanish words and phrases used in this essay. You might have native speakers of Spanish pronounce these words and phrases for the rest of the class.

Suggested Reading Options

- An oral reading of "Names/Nombres" is available in *The Language of Literature* Audio Library.
- Independent Reading (see page 8 of this Guide).
- Additional options are described on page 8 of this Guide.

RECIPROCAL TEACHING SUGGESTION ➡ Clarifying

Teacher Modeling *Pause & Reflect, page 29* If students are unsure why Julia's feelings about her "new names" change, model using the clarifying strategy.

You could say *At first I wasn't sure why Julia began to like her new Americanized names. When I reread lines 33–44, I saw that her nicknames gave her a sense of belonging and made her feel that she fit in at school.*

Student Modeling *Pause & Reflect, page 31* Have several students model using the clarifying strategy to understand the author's point about the pronunciation of her sister Ana's name. Offer these prompts: *How does Julia Alvarez pronounce Ana's name on the phone? Why is Ana's roommate confused by this pronunciation? Why does the author tell this story?*

Encourage students to use the other five reading strategies when appropriate as they proceed through the rest of the essay. (See page 10 of this Guide.)

After Reading

Recommended Follow-Up

- Thinking Through the Literature, page 43, *The Language of Literature*
- Choices & Challenges, pages 44–45, *The Language of Literature*
- SkillBuilders, pages 35–37, *The InterActive Reader*™

Informal Assessment Options

Retell Have students work in pairs to retell the events in this essay as an imaginary conversation between the author and one of the minor characters, such as Alvarez's mother or a high school friend.

Spot Check Look at the notes students made in the margins. Make sure their answers show an understanding of what they read.

Formal Assessment Options in *The Language of Literature*

Selection Quiz, page 27, Unit One Resource Book

Selection Test, pages 9–10, Formal Assessment Book

For more teaching options, see pages 37–45 in *The Language of Literature* Teacher's Edition.

Additional Challenge

1. ‖ MARK IT UP ⟩ **Compare and Contrast**
   Ask: *How did the author's attitude toward her name change during her high school years?* Have students mark passages in the essay to support their view.

2. **Analyzing the Essay**
   Ask: *What did you learn about the problems of immigrant students from reading this essay? Explain.*

Before Reading

Direct students' attention to the Connect to Your Life and Key to the Story activities on page 38 of *The InterActive Reader.*™ Use the following suggestions to prepare students to read the story.

Connect to Your Life
Discuss the power of the human imagination with students. Ask: *What is the imagination? When do you use your imagination? What do you like to create with your imagination?* Then have students complete their webs, and invite them to share their ideas.

Key to the Story
Tell students that one of the characters in "Zebra" is a Vietnam veteran. If possible, display a photo of the Vietnam Veterans Memorial in Washington, D.C. Discuss its appearance, especially its quality of somber simplicity. Then ask: *Why do people build memorials? What memorials have you seen or heard about?* Finally, have students write their responses on the line.

BUILD BACKGROUND Connect to Social Studies Tell students that the United States entered the Vietnam War to try to stop Communist-ruled North Vietnam from taking over South Vietnam. Point out that the country's terrain and the enemy's guerrilla-like tactics made fighting difficult for the American troops. In 1973, the last U.S. ground forces left Vietnam. The war ended when South Vietnam surrendered to North Vietnam in April 1975. After the war, many veterans, like John Wilson in "Zebra," struggled to readjust to life at home. Discuss the difficulties a war veteran might face when he or she comes home. Encourage students to consider how war experiences can harm people mentally as well as physically.

WORDS TO KNOW

- disciplinarian
- encrusted
- exuberantly
- gaunt
- intricate
- jauntily
- menacing
- poised
- tensing
- wince

VOCABULARY PREVIEW: Words to Know in Context

You can help students learn the Words to Know by reading aloud the following sentences or writing them on the board. Then show students how to use context clues to help them figure out the meaning.

disciplinarian: My mother, a strict *disciplinarian,* sets up many rules and makes sure that I follow them.

encrusted: After the snowstorm, the car windows were *encrusted* with ice and had to be scraped.

exuberantly: The children played *exuberantly,* laughing and running around the gym.

gaunt: During his long illness, Marco became *gaunt*—all skin and bones.

intricate: On her notebook cover, Marie-Rose drew an *intricate* design that was too complicated to copy.

jauntily: Ernie walked *jauntily* onto the court, swinging his arms and waving happily to the other players.

menacing: He looked so *menacing* in his monster costume that the children were afraid to go near him.

poised: *Poised* on one foot, Mattie shot the basketball at the hoop.

tensing: I could see the *tensing* of his arm muscles as he lifted the heavy weight.

wince: Evie tried not to *wince* as the dog stepped on her hand, but she could not hide her pain.

VOCABULARY FOCUS Word Parts: Roots

Teacher Modeling Remind students that they can sometimes use familiar roots to figure out the meaning of an unfamiliar word. Then use the following modeling suggestions for the word *descend* (page 41, line 43).

You could say The word descend *looks similar to* ascend, *which means "to go upward." I know the prefix* de- *can mean "down." Therefore,* descend *might mean "to go downward."*

Student Modeling Now have students follow your lead. Ask a volunteer to model the strategy to determine the meaning of *situated* (page 57, line 574).

A student might say I don't know the meaning of situated, *but the first part of the word is similar to both* sit *and* site. *The sentence doesn't have anything to do with sitting. Maybe* situated *and* site *have the same root. I know* site *means "the place where something is," and in this sentence the author describes how lines are placed on a page. I think* situated *must mean "placed" or "located."*

Mini-Lesson
See pages 103–104 of this Guide for additional work on **Word Parts: Roots.**

During Reading

COMPREHENSION FOCUS

Key Points	Strategies for Success
Target Skill ➡ Making Inferences In order to understand the story, readers must make crucial inferences about how the characters feel—about themselves, each other, and various events.	**Mini-Lesson** Before students read "Zebra," you may want to teach or review the **Making Inferences** lesson on pages 137–139 of this Guide. • Read aloud lines 194-202 on pages 45–46. Then help students infer what Zebra thinks of Mr. Wilson. Ask: *Whom does Zebra tell Mr. Wilson to see? How will she treat Mr. Wilson? Why do you think Zebra wants to help Mr. Wilson?* • As students read the story, have them complete the **Active Reading SkillBuilder** on page 67.
Cause and Effect "Zebra" is about healing, both psychologically and physically. Students must be able to understand how John Wilson helps Zebra cope with his injury.	After the *Pause & Reflect* on page 61, have students discuss how John Wilson and the art class are helping Zebra overcome the trauma of his accident. Ask: *How did Zebra's hand feel before the class began? How does it feel now? How do you think Mr. Wilson is helping Zebra?*

Suggested Reading Options

• An oral reading of "Zebra" is available in *The Language of Literature* Audio Library. ◯
• Partner/Cooperative Reading (see page 8 of this Guide).
• Additional options are described on page 8 of this Guide.

RECIPROCAL TEACHING SUGGESTION ➡ Visualizing

Teacher Modeling *Pause & Reflect, page 41* Model for students how to use sensory details to visualize Zebra running down the hill on Franklin Avenue.

You could say *I can picture Zebra running down the hill in lines 40–49. He feels light and free as he runs, with a cool wind blowing on his arms, legs, and neck. From this description, I can visualize Zebra running at full speed and feeling like a soaring eagle as he flies down the hill.*

Student Modeling *Pause & Reflect, page 44* Have several students model visualizing what John Wilson looks like. Offer this prompt: *What details describe Mr. Wilson's appearance and clothing? What details describe what he is doing?*

Encourage students to use the other five reading strategies when appropriate as they proceed through the rest of the story. (See page 10 of this Guide.)

ENGLISH LEARNERS

1. Help students understand that the "class in the *imagination*" (page 47, line 259) is a special class taught by a special teacher. Point out that each student in the class has a physical problem or challenge, such as poor vision or impaired speech.
2. Students might benefit from reading along with the recording of "Zebra" provided in *The Language of Literature* Audio Library. ◯

After Reading

Recommended Follow-Up

- Thinking Through the Literature, page 62, *The Language of Literature*
- Choices & Challenges, pages 63–64, *The Language of Literature*
- SkillBuilders, pages 67–69, *The InterActive Reader*™

Informal Assessment Options

Retell! Have students retell certain scenes in the story from John Wilson's point of view. Offer these prompts:

- *What did you think of Zebra when you first met him? How did you know that he had been injured?*
- *How did you feel about Zebra after you talked to Mrs. English?*
- *Why did you display the helicopter that Zebra made?*
- *Why did you place his drawing by your friend's name at the Vietnam Veterans Memorial?*

Spot Check Review the notes students made in the margins of the story. Invite volunteers to explain their answers and discuss any questions they still have about the story.

Formal Assessment Options in *The Language of Literature*

Selection Quiz, page 34, Unit One Resource Book

Selection Test, pages 11–12, Formal Assessment Book

For more teaching options, see pages 46–64 in *The Language of Literature* Teacher's Edition.

Additional Challenge

1. Give Advice
Have students write some advice, from Zebra's point of view, to a child who must cope with a physical challenge. To get students started, ask: *What might Zebra advise a child to do who has lost the ability to do something he or she loves?*

2. ▢▢ MARK IT UP ⬦ Analyze Character
Have students underline passages in the story that reveal Zebra's imagination at work. Then have students discuss how the boy's imagination helps him cope with his injuries. Ask: *How does Zebra feel when he begins creating drawings and sculptures for Mr. Wilson's art class? How does he feel when he works on art projects at camp?*

Before Reading

Direct students' attention to the Connect to Your Life and Key to the Biography activities on page 70 of *The InterActive Reader.*™ Use the following suggestions to prepare students to read the biography.

Connect to Your Life Guide students in a discussion of ways in which their community, their nation, or the world might change for the better. You might ask: *What problems exist in these places that you would like to see solved? Which problem do you think is most important?* After students complete the activity on page 70, invite volunteers to tell what they wrote and why.

Key to the Biography Read aloud the Key to the Biography. Then invite a volunteer to read the PREVIEW aloud. Have students fill out their webs. After they finish, invite them to share their information with the class.

BUILD BACKGROUND Connect to History Explain to students that Eleanor Roosevelt, wife of President Franklin D. Roosevelt, was born into a wealthy, respected New York family in 1884. She lived through a period of dramatic changes, including World War I, the Great Depression, and World War II. In 1932, in the midst of the Great Depression, Franklin Roosevelt was elected president. As First Lady, Eleanor spoke out against economic and social injustice. In later years, she became a champion of international human rights as the first American delegate to the United Nations.

WORDS TO KNOW

brooding

combatant

migrant

priority

prominent

Additional Words to Know

dynamic
    page 78, line 222

refugees
    page 86, line 444

VOCABULARY PREVIEW: Words to Know in Context

You can help students learn the Words to Know by reading aloud the following sentences or writing them on the board. Then show students how to use context clues to help them figure out the meaning.

brooding: After he lost all his money, his *brooding* silence showed that he was worried and upset.

combatant: I served in the Army as a *combatant,* fighting on many battlefields.

migrant: Ours was a *migrant* family, moving to a new town every year.

priority: Your homework is your *priority;* you must finish it before going outside to play.

prominent: Maya comes from a *prominent* family in town; her mother is the mayor and her father is the school principal.

dynamic: We need a *dynamic* speaker instead of one with no energy.

refugees: During the war, the United States took in thousands of *refugees,* who were fleeing poverty and certain death in their own countries.

VOCABULARY FOCUS: Using Context Clues

Teacher Modeling Remind students that authors sometimes restate the meaning of a difficult word within a sentence, defining it for the reader. Restatements or definitions are often signaled by a dash or by phrases such as *that is* and *also called*. Model using this type of context clue to determine the meaning of **debutante** (page 77, line 178).

You could say I'm not sure what debutante *means, but I see that the author includes a dash followed by additional information about the word. A* debutante *seems to be a wealthy young woman who attends parties and dances in order to take her place in the social world.*

Student Modeling Ask a volunteer to apply this strategy to figure out the meaning of the term **infantile paralysis** (page 80, line 287).

A student might say I've never heard of infantile paralysis, *but I see the term is followed by a dash and the word* polio, *which is followed by a dash and a restatement, or definition. According to the restatement,* infantile paralysis *is the same as polio, which is a crippling and deadly disease.*

Mini-Lesson See pages 95–98 of this Guide for additional work on **Using Context Clues.**

During Reading

COMPREHENSION FOCUS

Key Points	Strategies for Success
Target Skill ➡ Main Idea and Supporting Details The author includes many factual details in this biography to show readers how Eleanor Roosevelt's personality was shaped and why she took part in public life. Students must be able to identify stated and unstated main ideas and the details that support them.	**Mini-Lesson** Before students read "Eleanor Roosevelt," teach the **Main Idea and Supporting Details** lesson on pages 122–125 of this Guide. • Read aloud lines 1–55 on pages 72–73. Then help students identify the main ideas and key details in this section. Discuss how events in Eleanor's childhood affected her.
Historical References Students may be unfamiliar with many of the references to social and political organizations, such as the League of Women Voters, and to national and world events. To understand the biography, students must be able to use the footnotes to help clarify meaning.	• Point out the footnotes at the bottom of pages 77, 81, 82, 83, and 87 and explain that students can use them for help with historical references. Model using the footnote on page 77 to clarify the meaning of *settlement house.* Discuss with students how knowing what a settlement house is helps them understand what kind of person Eleanor Roosevelt was. • As they read, have students use the **Active Reading SkillBuilder** on page 89 of *The InterActive Reader.*™

Suggested Reading Options

- An oral reading of "Eleanor Roosevelt" is available in *The Language of Literature* Audio Library. ◠
- Partner/Cooperative Reading (see page 8 of this Guide).
- Additional options are described on page 8 of this Guide.

RECIPROCAL TEACHING SUGGESTION ➡ Questioning

Teacher Modeling *Pause & Reflect, page 81* Model using the questioning strategy to help students understand Eleanor's reasons for wanting her husband to remain in public life.

You could say *I am confused by the sentence "This time, Eleanor . . . stood up for her ideas." I ask myself: What made her suddenly stand up for herself? Then I remember that even as a teenager, Eleanor encouraged people to work for political and social justice. She must have valued a politically active life enough to urge her husband not to retire.*

Student Modeling *Pause & Reflect, page 85* Have several students model using the questioning strategy to better understand Eleanor's influence on Franklin. Offer this prompt: *How did Eleanor serve as the president's conscience?*

Encourage students to use the other five reading strategies when appropriate as they proceed through the rest of the biography. (See page 10 of this Guide.)

ENGLISH LEARNERS

1. Make sure students have a basic understanding of the American political process and an understanding of these terms in particular: **elected, Senate, Secretary of the Navy, Democratic Party, vice president, Republicans** (page 80); **governor, president** (page 81).

2. Students might benefit from reading along with the recording of "Eleanor Roosevelt" provided in *The Language of Literature* Audio Library. ◯

After Reading

Recommended Follow-Up

- Thinking Through the Literature, page 98, *The Language of Literature*
- Choices & Challenges, pages 99–100, *The Language of Literature*
- SkillBuilders, pages 89–91, *The InterActive Reader*™

Informal Assessment Options

Retell Have students work in groups of five to summarize events from the different phases of Eleanor's life, taking her perspective in each case: Eleanor as a child, Eleanor as a young adult, Eleanor as a new wife, Eleanor as First Lady, Eleanor as Ambassador to the United Nations.

Spot Check Look at the notes students made in the margins of the biography. Invite them to explain their answers and ask any questions they still have about Eleanor Roosevelt.

Formal Assessment Options in *The Language of Literature*

Selection Quiz, page 51, Unit One Resource Book

Selection Test, pages 15–16, Formal Assessment Book

For more teaching options, see pages 87–100 in *The Language of Literature* Teacher's Edition.

Additional Challenge

1. **Evaluate Childhood Influences**
   Ask: *How do you think Eleanor's childhood pains and struggles influenced her development as a person? What effect do you think they might have had on her life work—helping others?* Have students discuss and support their opinions.

2. **|||MARK IT UP ⟩ Examine the Biography**
   Ask: *If Eleanor could read Jacobs's biography of her, what might her reaction be?* Have students mark passages in the biography to support their views.

Before Reading

Direct students' attention to the Connect to Your Life and Key to the Story activities on page 92 of *The InterActive Reader.*™ Use the following suggestions to prepare students to read the story.

Connect to Your Life Invite volunteers to describe places in their neighborhood where they like to spend time with their friends. Encourage students to explain what makes these places special. Then have all students complete the activity on page 92.

Key to the Story Ask students to describe statues or monuments that honor heroes or other memorable people. Explain that murals, or wall paintings, can also commemorate important people, places, and events. Then have students complete their lists. Invite students to share the names they chose.

BUILD BACKGROUND **Connect to History** Tell students that this story mentions four important leaders in the American civil rights movement. Students may recognize the name of Harriet Tubman (1820–1913), the escaped slave who helped smuggle more than 300 enslaved persons out of slave states. She was also a spy for the Union army during the Civil War. Explain that Dr. Martin Luther King, Jr. (1929–1968) and Malcolm X (1925–1965) were civil rights leaders of the 1960s who were assassinated. King used nonviolent tactics such as boycotts to oppose segregation and was awarded the Nobel Prize for Peace. For most of his life, Malcolm X preached a militant and separatist philosophy. Fannie Lou Hamer (1917–1977) was a sharecropper's daughter who repeatedly risked her life so that she and other African Americans could gain the right to vote.

WORDS TO KNOW

beckon

drawl

inscription

liberation

scheme

Additional Words to Know

chisel
  page 94, line 21

rearing
  page 96, line 82

VOCABULARY PREVIEW: Words to Know in Context

You can help students learn the Words to Know by reading aloud the following sentences or writing them on the board. Then show students how to use context clues to help them figure out the meaning.

beckon: Elisabeth *beckoned* to me from across the gym, waving me toward her with her hand.

drawl: I had trouble understanding Bill's *drawl*—his slow, drawn-out way of speaking.

inscription: The *inscription* on the statue dedicated it to the fallen soldiers in Vietnam.

liberation: The president demanded the *liberation* of the prisoners, saying that it was wrong to keep them in jail now that the war was over.

scheme: As soon as the babysitter arrived, the twins began to *scheme* up ways to annoy her.

chisel: A few people *chiseled* their names into the big rock, using a penknife.

rearing: The frightened horse started *rearing* up on its hind legs.

VOCABULARY FOCUS: Understanding Idioms

Teacher Modeling Remind students that they can often determine the meaning of an unfamiliar idiom by looking for context clues. Model using the idiom *paid us no mind* (page 94, line 29).

You could say I've never heard the expression paid us no mind *before. From reading the surrounding sentences, I can see that the painter ignores Lou's comments.* Paid us no mind *probably means "paid no attention to us."*

Student Modeling Ask a student to model the strategy using the idiom *hanging back* (page 95, line 49).

A student might say I wonder what the author means by hanging back? *When I read on, I see that the Morris twins do not speak to the painter but just stand there watching her at work. They wait until Side Pocket speaks to her before offering her the food they have brought.* Hanging back *probably means "waiting cautiously or shyly."*

Mini-Lesson
See pages 105–106 of this Guide for additional work on **Understanding Idioms.**

During Reading

COMPREHENSION FOCUS

Key Points	Strategies for Success
Target Skill → Cause and Effect Students must understand the cause-and-effect relationships that drive this story.	**Mini-Lesson** Before students read "The War of the Wall," teach or review the **Cause and Effect** lesson on pages 129–133 of this Guide. • Read aloud lines 104–125 on page 97. Then have students discuss the painter's actions and how they affect the narrator, Lou, and the other characters. • As students read, have them complete the **Active Reading SkillBuilder** on page 105 of *The InterActive Reader.*™
Dialect The author makes her story more realistic by having the narrator and the other characters use expressions from a particular dialect. Students may need help understanding the unfamiliar expressions.	Explain that, as students read, they should put a check mark next to any words or phrases they don't understand. At each *Pause & Reflect,* encourage them to ask questions or work with a partner to figure out the meaning of confusing bits of dialect.

Suggested Reading Options

• An oral reading of "The War of the Wall" is available in *The Language of Literature* Audio Library. ◠
• Shared Reading (see page 8 of this Guide).
• Additional options are described on page 8 of this Guide.

RECIPROCAL TEACHING SUGGESTION ➡ Evaluating

Teacher Modeling *Pause & Reflect, page 99* Model using the evaluating strategy to help students form opinions about Mama's attitude toward the painter.

You could say *In the last paragraph on page 99, Mama seems annoyed and impatient. I guess she thought it was rude of the painter to ask so many questions about the food and to show her dissatisfaction with it. I can understand Mama's feelings, but I still think she shouldn't have spoken so sharply.*

Student Modeling *Pause & Reflect, page 101* Have several students model using the evaluating strategy to form opinions about the narrator and Lou's plan. Offer these prompts: *What do the narrator and Lou plan to do with the epoxy paint? Why? Do you think this is a good solution to the problem? Why or why not?*

Encourage students to use the other five reading strategies when appropriate as they proceed through the rest of the story. (See page 10 of this Guide.)

ENGLISH LEARNERS

1. Make sure students understand the following terms:
   pitching pennies, page 94
   the once-over, page 96
   by-and-by, page 98
   open fire on, page 100
2. Students might benefit from reading along with the recording of "The War of the Wall" provided in *The Language of Literature* Audio Library. ◯

After Reading

Recommended Follow-Up

- Thinking Through the Literature, page 118, *The Language of Literature*
- Choices & Challenges, pages 119–120, *The Language of Literature*
- SkillBuilders, pages 105–107, *The InterActive Reader*™

Informal Assessment Options

Retell Have students work in pairs to role-play the narrator and Lou and to tell how their impressions of the painter lady change in the story.

Spot Check Read the notations students wrote in the margins, paying particular attention to their responses to the *Pause & Reflect* questions. Discuss the predictions students made in response to question 2 on page 99. Invite them to ask any questions they still have about the story.

Formal Assessment Options in *The Language of Literature*

Selection Quiz, page 65, Unit One Resource Book

Selection Test, pages 19–20, Formal Assessment Book

For more teaching options, see pages 109–120 in *The Language of Literature* Teacher's Edition.

Additional Challenge

1. **Discuss the Ending**
   Ask: *What important fact does the dedication tell you about the painter? Why do you think the author ends this story with the dedication? How do you think the narrator and Lou might have responded to it, and why?*

2. **MARK IT UP ⟩ Evaluate a Character**
   Ask: *How would you evaluate the way the painter lady treats the people in the neighborhood?* Have students mark details in the story to support their opinions.

Before Reading

Direct students' attention to the Connect to Your Life and Key to the Story activities on page 108 of *The InterActive Reader.*™ Use the following suggestions to prepare students to read the story.

Connect to Your Life
Discuss the meanings of the words *predator* and *prey* with students, and invite volunteers to name some examples of each in the animal kingdom. Discuss strategies animals use to defend themselves against predators, including camouflage, running away, and fighting back. Then ask students to complete the matching activity and explain their choices.

Key to the Story
Help students locate India on a map, and explain that this country is the setting for the story. Tell students that both the cobra and the mongoose are animals found in India. Invite students to share what they know about these animals; if possible, display a picture of each from a book or magazine. Then read aloud the Key to the Story. Ask students what they think this story might be about, based on what they've learned.

BUILD BACKGROUND Rescue Animals
Ask students to share examples of animals who help to protect or rescue people in danger. *(Possible responses: dogs who warn their owners of intruders; dogs who locate people trapped in avalanches or collapsed buildings.)* Ask students what qualities the animals demonstrate in such cases (*e.g.,* loyalty; good training; special skills or abilities). Encourage students to keep these qualities in mind as they read the story.

WORDS TO KNOW

consolation

cower

cunningly

revive

scuttle

Additional Words to Know

thickets
  page 113, line 103

savage
  page 114, line 162

gait
  page 116, line 212

VOCABULARY PREVIEW: Words to Know in Context

You can help students learn the Words to Know by reading aloud the following sentences or writing them on the board. Then show students how to use context clues to help them figure out the meaning.

consolation: The flowers you gave me are no *consolation;* I don't know if anything could make me feel better after losing that race.

cower: When I reached into the mouse's cage, it *cowered,* shivering in the far corner.

cunningly: The spy was very clever; she *cunningly* disguised herself as a security guard so that no one would notice her.

revive: We tried desperately to *revive* Joe after he passed out during the basketball game.

scuttle: The crab *scuttled* quickly across the beach.

---

thickets: In the middle of the dirt yard, there were a few *thickets* of grass and weeds.

savage: The villagers were all terrified of the *savage* beast living in the woods.

gait: The soldier walked with a steady *gait,* planting one foot firmly in front of the other.

VOCABULARY FOCUS Word Parts: Suffixes

Teacher Modeling Tell students that they can sometimes use their knowledge of suffixes to figure out the meaning of an unfamiliar word. Model using the word **restless** (page 110, line 15).

You could say I'm not sure what restless *means. I've seen the suffix -less before in words like* hopeless *and* helpless. *I know it means "without." I also know that* rest *can mean "sleep," "relaxation," or "the stopping of activity." I think* restless *is an adjective. It means "without rest," "always moving," or "unable to relax."*

Student Modeling Ask a volunteer to model how to use the strategy to figure out the meaning of **sorrowful** (page 113, line 107).

A student might say I'm not sure what sorrowful *means. I know* sorrow *means "sadness" or "suffering." I also know that the suffix -ful can mean "full of." Sorrowful is an adjective that must mean "full of sadness or suffering." That makes sense here because the birds with the sorrowful voices have lost one of their babies.*

Mini-Lesson See pages 99 and 101 of this Guide for additional work on **Word Parts: Suffixes**.

During Reading

COMPREHENSION FOCUS

Key Points	Strategies for Success
Target Skill ➡ Predicting The author uses foreshadowing and other narrative elements to build suspense in this story. Students who can use the story clues to make predictions will have a richer understanding and enjoyment of the story.	**Mini-Lesson** Before students read "Rikki-tikki-tavi," you may want to teach the **Predicting** lesson on pages 140–142 of this Guide. • At the *Pause & Reflect* on page 115, have students make predictions about what Rikki-tikki might do next and explain why they think so. • As they read, students can complete the **Active Reading SkillBuilder** on page 131 of *The InterActive Reader.™*
The Author's Style The long sentences and unusual vocabulary in "Rikki-tikki-tavi" may confuse or frustrate some readers.	Draw students' attention to the Reading Tip on page 110 and read it aloud. Then read aloud the first two paragraphs of the story, having students follow along in their books. Discuss with students how the semicolons in the second paragraph separate complete ideas. Also, encourage students to read the story for key events and not let the details bog them down. Suggest that students underline unfamiliar or difficult words as they read and return to them later to figure out their meanings.

Suggested Reading Options

• An oral reading of "Rikki-tikki-tavi" is available in *The Language of Literature* Audio Library. ◠
• Shared Reading (see page 8 of this Guide).
• Additional options are described on page 8 of this Guide.

RECIPROCAL TEACHING SUGGESTION ➡ Visualizing

Teacher Modeling *Pause & Reflect, page 112* Model for students how to use sensory details to visualize Rikki-tikki's actions as he explores the house.

You could say When I read lines 67–71, I can picture the little mongoose full of curiosity and wanting to take in his new surroundings. I see him plop himself down in Teddy's father's lap and dip his nose into a bottle of ink. I see him rub his inky nose against the man's glowing cigar. I see Rikki-tikki getting into all kinds of mischief.

Student Modeling *Pause & Reflect, page 115* Have students model visualizing the scene described in the first full paragraph on page 113. Offer this prompt: *What details tell you what the garden looks like and what sounds are heard there? What details tell you what Rikki-tikki looks like as he explores?*

Encourage students to use the other five reading strategies when appropriate as they proceed through the rest of the story. (See page 10 of this Guide.)

ENGLISH LEARNERS

1. Make sure students understand the following idioms:

   single-handed (on one's own), page 110, line 4

   lost his senses (became unconscious), page 110, line 25

   off his guard (not paying attention), page 114, line 152

   stole off (sneaked away), page 119, line 302

   odds are in his favor (he is likely to win), page 120, line 339

   settle accounts with (get even with, get revenge on), page 124, line 470

2. Students might benefit from reading along with the recording of "Rikki-tikki-tavi" provided in *The Language of Literature* Audio Library. 🎧

After Reading

Recommended Follow-Up

- Thinking Through the Literature, page 135, *The Language of Literature*
- Choices & Challenges, pages 136–137, *The Language of Literature*
- SkillBuilders, pages 131–133, *The InterActive Reader™*

Informal Assessment Options

Retell Have groups of four or five students work together to present oral summaries of the story. Explain that group members should divide the story into sections, and each group member should retell the main events in his or her section.

Spot Check Look at the notes students made in the margins of the story. Invite them to explain their answers and discuss any questions they still have about the story.

Formal Assessment Options in *The Language of Literature*

Selection Quiz, page 72, Unit One Resource Book

Selection Test, pages 21–22, Formal Assessment Book

For more teaching options, see pages 121–137 in *The Language of Literature* Teacher's Edition.

Additional Challenge

1. **Examine Suspense**
   Have students discuss how Kipling builds suspense in this story. Students should provide details from the story to explain their ideas.

2. **MARK IT UP ⟩ Evaluate Character**
   Ask: *What is more important to Rikki-tikki in his battles with his enemies—his physical strength or his strategy?* Have students mark passages in the story to support their views.

Before Reading

Direct students' attention to the Connect to Your Life and Key to the Story activities on page 134 of *The InterActive Reader.*™ Use the following suggestions to prepare students to read the story.

Connect to Your Life

Discuss books or stories in which a character undergoes a change. You might get students started by naming a couple of stories, such as *A Christmas Carol* and *The Wizard of Oz.* After students have named a couple of other books or stories, ask: *What caused the characters to change? Did the changes seem realistic? Why or why not?* Then have students do the activity on page 134 and share their answers with the class.

Key to the Story

Write the word *reformation* on the board and read aloud the explanation of this term on page 134. Then have students work in pairs to find words related to *reformation* in the dictionary and add the words to their webs. Call on volunteers to share their words. List them on the board and discuss their meanings. Before students read the story, explain that *retrieve* means "to get back or regain." Finally, encourage students to read to find out whose reformation is retrieved, and how.

BUILD BACKGROUND

Connect to History Tell students that banks played an important role in the economy of small towns in the late 19th and early 20th centuries. The National Banking Act of 1863 helped establish a system of federally chartered banks. In the late 1800s, Will Porter, who would later take the pen name O. Henry, worked as a teller for the First National Bank in Austin, Texas. Like the main character in this story, Will Porter also spent some time in jail. Then explain to students that the main character is a safecracker—a burglar who breaks into safes in order to steal the contents.

WORDS TO KNOW

- assiduously
- balk
- compulsory
- elusive
- eminent
- rehabilitate
- retribution
- unobtrusively
- unperceived
- virtuous

VOCABULARY PREVIEW: Words to Know in Context

You can help students learn the Words to Know by reading aloud the following sentences or writing them on the board. Then show students how to use context clues to help them figure out the meaning.

assiduously: Jericho worked *assiduously* on his project, never taking a break.

balk: When I tried to get the horse to come back into the barn, she *balked,* refusing to move for twenty minutes.

compulsory: Class attendance is *compulsory;* that is, you must show up whether you like it or not.

elusive: The *elusive* bank robbers slipped away from the police every time.

eminent: The *eminent* brain surgeon is well-known in every hospital in the country.

rehabilitate: Prisons should work harder to *rehabilitate* criminals and prepare them for jobs in the outside world.

retribution: As *retribution* for the robbery, the judge put him in jail for five years.

unobtrusively: Unnoticed by the family, the neighbor's cat slipped *unobtrusively* through the back door.

unperceived: *Unperceived* by the guard, the prisoner picked the lock on his cell door.

virtuous: This man is not a criminal, but a good and *virtuous* citizen.

VOCABULARY FOCUS Word Parts: Prefixes

Teacher Modeling Remind students that sometimes they can use their knowledge of prefixes and other word parts to help them figure out the meaning of unfamiliar words. Then use the following modeling suggestions for the word *disregarding* (page 137, line 48).

Mini-Lesson See pages 99–100 of this Guide for additional work on **Word Parts: Prefixes.**

You could say I'm not sure what disregarding *means, but I can try breaking the word into parts. I recognize the prefix* dis- *from words such as disappear. I know that* dis- *can mean "not" or "the opposite of." I also know that the base word* regard *can mean "to look at or observe closely." Using these word parts, I think* disregarding *probably means "not noticing or paying attention to." This meaning makes sense in the sentence.*

Student Modeling Now have students follow your lead. Ask a volunteer to model using the strategy to figure out the meaning of *immovable* (page 146, line 329).

A student might say I'm not familiar with the word immovable. *However, I recognize the prefix* im- *from words such as* impossible. *I know* im- *means "not." I also know that* movable *means "able to be moved." So* immovable *must describe someone who cannot be moved.*

During Reading

COMPREHENSION FOCUS

Key Points	Strategies for Success
Target Skill ➡ Sequence Students' ability to follow the order of events is crucial to their understanding of the story.	**Mini-Lesson** Before students read "A Retrieved Reformation," you may want to teach the **Sequence** lesson on pages 126–128 of this Guide. • Read aloud lines 36–59 on page 137. Ask students to list in order the events described in these lines. • As students read "A Retrieved Reformation," encourage them to record the story's events in the **Sequence Flow Chart** on page 127.
Surprise Ending The story concludes with a surprise ending. To fully appreciate the story, it is important that students understand what happens at the end and why it is a surprise.	Read aloud lines 337–349 on page 146. Have students discuss what happens at the end of the story. Ask: *Why did Ben Price come to Elmore? What did he plan to do there? What does he do instead? Why do you think he changes his mind?*

Suggested Reading Options

• An oral reading of "A Retrieved Reformation" is available in *The Language of Literature* Audio Library. 🎧
• Partner/Cooperative Reading (see page 8 of this Guide).
• Additional options are described on page 8 of this Guide.

RECIPROCAL TEACHING SUGGESTION ➡ Evaluating

Teacher Modeling *Pause & Reflect, page 140* Model how to use the evaluating strategy to help students form opinions about Jimmy Valentine's behavior.

You could say *When I reread lines 97–107 on page 139, it seems clear that Jimmy is burglarizing safes again. Although Ben Price's comments in lines 113–120 suggest that Jimmy is very good at what he does, safecracking is illegal. The fact that he starts robbing banks immediately after being released from jail shows that he really hasn't changed—he still chooses wrong over right.*

Student Modeling *Pause & Reflect, page 142* Have several students model the evaluating strategy to form opinions about Jimmy's decision to give up safecracking. Offer this prompt: *What has caused Jimmy to give up robbing banks? Do you think he'll keep his promise to lead a "straight" life? Why or why not?* Students can use the **Active Reading SkillBuilder** on page 147 to form opinions about Jimmy and the other characters in the story.

Encourage students to use the other five reading strategies when appropriate as they proceed through the rest of the story. (See page 10 of this Guide.)

ENGLISH LEARNERS

1. Students acquiring English may find the vocabulary in this story difficult. Encourage them to think of cognates, or words in their own language that are similar in spelling and meaning to these difficult words. For example, speakers of Romance languages may understand the word *reformation* in the title. Other cognates in the story include *pardon, represent, community,* and *combination.*

2. Students might benefit from reading along with the recording of "A Retrieved Reformation" provided in *The Language of Literature* Audio Library. ◠

After Reading

Recommended Follow-Up

- Thinking Through the Literature, page 171, *The Language of Literature*
- Choices & Challenges, pages 172 and 176, *The Language of Literature*
- SkillBuilders, pages 147–149, *The InterActive Reader™*

Informal Assessment Options

Retell Have groups of four students give oral summaries of the story. One student should summarize Jimmy Valentine's prison experience. Another should summarize the life of crime he begins again as soon as he is released from prison. Two students should work together on presenting a summary of Jimmy's experiences in Elmore.

Spot Check Review the notes students made in the margins to make sure they have understood what they read. Pay particular attention to their answers to the *Pause & Reflect* questions.

Formal Assessment Options in *The Language of Literature*

Selection Quiz, page 87, Unit One Resource Book

Selection Test, pages 25–26, Formal Assessment Book

For more teaching options, see pages 163–177 in *The Language of Literature* Teacher's Edition.

Additional Challenge

1. **Evaluate Character**
Point out that at the end of the story, Jimmy Valentine uses his safecracking skills for a good purpose. Then ask students whether they think Jimmy would have performed such an action before he met Annabel. Have students write a brief paragraph in which they support their opinion. To get students started, ask: *Why does Jimmy crack safes before he meets Annabel? Why does Jimmy give up cracking safes after he meets Annabel? Why does he open the safe in her father's bank?*

2. ▐║ **MARK IT UP** ✎⟩ **Explain the Title**
Tell students that the title of a story can summarize its main idea. Then have students explain the title "A Retrieved Reformation" and tell how it relates to the story. Students should mark passages in the story to explain their ideas.

Before Reading

Direct students' attention to the Connect to Your Life and Key to the Poems activities on page 150 of *The InterActive Reader.*™ Use the following suggestions to prepare students to read the poems.

Connect to Your Life
Ask students: *How often do you spend time with your friends? Do you ever wish you could spend more time with friends or family?* Discuss with students why they think spending time with people they care about is important. Then read aloud the directions for the activity and have students complete their webs.

Key to the Poems
Ask students to compare the feeling of rushing to get a task done to that of completing a task at a slow, steady pace. Then read aloud the lines from "The Pasture." Ask: *What chore does the speaker plan to do? Does he or she seem to be in a hurry? How can you tell?* Discuss how the simple language and slow, flowing rhythm create a relaxed pace as well as a clear visual image.

BUILD BACKGROUND Connect to Geography Explain to students that Robert Frost spent much of his adult life in New England, where he worked for a time as a farmer. The region's uneven, rocky soil and long, cold winters have long made farming a challenge there. Many of Frost's poems are set in this landscape and convey the details of everyday life while exploring deeper themes.

Strategies for Reading Poetry

- Notice the form of the poem: the number of lines and their shape on the page.
- Read the poem aloud a few times. Listen for rhymes and rhythms.
- Visualize the images and comparisons.
- Mark words and phrases that appeal to you.
- Ask yourself what message the poet is trying to send.
- Think about what the poem is saying to you.

FOCUS ON POETRY

Before having students read "The Pasture" and "A Time to Talk," you may want to have them read or review the lesson "Poetry" on pages 191–195 of *The Language of Literature.* That lesson shows how the key elements of poetry work together in a poem to produce emotion and meaning. It also suggests some useful strategies students can use when reading poetry. The activities below will help prepare students for reading "The Pasture" and "A Time to Talk."

- **Rhythm** Remind students that **rhythm** is the pattern of stressed and unstressed syllables in a poem's lines. Explain that some poems have a regular arrangement of stressed and unstressed syllables. This arrangement, called **meter,** can help convey the poem's mood. Poets sometimes use shifts in rhythm to make a point. Encourage students to listen for both regular patterns and shifts in rhythm as they read these poems.

- **Theme** Both poems describe ordinary experiences on a New England farm. Work with students to generate a list of themes that might be associated with farm life, such as the importance of work, land, weather, and companionship. Ask students to write these themes in the margin of *The InterActive Reader*™ and keep them in mind as they read.

VOCABULARY FOCUS: Using Context Clues

Teacher Modeling Remind students that they can often use context clues to help them figure out the meaning of unfamiliar words. Model the strategy using the word *totters* (page 152, line 7).

You could say *I'm not sure what* totters *means, so I look for clues in the surrounding words and phrases. The words* little *and* so young *tell me that the calf is probably a newborn and may be very unsteady on its feet. When the mother licks the calf, it probably sways back and forth as if it is about to fall. That must be what* totters *means.*

Student Modeling Ask a student volunteer to use context clues to figure out the meaning of *thrust* (page 153, line 7).

A student might say *I know the speaker is hoeing when a friend calls out, and that the speaker stops working to talk.* Thrust *is what the speaker does with the hoe before taking a break. The phrases* in the mellow ground *and* blade end up *suggest that the speaker pushes the hoe into the ground so it stands straight up.* Thrust *must mean "to push in or down."*

Mini-Lesson See pages 95–98 of this Guide for additional work on **Using Context Clues.**

During Reading

COMPREHENSION FOCUS

Key Points	Strategies for Success
Target Skill ➡ Making Inferences The poet does not directly state how the speaker of each poem feels about work and companionship. Students must make inferences based on details in the poem to understand the speaker's viewpoint and attitude.	**Mini-Lesson** Before students read the poems, you may want to teach or review the **Making Inferences** lesson on pages 137–139 of this Guide. • Draw students' attention to the repeated line at the end of each stanza of "The Pasture." Then review what the speaker does when a friend visits in "A Time to Talk." Ask students what they can tell about the speaker's attitude toward companionship. Also help students note the details in each poem that reveal the speaker's unhurried and positive attitude toward work. • Have students complete the **Inference Chart** on page 138 of this Guide.
Images It is important for students to identify and picture the images in each poem.	• Read aloud each poem at least twice. Then have individual students identify descriptive words and phrases and tell the sense or senses they appeal to. For example, in lines 5–7 of "The Pasture," the descriptive words and phrases appeal to the senses of sight and touch. • Have students work in pairs to complete the **Active Reading SkillBuilder** on page 154 of *The InterActive Reader.*™

Suggested Reading Options

• Oral readings of the poems are available in *The Language of Literature* Audio Library. ◯
• Oral Reading (see page 8 of this Guide).
• Additional options are described on page 8 of this Guide.

RECIPROCAL TEACHING SUGGESTION ➡ Connecting

Teacher Modeling *Pause & Reflect, page 152* Model for students how to connect the experiences described in "The Pasture" to their own lives.

You could say *The speaker doesn't seem to be in a hurry about the chores. Instead, the speaker will take time to notice the details of his or her environment. That's what I do when I'm working on a task I like, so I think the speaker enjoys his or her work.*

Student Modeling *Pause & Reflect, page 153* Have volunteers model connecting to the experiences described in "A Time to Talk." Offer these prompts: *What does the speaker NOT do when a friend interrupts? What does the speaker do instead? How do you react in similar situations?*

Encourage students to use the other five reading strategies when appropriate as they proceed through the poems. (See page 10 of this Guide.)

ENGLISH LEARNERS

1. Help students understand the following terms and expressions: "The Pasture" (page 152)— **pasture, spring, rake, watch the water clear, shan't, fetch, calf;** "A Time to Talk" (page 153)— **a meaning walk, hoed, mellow ground, plod.**

2. Students might benefit from reading along with the recordings of "The Pasture" and "A Time to Talk" provided in *The Language of Literature* Audio Library. ◯

After Reading

Recommended Follow-Up

- Thinking Through the Literature, page 199, *The Language of Literature*
- Choices & Challenges, page 200, *The Language of Literature*
- SkillBuilders, pages 154–155, *The InterActive Reader*™

Informal Assessment Options

Retell Have partners role-play the interaction that occurs in each poem. They can take turns playing the speaker and the unnamed friend. Then have each pair think of three adjectives that describe the mood of each poem.

Spot Check Look at the notes students made in the margins. Make sure their answers show an understanding of what they have read. Discuss students' responses to question 1 on page 153, which tests students' understanding of the message of "A Time to Talk."

Formal Assessment Options in *The Language of Literature*

Selection Test, pages 29–30, Formal Assessment Book

For more teaching options, see pages 196–200 in *The Language of Literature* Teacher's Edition.

Additional Challenge

1. **Understanding Theme**
   Ask: *What message about human relationships do the speakers of these poems convey?* Have students write a paragraph to explain their ideas.

2. **MARK IT UP ⬦ Analyzing Word Choice**
   Tell students that poets choose precise words to create vivid experiences for their readers. For example, in "A Time to Talk," Frost uses the word "shout" instead of "say" and "thrust" instead of "put." Have students circle other examples of precise language in "The Pasture" and "A Time to Talk." Then have students explain what makes each example so effective.

Before Reading

Have students do the Connect to Your Life and Key to the Autobiography activities on page 156 of *The InterActive Reader.*™ Use the following suggestions to prepare students to read the autobiography.

Connect to Your Life
Guide students in a discussion about responding to insult or injury. Ask students to comment on the advantages and disadvantages of letting an insult slide, discussing it, or losing one's temper. After students fill out the checklists, let them share their responses with the class.

Key to the Autobiography
The excerpt is about how Jackie Robinson came to be the first African American to play in major league baseball. Have a brief discussion about Jackie Robinson as a pioneer black athlete. You might ask: *How well are professional sports teams integrated today?*

BUILD BACKGROUND
Connect to History Explain to students that in the 1940s, African Americans faced many barriers created by prejudice. Segregation kept blacks from using schools, restaurants, and hospitals used by whites. In baseball, the Negro League was completely separate from the white league. Jackie Robinson would help change that.

WORDS TO KNOW

cynical

eloquence

incredulous

insinuation

integrated

retaliate

shrewdly

speculating

taunt

ultimate

Additional Words to Know

contradiction
   page 160, line 81

indebted
   page 162, line 148

VOCABULARY PREVIEW: Words to Know in Context

You can help students learn the Words to Know by reading aloud the following sentences or writing them on the board. Then show students how to use context clues to help them figure out the meaning.

cynical: I'm sorry to be so *cynical,* but I just don't believe that Dan plans to do what he says.

eloquence: The man spoke with such *eloquence* that the audience was moved to tears.

incredulous: Although we tried to convince him that it was true, Julio was *incredulous* when he heard the news.

insinuation: Are you trying to say that I am not doing my job properly? I resent that *insinuation.*

integrated: Our neighborhood has become much more *integrated* in the past ten years; we have people of many different races now.

retaliate: If you pull a prank on your neighbor, she will surely *retaliate;* she might turn over your trash cans or let your dog out of the yard.

shrewdly: Janina *shrewdly* sensed that her brother would be more willing to help her if there was something in it for him.

speculating: There's no use *speculating* about the results; we can guess all we want, but we still won't know until the test comes back.

taunt: Ricky's classmates used to *taunt* him for being the smallest boy in the class, making him angry and miserable.

ultimate: Our next goal is to win this game; our *ultimate* goal is to win the championship.

contradiction: A snowstorm in July sounds like a *contradiction,* but it's been known to happen.

indebted: Tom feels *indebted* to his cousin Jenny for her help with his schoolwork; so he has promised to mow her lawn all summer.

VOCABULARY FOCUS: Using Context Clues

Teacher Modeling Remind students that they can often use context clues to figure out the meanings of words. Then use the following modeling suggestion for the word *accommodations* (page 158, line 16).

You could say I don't know the word accommodations, *but I can get clues from reading the paragraph where the word appears. In this paragraph, a hotel has refused to let a black player have a room. Branch Rickey threatens to take the team to stay at another hotel, but "the threat was a bluff because he knew the other hotels also would have refused accommodations to a black man." If other hotels "also" would have refused accommodations, that must mean that this hotel refused accommodations too. Since I already know that this hotel refused a room to the black player, I think that accommodations must be a restatement of "hotel room" or "place to stay."*

Student Modeling Now have students follow your lead. Ask a volunteer to model using context clues to determine the meaning of *exhaustive* (page 166, line 251).

A student might say After saying that Rickey's search had been exhaustive, Robinson goes on to say that it had "spanned the globe and narrowed down to a few candidates." I think that the phrase "spanned the globe" is a clue that exhaustive means "very broad and complete."

Mini-Lesson
See pages 95–98 of this Guide for additional work on **Using Context Clues.**

During Reading

COMPREHENSION FOCUS

Key Points	Strategies for Success
Target Skill ➡ Main Idea and Supporting Details Students must realize that although Robinson gives many details about the politics of baseball and his own feelings about Branch Rickey, the main idea of this selection has to do with Rickey's search for the unique individual who can both play great baseball and maintain his dignity in the face of abuse.	**Mini-Lesson** Before students read "The Noble Experiment," you may want to teach the **Main Idea and Supporting Details** lesson on pages 122–125 of this Guide. • After students have read through page 160, ask them to go back and circle details that support this main idea: *Next, he had to find the ideal player for his project.* • After reading, students can complete the **Active Reading SkillBuilder** on page 171 of *The InterActive Reader.*™
Historical Context Students may not realize the full extent of the racial hatred and abuse faced by Jackie Robinson. Unlike today, when professional baseball, basketball, and football teams are integrated, the early 1940s was a time of strict segregation. Many white people strongly opposed the integration of professional baseball, and when Jackie Robinson came to play for the Dodgers, he received loads of hate mail, constant insults, and even death threats.	Explain to students that Branch Rickey was not exaggerating when he tried to prepare Jackie Robinson for the kind of abuse he would have to endure. Point out to students that Robinson was well aware of the overt racism that was so prevalent in that day, and that by accepting Rickey's offer, he showed that he was willing to brave public hatred for the sake of racial justice.

Suggested Reading Options

• An oral reading of "The Noble Experiment" is available in *The Language of Literature* Audio Library. ◯
• Partner/Cooperative Reading (see page 8 of this Guide).
• Additional options are described on page 8 of this Guide.

RECIPROCAL TEACHING SUGGESTION ➜ Clarifying

Teacher Modeling *Pause & Reflect, page 170* Have students reread the previous section, from lines 308–335. Model using the clarifying strategy to understand what Branch Rickey means when he says "Robinson, I'm looking for a ballplayer with guts enough not to fight back."

You could say I wonder why Branch Rickey seems to think that not *fighting back would be a sign of courage rather than of fear. I think he means that it would be easier for Robinson to fight back, but if he fought back, he would be lowering himself to the level of his attackers. Also, the white crowds, prejudiced against Robinson from the start, would pay more attention to the fights than to Robinson's baseball abilities. I think that Rickey wants Robinson to have faith that he will actually gain dignity by refusing to fight back, rather than lose it.*

Student Modeling *Pause & Reflect, page 170* Ask several students to model how to clarify what Robinson means in lines 361–365 when he says that he must "turn the other cheek." Offer these prompts: *Why does Robinson feel he must turn the other cheek? How will it benefit black youth, his mother, and Rae for him to do so?*

Encourage students to use the other five reading strategies when appropriate as they proceed through the rest of the selection. (See page 10 of this Guide.)

After Reading

Recommended Follow-Up

- Thinking Through the Literature, page 296, *The Language of Literature*
- Choices & Challenges, page 297, *The Language of Literature*
- SkillBuilders, pages 171–173, *The InterActive Reader*™

Informal Assessment Options

Retell Have students retell this selection from Branch Rickey's point of view. Prompt students with questions like these:

- *Why did you want to integrate the major leagues?*
- *What made you choose Jackie Robinson as the first African American to play in the major leagues?*
- *What was your impression of Robinson during your first interview with him?*

Spot Check Look at the notes students made in the margins, paying special attention to their responses to the *Pause & Reflect* questions. Invite students to discuss their answers and any questions they still have.

Formal Assessment Options in *The Language of Literature*

Selection Quiz, page 52, Unit Two Resource Book

Selection Test, pages 43–44, Formal Assessment Book

For more teaching options, see pages 287–298 in *The Language of Literature* Teacher's Edition.

Additional Challenge

1. Write a Sequel
Ask students to write a scene in which Robinson tells Rachel and his mother about this opportunity, explaining the benefits and the risks involved. Encourage students to imagine the range of emotions the two women might have experienced, from pride and enthusiasm to concern for Robinson's safety.

2. ⫿⫿⫿ MARK IT UP ⟩ Analyze Conflict
Ask students: *What is Robinson's main problem in this selection? Who or what is he struggling against?* Have students look for passages where Robinson expresses discomfort or frustration; these passages will help them identify the people or forces opposing him. You might also remind students of some of the common types of conflict: person *vs.* person, person *vs.* society, and person *vs.* self.

Before Reading

Direct students' attention to the Connect to Your Life and Key to the Poem activities on page 174 of *The InterActive Reader.*™ Use the following suggestions to prepare students to read the poem.

Connect to Your Life
Have students discuss athletes they admire. Ask: *Which athletes do you admire most? What do you admire about them? How do they respond to tough challenges?* Then have students read the directions for the activity, complete the sentences, and share their responses in small groups.

Key to the Poem
Ask students if they have ever participated in or seen a game in which the outcome ultimately depended on the actions of one person. Ask students to describe these moments and share how they think they would feel if they were under that kind of pressure. Then have students read the directions to the Key to the Poem activity and jot down their thoughts on the lines.

BUILD BACKGROUND Connect to Social Studies
Explain to students that baseball began in the United States in the mid-1800s. By the early 1900s, the sport was so popular that people began calling it America's national pastime. Mighty Casey has been a popular figure since Ernest Lawrence Thayer wrote the poem in 1888. Suggest that, as students read the poem, they compare and contrast Casey with ballplayers today.

Strategies for Reading Poetry

- Notice the form of the poem: the number of lines and their shape on the page.
- Read the poem aloud a few times. Listen for rhymes and rhythms.
- Visualize the images and comparisons.
- Think about the poet's choice of words.
- Ask yourself what message the poet is trying to send.
- Think about what the poem is saying to you.

FOCUS ON POETRY

The discussion points below and the tips shown at the left will help prepare students for reading "Casey at the Bat." If your students need more detailed instruction on how to read and interpret poems, have them read "Poetry" on pages 191–195 of *The Language of Literature.*

- **Speaker** Read aloud the first stanza of "Casey at the Bat" on page 176. Discuss who the speaker might be. (He or she might be an announcer or an outside observer.) Invite volunteers to share their impressions of the hyperbolic, vivid language and tone often used by sports announcers, commentators, and writers. As students read "Casey at the Bat," have them listen for words and phrases that capture the excitement of the game in an exaggerated way.

- **Theme** "Casey at the Bat" explores the impact that glorifying one player can have on a team and its fans. After students have read the Preview, work with them to list both the positive and negative aspects of having a star player on a team. Have them consider how pinning all hopes on the performance of a single talented player can help and hurt a team.

VOCABULARY FOCUS: Using Words with Multiple Meanings

Teacher Modeling Remind students that some words have more than one meaning. Students can use context clues to help them figure out the intended meaning of such a word. Model the strategy using *springs* (page 176, line 6).

You could say I know that springs *can be used as a noun or a verb. As a noun,* springs *can mean "sources of water." As a verb,* springs *can mean "arises from a source." In this sentence, hope is an emotion that "springs" inside the human heart. Springs must mean "arises" here.*

Student Modeling Ask a student volunteer to use the strategy to figure out the meaning of *ground* (page 178, line 27).

A student might say I know ground *can be used as a noun or a verb. As a noun, it can mean "earth." As a verb, it can mean "hit a ground ball" or "rubbed or pushed harshly." In this sentence the "pitcher* ground *the ball into his hip." I think* ground *is a verb that means "pushed harshly."*

> **Mini-Lesson**
> See pages 107–108 of this Guide for additional work on **Using Words with Multiple Meanings**.

During Reading

COMPREHENSION FOCUS

Key Points	Strategies for Success
Target Skill ➡ Cause and Effect Students' ability to recognize cause-and-effect relationships in this narrative poem will help them understand the events and appreciate the dramatic tension.	**Mini-Lesson** Before students read "Casey at the Bat," you may want to teach the **Cause and Effect** lesson on pages 129–133 of this Guide. • Reread aloud lines 3 and 4, or have a volunteer reread them. Ask students to identify what Cooney and Burrows did and how the fans reacted. • Have students list additional cause-and-effect relationships in the **Cause-and-Effect Chart** on page 130 of this Guide.
Unusual Syntax and Difficult Language Some students may become frustrated or confused by the unfamiliar syntax used in some lines of this poem. Knowing how to reorder inverted sentences will help students make better sense of the text. Also, the diction used in this poem will be challenging for many students.	• Work with students to restate lines 11, 17, 31, 33, and 39. For example, help students restate line 11 as follows: "So a deathlike silence sat on that stricken multitude." • Tell students to refer to the Guide for Reading for help with difficult vocabulary.

Suggested Reading Options

• An oral reading of "Casey at the Bat" is available in *The Language of Literature* Audio Library. 🎧
• Oral Reading (see page 8 of this Guide).
• Additional options are described on page 8 of this Guide.

RECIPROCAL TEACHING SUGGESTION ➡ Questioning

Teacher Modeling *Pause & Reflect, page 177* Model using the questioning strategy to help students understand events in the narrative poem.

You could say *When I read the last stanza on page 176, I'm confused when the crowd becomes "joyous." I ask myself: What has happened to cheer them up? When I reread, I see that the fans believe that only Casey can help the team win. When the two batters before him surprise everyone by getting hits, Casey will get a turn at bat.*

Student Modeling *Page 178* Have several students model questioning the events in "Casey at the Bat." Offer these prompts: *Why doesn't Casey swing at the first pitch? Why does the crowd get angry at the umpire?* Students can also complete the **Active Reading SkillBuilder** on page 182 as they read.

Encourage students to use the other five reading strategies when appropriate as they read the rest of the poem. (See page 10 of this Guide.)

ENGLISH LEARNERS

1. Read the entire poem aloud to the class, using your voice and gestures to help convey the events in the poem. Encourage students to strive to understand and enjoy the basic story. Afterwards, have English learners work with English-proficient partners to paraphrase each stanza.

2. Students might benefit from reading along with the recording of "Casey at the Bat" provided in *The Language of Literature* Audio Library. ◌

After Reading

Recommended Follow-Up

- Thinking Through the Literature, page 303, *The Language of Literature*
- Choices & Challenges, page 304, *The Language of Literature*
- SkillBuilders, pages 182–183, *The InterActive Reader*™

Informal Assessment Options

Retell Have students work in pairs to retell the events in the poem from Casey's point of view. Offer these prompts: *Based on your reading of the poem, how do you think Casey feels about the opposing team? How do you think he feels about his abilities as a ballplayer as he faces the pitcher?*

Spot Check Look at the notes students made in the margins. Make sure their answers show an understanding of what they have read. Discuss students' answers to question 2 on page 181.

Formal Assessment Options in *The Language of Literature*

Selection Test, pages 45–46, Formal Assessment Book

For more teaching options, see pages 299–304 in *The Language of Literature* Teacher's Edition.

Additional Challenge

1. **Evaluate the Ending**
   Ask: *Would you have liked the ending more if Casey had hit a home run? Why or why not?*

2. **MARK IT UP ▷ Examine Character**
   Ask: *What are Casey's most important character traits?* Have students mark details in the poem to support their views.

Before Reading

Direct students' attention to the Connect to Your Life and Key to the Story activities on page 184 of *The InterActive Reader.*™ Use the following suggestions to prepare students to read the story.

Connect to Your Life
Ask students to describe how it feels to compete for something they care about, such as a sports trophy or a class award. Then ask: *How might your experience be different if you were competing against a close friend? How would you feel about doing that?* After students complete the activity, invite them to share their sentences with the rest of the class.

Key to the Story
Read aloud the quote from the story. Ask: *What does this statement seem to show about the speaker's values? Do you agree or disagree with what he says?* Then have students write their responses on the lines.

BUILD BACKGROUND Connect To History Explain that in "Amigo Brothers," two good friends compete against each other in a boxing tournament. Boxing was popular in Sumeria more than 5,000 years ago. It was later included as an event in the Olympic games of ancient Greece. Today, boxers are classified and matched in different divisions according to their weights. Amateur boxers compete without pay in local and national tournaments, such as the annual Golden Gloves competition.

WORDS TO KNOW

barrage
bedlam
dispel
evading
feint
game
improvise
pensively
perpetual
unbridled

Additional Words to Know

forcibly
   page 191, line 172
restrained
   page 191, line 172

VOCABULARY PREVIEW: Words to Know in Context

You can help students learn the Words to Know by reading aloud the following sentences or writing them on the board. Then show students how to use context clues to help them figure out the meaning.

barrage: Lucas covered his head to protect himself from the *barrage* of hailstones falling from the sky.

bedlam: He closed the window to shut out the *bedlam* on the streets; people were screaming, pushing each other, and throwing empty bottles.

dispel: The baseball star tried to *dispel* the rumors that he was injured; he kept playing and would not admit that he was in pain.

evading: The actress ducked into her limousine, *evading* the fans and photographers.

feint: The boxing coach taught his students how to *feint,* or fake a punch in order to trick their opponents.

game: Ask Lindsay to go along on your hiking trip; she's always *game* for an outdoor adventure.

improvise: Some public speakers work from a carefully written script, but others prefer to *improvise,* making up the speech as they go along.

pensively: Ana sat *pensively* in the waiting room, deep in thought about her dad's injury.

perpetual: Ever since his cat disappeared, Alex has been in a state of *perpetual* worry.

unbridled: With *unbridled* rage, the dog barked, snarled, and snapped at the rattlesnake.

forcibly: The rioting crowds were *forcibly* removed from the stadium by the police.

restrained: The prisoner had to be *restrained* with handcuffs when he grew violent.

VOCABULARY FOCUS Word Parts: Compound Words

Teacher Modeling Remind students that sometimes they can figure out the meaning of an unfamiliar compound word by thinking about the two words that make it up. Model the strategy, using the word *lightweight* (page 186, line 17).

Mini-Lesson See pages 99 and 102 of this Guide for additional work on **Word Parts: Compound Words.**

You could say I don't recognize the word lightweight, *but I see that it is made up of the two words* light *and* weight. Weight *refers to how heavy something is, so* lightweight *probably describes a person who is not very heavy. The words "lightweight champion" in line 17 probably refer to the boxing division for boxers who do not weigh very much.*

Student Modeling Ask a volunteer to model how to use compound words to determine the meaning of the word *knockouts* (page 186, line 33).

A student might say I can see that this word is made up of two smaller words, knock *and* outs. Knock *can mean "a hard blow."* Out *can mean many things, including "unconscious." In boxing,* knockouts *must be hard punches that leave an opponent unconscious or unable to continue fighting.*

During Reading

COMPREHENSION FOCUS

Key Points	Strategies for Success

Target Skill ➡ Predicting

The author of this story gives clues to help readers make predictions about how the main conflicts will be resolved. Students' ability to identify and use these clues is crucial to their understanding of the plot.

Mini-Lesson Before students read "Amigo Brothers," teach or review the **Predicting** lesson on pages 140–142 of this Guide.

- Read aloud lines 35–47 on page 187. Ask students to predict whether or not the two friends will fight one another and what will happen to the boys' friendship.

- Have students list their predictions and the details that support them in the **Active Reading SkillBuilder** on page 201.

Internal Conflict

Students must be aware of the internal conflict that the main characters experience between their goals as boxers and their feelings as friends.

At the *Pause and Reflect* on page 190, have students identify and read aloud details that illustrate each boy's internal conflict. Then ask: *What pact do they make? Do you think the pact is a good one? Why or why not?*

Suggested Reading Options

- An oral reading of "Amigo Brothers" is available in *The Language of Literature* Audio Library. ◯
- Shared Reading (see page 8 of this Guide).
- Additional options are described on page 8 of this Guide.

RECIPROCAL TEACHING SUGGESTION → Connecting

Teacher Modeling *Pause & Reflect, page 190* Model for students how to connect what they are reading with their own experience.

You could say *Tony and Felix are best friends, and they are both very serious about achieving their goals. If I had to compete against my best friend for something important, I would have mixed feelings too. I can understand why the upcoming fight puts a strain on their friendship.*

Student Modeling *Pause & Reflect, page 192* Have several students model connecting their experiences with what they read. Offer this prompt: *Have you ever felt nervous about the outcome of a sporting event or other activity you were involved in? How did you prepare for the event?*

Encourage students to use the other five reading strategies when appropriate as they proceed through the rest of the story. (See page 10 of this Guide.)

ENGLISH LEARNERS

1. Make sure that students understand the meanings of these idioms:

   blasting . . . each other, page 188

   psyching up, page 190

   Finding no takers, page 191

   passing some heavy time, page 191

   playing possum, page 197

   giving an inch, page 198

2. Students might benefit from reading along with the recording of "Amigo Brothers" provided in *The Language of Literature* Audio Library. ☊

After Reading

Recommended Follow-Up

- Thinking Through the Literature, page 372, *The Language of Literature*
- Choices & Challenges, pages 373–374, *The Language of Literature*
- SkillBuilders, pages 201–203, *The InterActive Reader™*

Informal Assessment Options

Retell Have pairs of students retell the events of the story as if they were Tony and Felix, now grown to adulthood, reminiscing together about their boxing competition.

Spot Check Look at the notes students made in the margins of the story. Invite them to explain their answers and discuss any questions they still have about the story.

Formal Assessment Options in *The Language of Literature*

Selection Quiz, page 17, Unit Three Resource Book
Selection Test, pages 55–56, Formal Assessment Book

For more teaching options, see pages 361–374 in *The Language of Literature* Teacher's Edition.

Additional Challenge

1. **Evaluate the Climax**
   Work with students to identify the climax of the story (lines 440–447). Have students discuss whether they find this scene realistic or not.

2. **MARK IT UP** ➤ **Connect to Life**
   Ask: *What do you think Felix and Tony learn from this experience?* Have students mark passages in the story to explain their views.

Before Reading

Direct students' attention to the Connect to Your Life and Key to the Drama activities on page 204 of *The InterActive Reader.*™ Use the following suggestions to prepare students to read the drama.

Connect to Your Life
Ask students to think about a time when they faced a strange, unexpected, or even dangerous situation. Invite volunteers to describe how they reacted. Then ask: *Have you ever been a part of or seen a group when it faced a frightening situation? How did the group react? How would you compare the group's reaction to your individual reaction to danger?* Have students fill out their lists. Then call on volunteers to share their examples.

Key to the Drama
With students, define and discuss the words *prejudices* ("preconceived judgments or opinions") and *suspicion* ("doubt or mistrust"). Then have partners work together to add related words to the web. Finally, read aloud the sentence in the Key to the Drama. Ask students what they think the sentence means. Ask: *When have prejudices killed people in the past? Who died? Why were they killed?*

BUILD BACKGROUND Connect to History Tell students that *The Twilight Zone* was a television series created by Rod Serling. Eerie and very suspenseful, the series became one of the most popular shows in television history during its 1959–1965 run. Its stories often involved ordinary people in suburban settings typical of the late 1950s. Point out that the events in the series were far from ordinary, however; they were a window into an imaginary world beyond ours—the twilight zone. As the characters faced the unknown, they reacted in both typical and unexpected ways. *The Monsters Are Due on Maple Street* originally aired on March 4, 1960.

WORDS TO KNOW

- antagonism
- contorted
- defiant
- flustered
- idiosyncrasy
- incriminate
- intense
- legitimate
- optimistic
- persistent

VOCABULARY PREVIEW: Words to Know In Context

You can help students learn the Words to Know by reading aloud the following sentences or writing them on the board. Then show students how to use context clues to help them figure out the meaning.

antagonism: Ever since their fight, David has continued to show *antagonism* toward Mina.

contorted: When he broke his ankle, the athlete's face was *contorted* with pain.

defiant: In a *defiant* move, Sean tore up the contract and threw it in his boss's face.

flustered: Jeannie gets very *flustered,* blushing and stammering whenever Renaldo talks to her.

idiosyncrasy: Wearing a heavy coat on a hot day is one of her many *idiosyncrasies.*

incriminate: Since there is no evidence to *incriminate* the suspect, the police cannot prove that he is guilty.

intense: Julia felt an *intense* pain in her knee, as if she'd been hit by a baseball bat.

legitimate: Spending the weekend at the beach is not a *legitimate* excuse for not doing your homework.

optimistic: Marcus worries before a test, but Jeremy feels *optimistic* and expects to get an "A."

persistent: If you want the job at the store, you'll have to be *persistent* and call the owner again and again.

VOCABULARY FOCUS Word Parts: Suffixes

Teacher Modeling Tell students that they can sometimes figure out the meaning of an unfamiliar word by thinking about the word parts it contains. Then use the following modeling suggestions for the word *reflective* (page 208, line 56).

You could say I'm not sure what the word reflective *means, but I can try breaking the word into parts. I recognize the suffix -ive from words like* combative *and* active. *From these words I can guess that –ive means "having the quality of." I also see the base word* reflect, *which can mean "to think in a careful way." I can figure out from these word parts that* reflective *must mean "having the quality of careful thought."*

Student Modeling Now have students follow your lead. Ask a volunteer to model using the strategy to figure out the meaning of *lighten* (page 214, line 240).

A student might say I'm not familiar with the word lighten. *However, I do know that the base word* light *can mean "not serious" or "carefree," and the suffix -en means "to cause to be." Since this sentence describes people who are laughing to try to hide their fears,* lighten *must mean "to make less serious."*

> **Mini-Lesson** See pages 99 and 101 of this Guide for additional work on **Word Parts: Suffixes.**

During Reading

COMPREHENSION FOCUS

Key Points	Strategies for Success
Target Skill ➡ Compare and Contrast It is essential for students to contrast the neighbors' behavior before and after the strange events begin to happen.	**Mini-Lesson** Before students read *The Monsters are Due on Maple Street,* teach or review the **Compare and Contrast** lesson on pages 134–136 of this Guide. • Read aloud lines 1–21 on page 206 and lines 411–427 on page 220. Ask: *What are the neighbors doing at the beginning of the drama? How do they act toward each other? How do they behave after Les Goodman's car starts by itself?* • Have students fill in the **Venn Diagram** on page 135 of this guide during or after reading.
Author's Purposes In order to understand the drama's message, it is important that students identify the author's purposes for writing.	• Read aloud lines 651–660 on page 228. Ask students to discuss the author's purpose for writing this passage. Ask: *What opinion does the author express? What does he try to persuade readers to believe? Do you agree with the author's message?* • Have students fill in the **Active Reading SkillBuilder** on page 229 and record details from the drama that reflect the author's purposes for writing.

Suggested Reading Options

• An oral reading of *The Monsters Are Due on Maple Street* is available in *The Language of Literature* Audio Library. ◯
• Partner/Cooperative Reading (see page 8 of this Guide).
• Additional options are described on page 8 of this Guide.

RECIPROCAL TEACHING SUGGESTION ➡ Evaluating

Teacher Modeling *Pause & Reflect, page 224* To help students form opinions about why Charlie shoots Pete Van Horn, model the evaluating strategy.

You could say *I was surprised when Charlie shoots Pete. I didn't understand why Charlie suddenly becomes so violent, but then I realized that he is very frightened. Charlie and some of the other neighbors have become so fearful that they aren't thinking logically. Charlie acts the way he does because he feels that his life is threatened. Even so, I think Charlie is reckless to shoot before he knows who is approaching.*

Student Modeling *Pause & Reflect, page 227* Have several students model the evaluating strategy to form opinions about why the neighbors turn on each other. Offer this prompt: *Why do the neighbors attack Charlie? What does Charlie accuse Tommy of? How do the neighbors react when their friends come under suspicion? Why do you think they are acting this way?*

Encourage students to use the other five reading strategies when appropriate as they proceed through the rest of the drama. (See page 10 of this Guide.)

ENGLISH LEARNERS

1. Point out that at the beginning of the drama, the narrator describes a typical suburban neighborhood in the 1950s or early 1960s. You may need to explain terms like "front-porch gliders," "hopscotch," and "the bell of an ice-cream vendor."

2. Students might benefit from reading along with the recording of *The Monsters Are Due on Maple Street* provided in *The Language of Literature* Audio Library. 🎧

After Reading

Recommended Follow-Up

• Thinking Through the Literature, page 429, *The Language of Literature*

• Choices & Challenges, pages 430–431, *The Language of Literature*

• SkillBuilders, pages 229–231, *The InterActive Reader*™

Informal Assessment Options

Retell Have pairs of students role-play the aliens as they describe the events on Maple Street to their leader. Offer these prompts:

• *How do the people act when Tommy talks about ships from outer space?*

• *What do the people do when Les Goodman's car starts by itself?*

• *Why does Charlie shoot Pete Van Horn? Why do the people turn on Charlie?*

• *What makes them start turning on their other neighbors?*

Spot Check Look at the notes students made in the margins. Invite them to explain their answers and discuss any questions they still have about the drama.

Formal Assessment Options in *The Language of Literature*

Selection Quiz, page 45, Unit Three Resource Book

Selection Test, pages 65–66, Formal Assessment Book

For more teaching options, see pages 415–431 in *The Language of Literature* Teacher's Edition.

Additional Challenge

1. Write a New Ending

Have students write a new ending to explain what happens after all the neighbors begin accusing each other. Ask students to tell what the neighbors do to each other. To get students started, ask: *How do the neighbors feel at the end of the drama? How do they treat each other? What do you think they will do to each other out of fear?*

2. ▐▌MARK IT UP ⟩ Understand Theme

Tell students that one of the themes of the drama is that fear can cause people to look for a scapegoat. Explain that a scapegoat is a person or group of people who are blamed for causing a particular problem. Discuss how the author develops this theme in this drama. Then have students underline passages in the drama in which the neighbors look for and find scapegoats.

Before Reading

Direct students' attention to the Connect to Your Life and Key to the Story activities on page 232 of *The InterActive Reader.*™ Use the following suggestions to prepare students to read the story.

Connect to Your Life
Discuss the meaning of the word *adapt* with students. Ask them to share examples of ways people adapt to new environments. Students may mention immigrants learning a new language or explorers eating native species of food. Discuss why adaptation can be an important survival skill. Then have students fill out their web. If students have difficulty thinking of a time when they had to adapt, encourage them to think about what it was like to start a new grade in school, spend a night away from home for the first time, or learn a new skill.

Key to the Story
Write the word *colonization* on the board and discuss its meaning with students. Explain that the main characters in this futuristic story try to colonize the planet Mars. (You may wish to point out the location of Mars on a map or model of the solar system.) Work with students to create a web of words related to *colonization*. Then have them complete the activity.

BUILD BACKGROUND The Red Planet Explain to students that in the 1800s, astronomers saw variations on the surface of Mars that gave the appearance of canals. People at that time wondered if these "canals" had been built by intelligent beings. We now know this theory is untrue, but Mars is still a popular setting for science fiction stories, novels, and films that depict alien life. Ask students who have read such stories and novels or seen such films to describe different ways in which Mars is portrayed.

WORDS TO KNOW

amiss

dwindle

flimsy

forlorn

recede

Additional Words to Know

submerged
   page 234, line 25

drenched
   page 237, line 113

dismay
   page 241, line 227

suspended
   page 251, line 575

VOCABULARY PREVIEW: Words to Know in Context

You can help students learn the Words to Know by reading aloud the following sentences or writing them on the board. Then show students how to use context clues to help them figure out the meaning.

amiss: Henry knew something was *amiss,* or wrong, when he saw that the front door was open and no one was home.

dwindle: Their savings *dwindled* because they spent more money than they made.

flimsy: We had only a *flimsy,* floppy little paper sign for our lemonade stand; it blew right off the table with the first strong wind.

forlorn: The abandoned puppy looked *forlorn;* it lay with its chin on the ground and its ears drooping.

recede: It took nine days for the flood waters to *recede;* before that, everyone was riding around town in rowboats.

---

submerged: Sea plants grow best when *submerged,* or placed under water.

drenched: After sitting in the rain for three hours, Betsy was *drenched.*

dismay: Gary felt *dismay,* or dread, when he read the first question on the test.

suspended: The wind chimes hung *suspended* from the top of the window.

VOCABULARY FOCUS: Using Words with Multiple Meanings

Teacher Modeling Remind students that many words have more than one meaning. They can often figure out which meaning of a word is intended in a sentence by looking for context clues. Model using this strategy for the word *draw* (page 234, line 23).

You might say I'm not sure which meaning of draw *is intended in this sentence.* Draw *can mean "sketch," or it can mean "to cause to flow forth." I can look for context clues in the surrounding words and phrases. The words "his soul from him, as marrow comes from a white bone" show that* draw *means "to cause to flow forth" here.*

Student Modeling Ask students to model figuring out the intended meaning of the word *seal* (page 235, line 61).

A student could say A seal *can be a type of aquatic mammal or a device used to keep something closed. The clues "morning paper" and "broke" help me figure out that in this sentence,* seal *means "a device used to keep something closed."*

Mini-Lesson See pages 107–108 of this Guide for additional work on **Using Words with Multiple Meanings.**

During Reading

COMPREHENSION FOCUS

Key Points	Strategies for Success
Target Skill ➡ Sequence It is crucial for students to keep track of events and recognize parallels within the circular plot structure.	**Mini-Lesson** Before students read "Dark They Were, and Golden-Eyed," you may want to teach or review the **Sequence** lesson on pages 126–128 of this Guide. • At the *Pause & Reflect* prompts on pages 235 and 245, have volunteers summarize events so far. • During or after reading, students can complete the **Literary Analysis SkillBuilder** on page 256 of *The InterActive Reader.*™
Foreshadowing Students must be able to identify examples of foreshadowing to appreciate the suspense of the story.	At the *Pause & Reflect* on page 235, work with students to identify words and phrases that help create the story's uneasy mood and menacing tone. In particular, draw students' attention to lines 22–26 and ask what they think this paragraph might **foreshadow,** or suggest about later events. Have students identify additional examples of foreshadowing as they read on. Students may mention the conversation between Mr. Bittering and David on page 236 and the changed plants and animal on page 240.

Suggested Reading Options

• An oral reading of "Dark They Were, and Golden-Eyed" is available in *The Language of Literature* Audio Library. ◯
• Independent Reading (see page 8 of this Guide).
• Additional options are described on page 8 of this Guide.

RECIPROCAL TEACHING SUGGESTION → Visualizing

Teacher Modeling *Pause & Reflect, page 235* Model for students how to use sensory details to form mental pictures of the landscape on Mars.

You could say The phrases "lying like children's delicate bones," "blowing lakes of grass," "deep dome of Martian sky," and "racing hiss of wind" help me picture how haunting and desolate the Martian landscape is. I can understand why Mr. Bittering feels uneasy here.

Student Modeling *Pause & Reflect, page 240* Have several students model how to visualize the details in lines 134–141. Offer these prompts: *What are the colors of the Martian landscape? What details show what the wind and sun feel like and their effects on the environment?*

Encourage students to use the other five reading strategies when appropriate as they proceed through the rest of the story. (See page 10 of this Guide.)

ENGLISH LEARNERS

1. Make sure students understand the basic story premise: that a group of humans set up a colony on Mars and are stranded there when war on Earth destroys their means of returning home. Slowly they find themselves turning into Martians.

2. Students might benefit from reading along with the recording of "Dark They Were, and Golden-Eyed" provided in *The Language of Literature* Audio Library. ◯

After Reading

Recommended Follow-Up

- Thinking Through the Literature, page 491, *The Language of Literature*
- Choices & Challenges, page 503, *The Language of Literature*
- SkillBuilders, pages 255–257, *The InterActive Reader*™

Informal Assessment Options

Retell Have students work in small groups to retell the story from Mrs. Bittering's perspective. Encourage students to skim the text for clues about how she looked and acted in the beginning of the story and how her appearance and opinions changed over time.

Spot Check Look at the notes students made in the margins. Make sure their answers show an understanding of what they have read. Pay particular attention to questions 1 and 2 on page 254, as these questions check students' comprehension of the ending and the circular plot structure.

Formal Assessment Options in *The Language of Literature*

Selection Quiz, page 76, Unit Three Resource Book

Selection Test, pages 75–76, Formal Assessment Book

For more teaching options, see pages 478–491 and pages 502–503 in *The Language of Literature* Teacher's Edition.

Additional Challenge

1. **Compare Viewpoints**
   Have students write two diary entries from the point of view of one of the Bittering children. One should be written just after the family's arrival on Mars, and the other should be written during their transformation.

2. ▮▮▮ **MARK IT UP** ⟩ **Analyze Character Changes**
   Ask: *How would you describe the ways that the Bitterings change in this story?* Have students underline details that describe the characters' gradual transformation. Encourage students to look for details about the characters' appearance, their likes and dislikes, their moods, and the language they speak.

Before Reading

Direct students' attention to the Connect to Your Life and Key to the Poem activities on page 258 of *The InterActive Reader.*™ Use the following suggestions to prepare students to read the poem.

Connect to Your Life
Ask students to describe examples of real or fictional people who have made great sacrifices for others. Ask: *What are some reasons people make such sacrifices?* Have students complete the activity and share their responses. Explain that this poem tells of a sacrifice made for love.

Key to the Poem
Discuss how people traveled before the invention of trains or cars. Students may mention that people traveled on foot, on horseback, or by stagecoach. Point out that one danger travelers faced in the 1700s was highway robbery. Have a volunteer read aloud the "What's the Big Idea?" paragraph. Discuss why some highwaymen might have stolen from the rich to give to the poor, and why stories about them and their adventures became popular. Have students make their lists and share their responses.

BUILD BACKGROUND
Connect to Legend Tell students that Robin Hood, a legendary highway robber, is still popular in stories and movies today. Explain that Robin Hood, who may or may not have actually existed, became the popular subject of many English ballads during the 12th century. Discuss both the negative and positive attributes of the image of the highwayman, and encourage students to keep these qualities in mind as they read the poem.

Strategies for Reading Poetry

- Notice the form of the poem: the number of lines and their shape on the page.
- Read the poem aloud a few times. Listen for rhymes and rhythms.
- Visualize the images and comparisons.
- Mark words and phrases that appeal to you.
- Ask yourself what message the poet is trying to send.
- Think about what the poem is saying to you.

FOCUS ON POETRY

The discussion points below will help prepare students for reading "The Highwayman."

- **Rhythm** Read aloud lines 1–2 of "The Highwayman" on page 260, and help students identify the rhythmic pattern by clapping on the stressed syllables. Point out that the beat mimics the gait of a galloping horse, and ask students why they think the poet used this rhythm. Then read aloud lines 3–5, and draw students' attention to the rhythmic shift in line 4. Discuss the effect this shift has on the poem's mood and tone. Students may mention that the repetition in line 4 adds emphasis and drama to the narrative.

- **Alliteration** The poet uses alliteration to make the language in the poem more musical. Direct students' attention to lines 2–3 on page 260, and call on volunteers to find examples of alliteration ("**g**hostly **g**alleon," "**r**oad was a **r**ibbon"). Suggest to students that as they read the poem, they should pay attention to examples of alliteration and other sound devices that help make the language vivid.

VOCABULARY FOCUS Word Parts: Compound Words

Teacher Modeling Remind students that they can often use the meanings of the smaller words within a compound word to help them figure out its meaning. Model using the word *landlord* (page 262, line 16).

You could say *I'm not sure what a landlord is, but I see the smaller words* land *and* lord *in it. I know* land *can mean "earth" or "territory." A* lord *is a man of high rank, usually someone who owns property. The inn's* landlord *must be its owner.*

Student Modeling Call on a volunteer to model figuring out the meaning of the word *madman* (page 272, line 85).

A student might say *I can see that this word is made up of two smaller words,* mad *and* man. Mad *can mean "insane" or "angry." I think a* madman *must be a man who is or seems to be insane.*

Mini-Lesson
See pages 99 and 102 of this Guide for additional work on **Word Parts: Compound Words.**

During Reading

COMPREHENSION FOCUS

Key Points	Strategies for Success

Target Skill ➡ Making Inferences

For students to understand the plot of this narrative poem, they must be able to make inferences about events and about the characters' feelings and actions.

Mini-Lesson Before students read the poem, you may want to teach or review the **Making Inferences** lesson on pages 137–139 of this Guide.

• Read aloud lines 16–30 on pages 262 and 264. Then have students infer how Tim the ostler feels toward the highwayman, and why.

• After reading, have students use the **Inference Chart** on page 138 of this Guide to make additional inferences. If students need more help, offer these prompts: *What clues are there on pages 262 and 264 that suggest that Bess and the highwayman are in love? Based on your reading of page 266, what inferences can you make about the character of the redcoats?*

Antiquated Language and Style

The antiquated language and unusual syntax in this poem may confuse students. They may need help to understand the dramatic events and to enjoy the vivid narration.

Point out the Reading Tip on page 261, and show students how to use the Guide for Reading, beginning on page 261, for help in understanding difficult words and passages. Tell students to read difficult lines aloud a few times. Then have pairs of students paraphrase each stanza to retell the story of the highwayman.

Suggested Reading Options

• An oral reading of "The Highwayman" is available in *The Language of Literature* Audio Library. ◠
• Oral Reading (see page 8 of this Guide).
• Additional options are described on page 8 of this Guide.

RECIPROCAL TEACHING SUGGESTION ➡ Predicting

Teacher Modeling *Pause & Reflect, page 266* Read aloud lines 49–54. Model for students how to make predictions based on story clues.

You could say *The highwayman and Bess, the landlord's daughter, seem to love each other very much. He seems determined to come back to her, no matter what. However, the soldiers are holding Bess hostage. I predict that the highwayman will return in the evening, and the soldiers will be waiting to capture or kill him.*

Student Modeling *Pause & Reflect, Page 270* Have several students model making predictions based on the clues in lines 55–60. Offer these prompts: *Why does Bess twist her hands? What is she trying to do? What do you think she will do now that she is able to reach the trigger of the musket?*

Encourage students to use the other five reading strategies when appropriate as they proceed through the rest of the poem. (See page 10 of this Guide.)

ENGLISH LEARNERS

1. The antiquated language and poetic structure of "The Highwayman" may make it especially challenging for English learners to understand. Summarize the poem before reading it aloud. Afterwards, have students work with English-proficient partners to paraphrase it.

2. Students might benefit from reading along with the recording of "The Highwayman" provided in *The Language of Literature* Audio Library. ◯

After Reading

Recommended Follow-Up

- Thinking Through the Literature, page 570, *The Language of Literature*
- Choices & Challenges, page 571, *The Language of Literature*
- SkillBuilders, pages 274–275, *The InterActive Reader™*

Informal Assessment Options

Retell Have students work in small groups to prepare and present pantomimed stagings of the events in the poem.

Spot Check Look at the notes students made in the margins. Make sure their answers show an understanding of what they have read. To check comprehension, pay particular attention to the cause-and-effect question on page 271.

Formal Assessment Options in *The Language of Literature*

Selection Test, pages 95–96, Formal Assessment Book

For more teaching options, see pages 564–571 in *The Language of Literature* Teacher's Edition.

Additional Challenge

1. **Examine a Character**
   Have students recall that highwaymen were armed thieves. Then ask students to write a paragraph that answers these questions: *In what ways does the poet make this highwayman seem noble? Do you think it is right to portray a thief as a heroic person?* Have students use details about the highwayman's appearance, actions, and love for Bess to explain their answers.

2. **◼‖‖ MARK IT UP ⟩ Analyze Images**
   "The Highwayman" is full of vivid images that refer to colors. Have students underline examples of these images. Then discuss how the color references affect the poem's mood. Ask: *How do the images of color help you picture the highwayman, Bess, and Tim more clearly?*

Before Reading

Direct students' attention to the Connect to Your Life and Key to the Informative Article activities on page 276 of *The InterActive Reader.*™ Use the following suggestions to prepare students to read the article.

Connect to Your Life
Tell students that in 1912, the *Titanic,* the world's largest luxury liner, struck an iceberg in the Atlantic Ocean and sank, killing approximately 1,522 people. Then ask students if they can think of other large-scale disasters (natural or caused by humans) they have heard about. Have students work in small groups to complete their web; then invite them to share their answers with the class.

Key to the Informative Article
Ask students what interesting facts or details they know about the *Titanic*. List their responses on the board. Have them write this information in the first column of their chart. Then have students complete the second column independently. Tell them to complete the third column after they finish reading the article.

BUILD BACKGROUND Connect To Technology Tell students that modern-day scientists use mini-submarines called submersibles to explore shipwrecks. A submersible named *Alvin* and its attached underwater robot, *Jason Junior,* explored the wreck of the *Titanic*. Seeing this haunting wreck up close enabled observers to vividly imagine what life was like for the passengers and crew on the ship, both before and during its awful final moments.

WORDS TO KNOW

- accommodations
- dazzled
- eerie
- feverishly
- indefinitely
- list
- novelty
- prophecy
- toll
- tribute

VOCABULARY PREVIEW: Words to Know in Context

You can help students learn the Words to Know by reading aloud the following sentences or writing them on the board. Then show students how to use context clues to help them figure out the meaning.

accommodations: We drove into town late at night and could find no *accommodations;* all of the motels were full.

dazzled: Esmerelda was so *dazzled* by the bright sunlight that she could hardly see.

eerie: As I stood outside in the dark, I had an *eerie* feeling that someone was watching me; it made me very nervous.

feverishly: He worked so *feverishly* to get the project done that he went without eating or sleeping for two days.

indefinitely: If we don't get directions to Harry's house, we could be driving around *indefinitely* trying to find it.

list: The tower of blocks had begun to *list* so far to one side that it looked like it might fall over.

novelty: To you, a key chain is nothing new, but to a little child, it's quite a *novelty*.

prophecy: The old man made a *prophecy* predicting that the town would be destroyed by fire.

toll: The death *toll* from the earthquake keeps rising as rescue teams find more bodies amid the rubble.

tribute: In a lovely *tribute* to their mothers, the children of the school read aloud their Mother's Day poems.

VOCABULARY FOCUS: Using Context Clues

Teacher Modeling Remind students that they can often use context clues to figure out the meaning of unfamiliar words. Then use the following modeling strategy for the word *gymnasium* (page 281, line 111).

You could say I'm not sure what gymnasium *means, but I see these clues in the sentence: "exercise equipment," "stationary bicycles," and "rowing machines." These items are all located in the gymnasium. I think a gymnasium must be an exercise room. The word* gym *must be a shortened form of this word.*

Student Modeling Now have students follow your lead. Ask volunteers to model how to use context clues to determine the meaning of *outfitted* (page 279, line 49).

A student might say I don't know what outfitted *means. I look for clues and see these words in the same sentence: "carefully prepared down to the last detail." The next paragraph describes some special features the* Titanic *was equipped with. I think* outfitted *means "equipped."*

Mini-Lesson See pages 95–98 of this Guide for additional work on **Using Context Clues.**

During Reading

COMPREHENSION FOCUS

Key Points	Strategies for Success
Target Skill ➡ Distinguishing Fact from Opinion Author Robert Ballard includes both facts and opinions in this article to engage readers and help them understand events. Students' ability to distinguish between facts and opinions is crucial to their comprehension and enjoyment of the article.	**Mini-Lesson** Before students read the excerpt from *Exploring the* Titanic, you may want to teach the **Fact and Opinion** lesson on pages 143–145 of this Guide. • Read aloud lines 55–76 on pages 279 and 280. Have volunteers identify facts and opinions in the passage. • After reading, students can complete the **Active Reading SkillBuilder** on page 297 of this Guide.
Cause and Effect The author carefully describes the cause-and-effect chain of events that led to the disaster. Students must be able to identify these causes and effects in order to understand what happened, and why.	At the *Pause & Reflect* on page 287, ask: *How did the captain and crew treat the initial iceberg warnings? What effect did this ultimately have?* As students continue reading, have them identify the reasons why the *Titanic* sank.

Suggested Reading Options

• An oral reading of the excerpt from *Exploring the* Titanic is available in *The Language of Literature* Audio Library. 🎧
• Partner/Cooperative Reading (see page 8 of this Guide).
• Additional options are described on page 8 of this Guide.

RECIPROCAL TEACHING SUGGESTION ➡ Evaluating

Teacher Modeling *Pause & Reflect, page 280* Model for students how to form an opinion about the builders' decision to build the *Titanic*.

You could say *The* Titanic's *builders seemed to be mostly interested in building a huge, floating palace that would be grander than any other ship in the world. One eyewitness said that the* Titanic *was built on a "nightmare scale." I think that the* Titanic's *builders were more interested in grandeur than safety.*

Student Modeling *Pause & Reflect, page 287* Have students evaluate how well the crew responded to the threat of icebergs. Offer this prompt: *How many iceberg warnings did the* Titanic *receive? Did the officers and crew pay enough attention to the warnings? What more could they have done to avoid the icebergs ahead?*

Encourage students to use the other five reading strategies when appropriate as they proceed through the rest of the article. (See page 10 of this Guide.)

ENGLISH LEARNERS

1. Make sure students understand how the following facts contributed to the scope of the disaster: the dismissal of the iceberg warnings, the size and speed of the ship, and the limited number and poor use of the lifeboats.
2. Students might benefit from reading along with the recording of the excerpt from *Exploring the* Titanic provided in *The Language of Literature* Audio Library. ◯

After Reading

Recommended Follow-Up

- Thinking Through the Literature, page 672, *The Language of Literature*
- Choices & Challenges, pages 673–674, *The Language of Literature*
- SkillBuilders, pages 297–299, *The InterActive Reader*™

Informal Assessment Options

Retell Have students work in small groups to retell events from this article as if they were survivors describing the experience. Have each group member role-play a passenger traveling in a different class.

Spot Check Look at the notes students made in the margins of the article. Invite them to explain their answers and discuss any questions they still have.

Formal Assessment Options in *The Language of Literature*

Selection Quiz, page 10, Unit Five Resource Book

Selection Test, pages 107–108, Formal Assessment Book

For more teaching options, see pages 658–674 in *The Language of Literature* Teacher's Edition.

Additional Challenge

1. **Evaluate Character**
   Have students work in teams to debate whether Captain Smith's actions aboard the *Titanic* were heroic or not. Tell students to mark passages in the article to support their opinion.
2. **|||MARK IT UP⟩ Draw Conclusions**
   Have students mark passages in the article that describe mistakes that could have been avoided. Then ask: *If a member of your family had died on the* Titanic, *would you have filed a lawsuit? If so, whom would you have sued and why?*

Before Reading

Direct students' attention to the Connect to Your Life and Key to the Memoir activities on page 300 of *The InterActive Reader.*™ Use the following suggestions to prepare students to read the memoir.

Connect to Your Life
Ask students: *What does the word* freedom *mean to you?* Record their responses on the board. Then have students work in small groups to brainstorm additional words related to the concept of freedom. Finally, have them complete the Connect to Your Life activity independently.

Key to the Memoir
Invite volunteers to share any facts they know about Nelson Mandela or the struggle against apartheid in South Africa. Ask a student to read aloud the Key to the Memoir paragraphs. Discuss questions students may have about the information, and ask: *What qualities do you think Nelson Mandela might have? How can you tell? What else would you like to learn about him?*

BUILD BACKGROUND Connect to History Explain to students that in 1948, the white-controlled government of South Africa established apartheid, a strict form of racial segregation. Under apartheid, the white minority had control of the government while black and other nonwhite South Africans—the majority of the population—had no political rights. Their freedom of movement was restricted, and they were required to live in designated areas and attend separate schools. Anti-apartheid leaders such as Nelson Mandela struggled to dismantle the repressive system, which was repealed in 1989. Today they continue to work towards equality for all South Africans.

WORDS TO KNOW

curtailed
incomprehensible
indivisible
resiliency
transitory

Additional Words to Know

comrade
   page 302, line 19
obstructed
   page 305, line 102
attorney
   page 305, line 113

VOCABULARY PREVIEW: Words to Know in Context

You can help students learn the Words to Know by reading aloud the following sentences or writing them on the board. Then show students how to use context clues to help them figure out the meaning.

curtailed: We hoped to play tennis for an hour, but our game was *curtailed* by a sudden thunderstorm; we played for only twenty minutes.

incomprehensible: Joe could not understand how he didn't win the class election after all his hard work; the defeat was just *incomprehensible* to him.

indivisible: The team members have such strong unity that they are *indivisible*; no one can tear them apart.

resiliency: I'm impressed by Ronnie's *resiliency*; she can bounce back from any defeat.

transitory: Wealth and fame are only *transitory* goods, but wisdom and love can last forever.

comrade: The two soldiers had been *comrades* for years, fighting together in battle after battle.

obstructed: Emily tried to see the stage, but a tall man with a large hat *obstructed* her view.

attorney: Yes, my mother is an *attorney*, but she practices business law; you'll need a criminal lawyer for your case.

VOCABULARY FOCUS Word Parts: Roots

Teacher Modeling Remind students that they can sometimes use familiar words or roots to figure out the meaning of a word. Model using the word *policy* (page 302, line 1).

You could say *I don't recognize this word, but it looks like the word* police, *which I know. Maybe the two words have the same root and similar meanings. I know that the police is the government agency or department that enforces laws. I think* policy *might also have to do with laws or regulations. When I look it up, I see that* policy *means "a government plan or course of action," and that both* policy *and* police *contain the Greek root* polis, *which has to do with cities and civic organizations.*

Student Modeling Ask a student volunteer to model figuring out the meaning of *inclinations* (page 304, line 63).

A student might say *I don't recognize this word, but the first part looks like another word I know,* incline, *which can mean "to lean" or "a slanted surface." Maybe these words have similar meanings. I think* inclinations *might mean "leanings" or "slants." When I look it up in the dictionary, I see that it does mean "leanings" and also "preferences." Both words come from the Latin root* clinare, *"to lean."*

Mini-Lesson See pages 103–104 of this Guide for additional work on **Word Parts: Roots.**

During Reading

COMPREHENSION FOCUS

Key Points	Strategies for Success

Target Skill ➡ Main Idea and Details

In this memoir, Mandela uses many details from his life to illustrate his ideas about freedom and the struggle against apartheid. To understand the memoir, students must see the links between main ideas and their supporting details.

Mini-Lesson Before students read the excerpt from *Long Walk to Freedom,* teach or review the **Main Idea and Supporting Details** lesson on pages 122–125 of this Guide.

• At each *Pause & Reflect,* work with students to identify the main idea and supporting details in each paragraph of that section.

• After reading, students can complete the **Active Reading SkillBuilder** on page 307 of *The InterActive Reader.*™

Making Inferences

Mandela alludes to the fact that he made choices that hurt his family, but he does not describe these choices or their consequences. Students must infer what these choices and consequences were in order to appreciate South Africa's struggle and Mandela's commitment to the cause of freedom.

At the *Pause & Reflect* on page 305, ask: *What "twin obligations" does Mandela refer to? Why was it difficult for him to fulfill both of these obligations? To which obligation did he give higher priority? How do you think his involvement in the anti-apartheid movement affected his wife and children?*

Suggested Reading Options

• An oral reading of the excerpt from *Long Walk to Freedom* is available in *The Language of Literature* Audio Library. ◠

• Independent Reading (see page 8 of this Guide).

• Additional options are described on page 8 of this Guide.

RECIPROCAL TEACHING SUGGESTION ➡ Evaluating

Teacher Modeling *Pause & Reflect, page 303* Model using the evaluating strategy to help students form opinions about Nelson Mandela's character.

You could say *Nelson Mandela writes that he often felt fear but did not let it stop him from acting boldly. Also, despite the difficulty and injustice he has faced, he maintains his faith in humanity. I think Mandela is a courageous, hopeful, and determined man. These qualities make him a great leader.*

Student Modeling *Pause & Reflect, page 305* Have students model forming opinions about Mandela's commitment to his people. Offer this prompt: *Why did Mandela choose to devote his life to his people rather than his family? Do you agree with his reasons for making this choice? Why or why not?*

Encourage students to use the other five reading strategies when appropriate as they proceed through the rest of the memoir. (See page 10 of this Guide.)

After Reading

Recommended Follow-Up

- Thinking Through the Literature, page 737, *The Language of Literature*
- Choices & Challenges, pages 738–739, *The Language of Literature*
- SkillBuilders, pages 307–309, *The InterActive Reader™*

Informal Assessment Options

Retell Have students work in groups of three to summarize the selection, emphasizing the main ideas. Explain that each group member should retell a separate section of the piece.

Spot Check Look at the notes students made in the margins. Ask students who used the **?** notation whether they were able to clear up their confusion, and if so, how.

Formal Assessment Options in *The Language of Literature*

Selection Quiz, page 41, Unit Five Resource Book

Selection Test, pages 115–116, Formal Assessment Book

For more teaching options, see pages 732–739 in *The Language of Literature* Teacher's Edition.

Additional Challenge

1. **Respond to a Quote**
   Read aloud the sentence "Man's goodness is a flame that can be hidden but never extinguished" (page 303, lines 43–44). Have students write a paragraph telling what this statement means, whether they agree, and why. Ask: *Do you think that human beings are inherently good? Do you think that people who do very bad things are capable of change? Why or why not?*

2. **MARK IT UP ⬦ Analyze Tone**
   Remind students that tone is an author's attitude toward his or her subject. Ask: *How would you describe Mandela's attitude toward the struggle for freedom? For example, would you say that his tone is serious or humorous, positive or bitter?* Have students mark phrases or passages in the memoir that support their views.

Before Reading

Direct students' attention to the Connect to Your Life and Key to the Biography activities on page 310 of *The InterActive Reader.*™ Use the following suggestions to prepare students to read the biography.

Connect to Your Life
Ask students to think about a time when they have faced a difficult challenge. Ask: *At such a time, who do you think about to help you deal with the situation?* Explain that Anthony Burns, the subject of this biography, tries thinking about home and family during an especially difficult experience.

Key to the Biography
Encourage students to discuss what they already know about slavery. Then read aloud the Key to the Biography. Explain to students that runaway slaves often sought freedom by fleeing to states where slavery was outlawed. However, in 1850 the newly enacted Fugitive Slave Law gave slave owners the legal right to track down, catch, and return slaves who had fled to antislavery states. Finally, have students complete their lists, adding two or three questions they have about Burns.

BUILD BACKGROUND Connect to History Tell students that under the Fugitive Slave Law, people caught helping slaves escape could be fined or imprisoned. Some antislavery states—such as Massachusetts—resisted, standing by their personal liberty laws and refusing to accept the federal government's jurisdiction in these matters. Point out that abolitionists, those who fought to abolish slavery, considered the practice of slave-catching to be kidnapping.

WORDS TO KNOW

- agitate
- alleged
- compliance
- contradict
- illustrious
- mobilize
- peer
- petty
- throb
- wretched

Additional Words to Know

- fugitive
  page 315, line 102
- inquiry
  page 326, line 444

VOCABULARY PREVIEW: Words to Know in Context

You can help students learn the Words to Know by reading aloud the following sentences or writing them on the board. Then show students how to use context clues to help them figure out the meaning.

agitate: They *agitated* for fair housing by speaking to large groups and handing out leaflets.

alleged: There is no proof that the *alleged* crime took place.

compliance: Since he was not in *compliance* with the dress code, he was sent home from school.

contradict: I didn't agree with the teacher's answer, so I *contradicted* her.

illustrious: Everyone knows and respects my grandmother, the most *illustrious* member of the town council.

mobilize: We *mobilized* everyone in the neighborhood to work together to clean up our park.

peer: A small pair of eyes *peered* through the hole in the wall.

petty: The police ignored the *petty* thieves and went after the really dangerous criminals.

throb: Michael's head began to *throb* with pain after he ran into the closed door.

wretched: Her fever, headache, and chills make her feel *wretched*.

---

fugitive: The two robbers became *fugitives* from the law, running from town to town and hoping to escape arrest.

inquiry: The principal will start an *inquiry* to find out what happened to the missing tests.

VOCABULARY FOCUS Word Parts: Roots

Teacher Modeling Remind students that they can sometimes figure out the meaning of an unfamiliar word if they recognize its root from other, familiar words. Then use the following modeling suggestions for the word *oppose* (page 322, line 316).

You might say I don't recognize the word oppose. However, it looks similar to opposite, which means "the complete reverse" or "contrary to." Maybe these words share the same root and are related in meaning. In this sentence, oppose could mean "stand against" or "hold a contrary position to."

Student Modeling Now have students follow your lead. Ask a volunteer to model the strategy to determine the meaning of *proceed* (page 322, line 336).

A student could say I don't know the meaning of proceed, but it looks similar to process, which means "a series of steps or actions." Maybe these words are related in meaning. I can tell that proceed is a verb in this sentence. I think it must mean "to take certain steps or actions."

Mini-Lesson
See pages 103–104 of this Guide for additional work on **Word Parts: Roots.**

During Reading

COMPREHENSION FOCUS

Key Points	Strategies for Success
Target Skill ➡ Narrative Elements This excerpt contains numerous people, settings, and shifting points of view. It is essential that students be able to keep track of the biography's narrative elements and follow the main events.	**Mini-Lesson** Before students read, teach or review the **Narrative Elements** lesson on pages 146–149 of this Guide. • Read aloud lines 534–558 on page 329. Have students identify the people, setting, and events in the passage. Ask: *Who are the people that want to help Anthony? Which people want to keep him in slavery? What does Anthony decide to do?* • As students read, have them use the **Story Map** on page 147 of this Guide to keep track of the selection's narrative elements.
Conflict It is important for students to understand the internal and external conflicts in this selection.	Read aloud lines 370–393 on pages 323–324. Ask students to identify Anthony's internal conflict as well as the external ones that involve him. If necessary, point out that Anthony is torn between his desire to ask for legal help and his fear of angering Colonel Suttle.

Suggested Reading Options

• An oral reading of the excerpt from *Anthony Burns: The Defeat and Triumph of a Fugitive Slave* is available in *The Language of Literature* Audio Library. ◠
• Shared Reading (see page 8 of this Guide).
• Additional options are described on page 8 of this Guide.

RECIPROCAL TEACHING SUGGESTION ➡ Clarifying

Teacher Modeling *Pause & Reflect, page 313* Model for students how to use the clarifying strategy to understand why Anthony feels sad when he retreats into the past.

You could say *When I carefully reread lines 17–28 on page 312, I see that Anthony doesn't know who his father is. He fears that Mars John, the slave owner, is his father. When Anthony studies his hand in lines 24–28, he notices that his skin is light brown. However, Mamaw—his mother—and Big Walker— the man who acts as Anthony's father—are very dark. Anthony's confusion about his past makes him feel sad.*

Student Modeling *Pause & Reflect, page 314* Ask several volunteers to model using the clarifying strategy to understand what Colonel Suttle means when he speaks to Anthony. Offer this prompt: *What promises might Suttle make to Anthony? What threats could the slave owner carry out?*

Encourage students to use the other five reading strategies when appropriate as they proceed through the rest of the biography. (See page 10 of this Guide.)

ENGLISH LEARNERS

1. At each *Pause & Reflect,* have English learners work with English-proficient partners to summarize events and add information to their story maps. Reassure students that they should strive for a basic understanding of the events described in this challenging biography.

2. Students might benefit from reading along with the recording of the excerpt from *Anthony Burns: The Defeat and Triumph of a Fugitive Slave* in *The Language of Literature* Audio Library. ◯

After Reading

Recommended Follow-Up

• Thinking Through the Literature, page 766, *The Language of Literature*

• Choices & Challenges, page 777, *The Language of Literature*

• SkillBuilders, pages 337–339, *The InterActive Reader™*

Informal Assessment Options

Retell Have pairs of students retell the events in the biography by taking on the roles of Colonel Suttle and Richard Dana. Offer these prompts:
• *Why is Anthony Burns in jail?*
• *What takes place in the courtroom?*
• *What do you think should be done with Anthony?*

Spot Check Review the notes students made in the margins of the story. Invite them to ask any questions they still have about the biography.

Formal Assessment Options in *The Language of Literature*

Selection Quiz, page 51, Unit Five Resource Book

Selection Test, pages 119–120, Formal Assessment Book

For more teaching options, see pages 750–777 in *The Language of Literature* Teacher's Edition.

Additional Challenge

1. ▐▐▐ **MARK IT UP** ⟩ **Illustrate a Scene**
   Have students select a passage that describes a dramatic moment during the trial, underline details that help them visualize it, and create an illustration of the scene.

2. ▐▐▐ **MARK IT UP** ⟩ **Compare Opinions**
   Point out that the people in this biography have different opinions about slavery. Some are radically opposed to slavery, while others believe strongly in the institution. Still others support slavery only in certain regions. Have students mark passages that directly or indirectly reveal the people's opinions. Then discuss how these conflicting opinions might have divided the nation.

End Unit
Lesson Plans

Reading a Magazine Article

Introducing the Concept

Students may have difficulty sorting out the headings, text, and visuals in some magazine articles. Tell students that using these strategies will help.

Teaching Tips for the Magazine Article

A **Visuals and Captions:** Suggest that students preview the visuals in a magazine article to get an idea of the topic before they begin reading. Previewing the visuals and captions on this magazine article should tell students that the article's topic is animal communications.

B **Title and Headings:** Read aloud the title of this article. Point out to students that "Say What?" uses a question and an idiomatic expression to grab the reader's attention.

C **Larger Typeface:** Point out that the introductory paragraph in this article is set in a larger, boldface type. The text introduces the main topic.

D **Italics and Boldface:** Remind students that boldface type is heavier than regular type and italic type is slightly slanted. The boldface and italic type signal to readers that definitions or explanations may follow. You might have students identify the two boldface words in the article.

E **Charts and Sidebars:** Tell students that the sidebar in this article introduces animals that can communicate with humans. Point out that a sidebar in a magazine article is always tied to the topic but often provides information on a related subtopic.

Additional Questions

1. Which communicating animals are covered in the article? **(dolphins, bees, and gorillas)**
2. Which animals use phonations to communicate? **(dolphins)**
3. Which animals use pheromones to communicate? **(bees)**

Additional Tips for Reading a Magazine Article

- **Read items in any order:** Tell students that they can read the items in a magazine article in any order they choose. After they preview the article, students can read the sidebars or the captions first—whatever catches their interest.

- **Ignore advertising:** Encourage students to screen out the eye-catching ads that appear in some articles. These ads are designed to grab their attention and entice them to buy.

- **Understand slang terms:** Point out that magazines aimed at teenagers often use informal language and popular slang. Students whose first language isn't English may have trouble understanding such slang as *hottie* (meaning "handsome man") and *real deal* (meaning "realistic"). You might suggest that students jot down any words and terms they don't understand and ask a friend to translate.

Reading a Textbook

Introducing the Concept

Many students are confused by the titles, subheadings, and features on a textbook page. Learning can be hindered if students cannot navigate their way through these items. Tell students that these skills and strategies will help them learn to read textbooks.

Teaching Tips for the Textbook Page

A **Title and Subheadings:** Have students note that the title of the lesson is "Scientific Measurement" and the subheading is "Length." Point out the different sizes and typeface of the two heads. Make sure students understand that subheadings are usually smaller than the broader subject headings.

B **Objectives:** Tell students that the objectives list the skills and knowledge they should acquire by reading the lesson. As students read the lesson, they may want to refer to the objectives and check off those they have achieved.

C **Vocabulary Terms:** Encourage students to scan the vocabulary words before they begin reading the lesson.

D **Italics and Boldface:** Suggest that students highlight or note unfamiliar italicized words as well as the boldfaced vocabulary words. You might read the italicized and boldfaced words on this page and ask students to locate the words' definitions.

E **Graphics:** Point out that the table on this page provides a list of prefixes for scientific units. Make sure students understand the value of each example given in the chart. Help them get started by explaining that a kilogram is equal to 1,000 grams.

F **Visuals and Captions:** Tell students that the visual on this page presents an image of a metric ruler. Point out that the image of the ruler is directly tied to the headings, table, and vocabulary on the textbook page. To underscore the fact that the visual presents the information more clearly than words could, ask volunteers to try to present the information orally.

Additional Questions

1. According to the lesson objectives, what will readers be able to identify after reading this lesson? **(standard units of measurements used in science)**
2. What does the prefix *hecto* mean? **(100)**
3. How many centimeters are shown in the picture of the metric ruler? **(ten)**

Additional Tips for Reading a Textbook

• **Recall prior knowledge:** Before students begin reading, have them get together in small groups and discuss what they know about the topic.

• **Follow the PACER method:** When students read a lesson in a textbook, encourage them to follow the PACER method: **P**review the entire lesson, use section subheadings to **A**nalyze the purpose of a passage, **C**arefully read the text, **E**valuate the material, and, finally, **R**eview their notes.

• **Use a graphic organizer:** As students read, suggest that they use a graphic organizer to help make sense of the material. For example, they might use an outline to list a lesson's main ideas and supporting details.

Reading Graphs and Charts

Introducing the Concept

Charts and graphs help convey a lot of information in a little space. They are effective because they can present data over a period of time and show relationships among items. Although charts and graphs present information in different ways, they each have some common elements.

Teaching Tips for the Chart

A **Title:** The title of a chart is a key element and should be as descriptive as possible.

B **Relationship:** Tell students that depending on the purpose, one visual may be more appropriate than the other. If an audience were interested in temperature peaks, then the line graph would be easier to read; if they wanted to know the average temperature for the month of June, then the chart would be more appropriate.

C **Headings:** Point out that in both examples the headings remain the same, but the information is presented differently.

D **Horizontal and Vertical Lines:** Show students that in the line graph the horizontal lines represent the temperature while the vertical lines represent the months. In the sample chart, the headings separate the information into columns.

E **Symbols or Abbreviations:** Another temperature abbreviation is °C (degrees Celsius).

F **Credit:** Tell students that the credit shows the reader that a source is reliable.

Additional Questions

1. Which month begins to show a decrease in temperatures after Juneau, Alaska, has reached the highest average temperatures? **(August)**

2. Use the chart to find the two months that show the greatest change in temperatures. **(April and May)**

3. If you wanted to quickly scan the lowest temperatures, which visual is best? **(line graph)**

Other Types of Charts and Graphs

Reproduce the following charts and graphs to show students the variety of visuals they will come across in their reading. When reading a pie chart, students should read each label. When they encounter a bar graph, remind them to read the headings on the horizontal and vertical axes before trying to understand the graph's content. In a flow chart, remind them to follow the arrows.

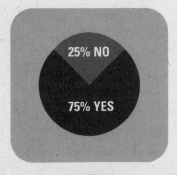

Pie Chart

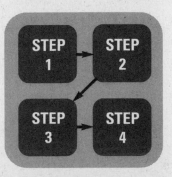

Bar Graph   **Flow Chart**

Reading a Weather Map

Introducing the Concept

Maps not only represent geographic information such as mountains and lakes, but they also show political and social information such as immigration in the New England States in the 1700s. You might want to show students examples of different types of maps (see examples below) and then explain to them that most maps share similar features.

Teaching Tips for the Map

A **Title:** Titles inform the reader of the type of information represented on the map. Many titles have dates reflecting a time period; others have names of specific regions or areas; and some have names of battles or economic activity.

B **Key or Legend:** Remind students that keys or legends can include arrows, symbols, colors, letters, numbers, and lines to represent an item or activity on the map. The key on this map shows symbols for precipitation and fronts, and it includes letters for pressure systems.

C **Geographic Labels:** Students should watch for type styles (for example, italic, all caps, boldface) and sizes in order to distinguish rivers, capital cities, state and country names, mountain ranges, etc.

D **Scale and Pointer:** Most maps will include a pointer to show which way the directions north (N), south (S), east (E), and west (W) point on the map. Some maps, but not all, also include a scale that is used to measure the distance between certain areas in miles and kilometers.

Additional Questions

1. What kind of precipitation is shown on the map? **(rain, snow, flurries, and showers)**
2. What do the symbols **H** and **L** represent? **(High and Low pressure)**
3. Is Boston a northern, southern, or western city? **(northern)**
4. What kind of precipitation is predicted for San Francisco? **(rain)**

Basic Types of Maps

• **Physical maps** show mountains, hills, plains, rivers, lakes, oceans, and other physical features of an area.

• **Political maps** show political units, such as countries, states, counties, districts, and towns. Each unit is typically shaded a different color, represented by a symbol, or shown with a different typeface.

• **Historical maps** illustrate such things as economic activity, migrations, battles, and changing national boundaries.

Reading a Diagram

Introducing the Concept

Diagrams can be an extremely useful means of illustrating and understanding written texts; however, they pose their own set of challenges for readers. After the first glance, some diagrams demand close study and interpretation. Explain to students that although diagrams may look easy because of the pictures, they sometimes contain complex information. These strategies should help students sort through many different kinds of diagrams.

Teaching Tips for the Diagram

A **Title:** Remind students that a diagram's title is not necessarily at the top; it might be at the bottom or on the side. Some diagrams don't even have titles.

B **Images:** Point out to students that, although the image in this diagram has many parts, the diagram itself is fairly simple. Its primary purpose is to label the different parts of the microscope, rather than show how the different parts work together.

C **Caption and Labels:** As in many diagrams, the captions and labels here contain critical information about the parts of the microscope.

More Practice with Diagrams

Reproduce the diagram and caption below for your students, asking them the following questions.

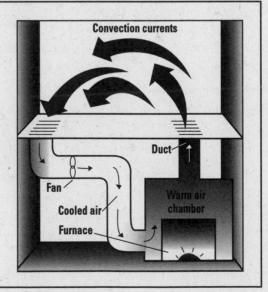

Vents located in the floor or near the base of a wall in each room allow air, heated by a furnace and pumped upward, to enter the room. The warm air rises, setting up a forced convection current. After the air cools and falls down the opposite wall of the room, it passes through a vent on the opposite side of the wall and is returned to the furnace for reheating.

Convection currents

Duct

Fan

Cooled air

Warm air chamber

Furnace

1. How does the warm air enter the room? (**The warm air enters the room through a duct in the floor.**)

2. What happens to the air in the room after it has cooled? (**It sinks back to the floor at the other end of the room, having moved across the room by convection current. It then leaves the room through another vent in the floor.**)

3. Where and how is the cool air reheated? (**It is reheated by the furnace in the warm-air chamber.**)

Main Idea and Supporting Details

Introducing the Concept

Students often have trouble identifying a paragraph's main idea. They may not always be able to distinguish the main point of a paragraph from the details that support it. Tell students that these strategies can help.

Teaching Tips for Main Idea and Support

- **Main Idea:** The main idea of a paragraph is presented in a general statement. The specific details contained in the other sentences in the paragraph support this general statement.
- **Summary:** Tell students that restating a main idea as a headline or title will help them summarize the paragraph.
- **Supporting Details:** Point out that types of supporting details include sensory details, specific examples, facts and statistics, reasons, and anecdotes.

Additional Questions

1. What types of details are used to support the first paragraph's main idea? (facts)
2. How might you restate the main idea in the second paragraph as a title? (Treating Illnesses in Columbus's Time)

Additional Tips

Tell students that not all main ideas are stated in the first sentence. Some main ideas appear in the middle of a paragraph; some are stated in the last sentence. Sometimes, especially in narrative or descriptive writing, a main idea is implied rather than stated. When the main idea is implied, students must figure out the major point that ties all the sentences together. In the following paragraph, for example, all of the sentences are tied together by the following implied main idea: Dina is sad.

> Dina sighed heavily as she looked out the window. The gloomy weather mirrored her mood. As raindrops dripped from the trees, Dina felt a tear slide down her cheek. She wiped it away and tried to smile, but her lips wouldn't curve upward. Finally surrendering to her mood, Dina lay down on her bed and cried.

Problem and Solution

Introducing the Concept

Students who are familiar with common text structures, such as problem and solution, generally find it easier to comprehend and mentally organize what they read. Explain to students that when they recognize that a text is describing a problem and solution, they can more easily break the text down into recognizable parts.

Teaching Tips for the Problem and Solution Text

- **Statement of Problem:** Explain to students that while the problem is often stated at the very beginning of a text, as in "After School Blues," this might not always be the case.
- **Explanation of Problem:** Point out to students that this text explains the problem from two points of view: that of the school neighbors and that of the students. Remind them that the explanation of a problem in a text may be balanced or unbalanced.
- **Proposed Solution:** Point out that in this case, the proposed solution is phrased as a question ("Why not open up the school gym . . ?").
- **Support for Proposal:** Explain to students that in giving support for a proposal, writers will often use persuasive language to convince their readers that this solution is a good one.
- **Evaluating the Solution:** Encourage students to make a habit of evaluating all of the proposals that they read in school and on their own.

Additional Example

The following paragraph contains another problem and proposed solution. Share it with students. Ask them to identify its different elements and evaluate the proposed solution.

> The Kowalski Community Center attracts people from all over the twin cities of Jonesville and Fort Hugo. Kids of all ages come for soccer and basketball practice, for arts and crafts classes, and for drama rehearsals. Because the center is at the outer edge of Jonesville, most people have to travel several miles to get there. This is hard for kids whose parents are not always available to drive them back and forth. It's also difficult for parents, especially if they have two or more children going to different practices at different times of the day.
>
> A local shuttle bus would solve this problem. The route could go through the two towns, to the Kowalski center, and back. It could run once or twice every hour. This would make it easier for kids to get to the center, and it would help parents save travel time and gasoline money. If more people took the bus to the center, it would also reduce local traffic and the pollution from extra cars on the road. It makes sense for everyone!

Answers
Statement of problem: "most people have to travel for several miles or more to get there"
Explanation of problem: *from* "This is hard for kids . . . " *to* "at different times of the day."
Proposed solution: "A local shuttle bus would solve this problem."
Support for proposal: The second paragraph, from the second sentence to the end.

Sequence

Introducing the Concept

Make sure that students understand the meaning of the word *sequence.* Ask for examples of when students need to use proper sequence in their reading, writing, and speaking. Answers may include writing an essay (introduction, body, and conclusion), describing a process, creating a storyboard, and telling a joke. Explain that active readers make sure they understand sequences so they can understand and remember material more easily.

Teaching Tips for Sequence

- **Main Steps:** Students may want to number the main steps as they read. Alternatively, they can jot down a word or phrase that describes each step. Reviewing these notations can help when students are preparing for a test.
- **Time Words:** Ask students to suggest other words and phrases that can signal time, such as *tomorrow, soon, in the 1700s, at the same time,* and *after 20 minutes.*
- **Order Words:** Have students think of more words and phrases that signal order, such as *begin by, after that, next,* and *finally.*

Additional Questions

1. How long does the egg stage last for most types of butterflies? **(about 10 days)**
2. Does a caterpillar molt once, a few times, or several times during its life? **(several times)**
3. In the third stage, what happens while the pupa is in its chrysalis? **(Its body changes—it grows wings, antennae, and other butterfly parts.)**
4. What does the adult butterfly look like right after breaking from the chrysalis? Why? **(soft and wrinkly; needs air and blood pumped through its body)**

Additional Tips for Recognizing Sequence

- **Sequence in the classroom:** Explain that understanding sequence is especially important when reading science and social studies materials. Recognizing the order in which historical events occurred can help readers understand how the events are related and why some events happened. In science class, altering the order of steps can change the outcome of a laboratory experiment. Encourage students to look for dates, times, and numbered steps when reading social studies and science books.
- **Sequence in everyday life:** Challenge students to think of written materials outside the classroom that often use sequence. Answers may include recipes, technical instructions, directions to a friend's home, the rules of most board games, and some news stories.
- **Events out of sequence:** Tell students that some writers deliberately present events out of order to emphasize certain steps or to build suspense. When students notice that a writer is using this technique, they may wish to write down the steps in their actual order to make sure they understand the material.
- **Graphic organizers:** Creating a flow chart or time line can help students understand a complicated chain of events.
- **Numbered items:** Encourage students to look for numbered items as well as signal words. Point out that the first paragraph of the butterfly article includes a numbered list.

Cause and Effect

Introducing the Concept

Writing organized by causes and effects shows that one event took place as a result of another event. Point out, however, that events following one another do not necessarily have a cause-and-effect relationship. The events may be sequential. Students can use these strategies to determine whether events have a causal relationship.

Teaching Tips for Cause and Effect

- **Effects:** Suggest that students look for effects in a piece of writing by posing a question based on the title of the piece, such as "What happened because African elephants are at risk?"
- **Causes:** Tell students that they can also look for causes by posing a question, such as "Why are African elephants at risk?"
- **Signal Words:** Point out that cause-and-effect writing does not always contain signal words. In such a case, students can use the "because test" to determine whether two events have a cause-and-effect relationship. Tell students to link the events with the word *because*. If the sentence still makes sense, the relationship is causal.

Additional Questions

1. What happened because the number of African elephants was so low? (**The African elephant was placed on the endangered species list.**)
2. Why did some African countries object to the law banning international ivory trade? (**because these countries depend on the ivory trade**)

Additional Tips

Tell students that not all events are linked by a series of causes and effects. Sometimes a single cause can have more than one effect. Also, several causes can result in a single effect. You might use the following chart to demonstrate a single effect with multiple causes.

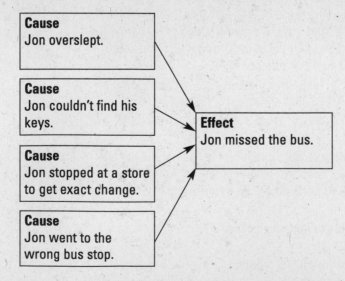

Comparison and Contrast

Introducing the Concept

Explain that although comparisons and contrasts can appear in all types of writing, they are especially common in science and social studies materials. Social studies textbooks often compare and contrast different periods in history, such as the Middle Ages and the Renaissance. A science textbook might help students understand the differences between plant cells and animal cells by comparing and contrasting the two.

Teaching Tips for Comparison and Contrast

- **Direct Statements:** Read aloud the first sentence of the article: "Annie and Elizabeth say they're alike in many ways and different in others." Point out that a direct statement such as this one is the most obvious way to signal a comparison or contrast. Mention that this sentence would be too vague without the specific examples that follow.
- **Comparison Signal Words:** Explain that there are other comparison signal words and phrases, such as *neither, as well as, additionally,* and *likewise.*
- **Contrast Signal Words:** Mention some other words and phrases that signal a contrast, such as *still, however, in contrast,* and *instead.*

Additional Questions

1. According to the third paragraph of the article, what difference do all twins have in common? **(All twins have different fingerprints.)**
2. What is the difference between "mirror-image twins" and other identical twins? **("Mirror-image twins" resemble a mirror image of each other; often one twin is right-handed and the other is left-handed.)**
3. Why are Annie and Elizabeth described as "identical but not the same"? **(They look alike but are different in many ways, including their tastes and habits.)**

Additional Tips for Recognizing Comparisons and Contrasts

- **Multiple items:** For texts that compare and contrast more than two people or things, have students make a chart with side-by-side columns instead of a Venn diagram. A chart can help students clarify the multiple elements.
- **No signal words:** Explain that some comparisons and contrasts do not use direct statements or signal words. Give students some examples of this kind of comparison or contrast, such as "My sister likes action movies. I like comedies." Discuss how adding signal words or a direct statement of comparison or contrast could make the connection between these ideas clearer.
- **Comparisons in everyday life:** Ask students to think about how often they see comparison-and-contrast structures in their daily lives. Here are some examples:
  - –charts, graphs, and tables in newspapers and magazines and on television
  - –reviews of movies, TV shows, video games, Web sites, and albums
  - –definitions in dictionaries, newspapers, magazines, and books
  - –advertisements in newspapers and magazines and on television

Argument

Introducing the Concept

Students may not be aware that they read arguments regularly. Some examples include a letter to the editor of a newspaper or magazine, a movie or book review, and a speech. Ask students to think about the last argument they read. Then ask them if they agreed or disagreed with the argument, or if they changed their mind based on an opinion a writer expressed.

Teaching Tips for the Argument

- **Signal Words:** Tell students that looking for signal words is an important strategy in helping them determine the writer's position or opinion. Some additional examples include *accept, agree, in my opinion, oppose,* and *disagree.*
- **Support:** Writers may use facts, statistics, examples, observations, narratives, or expert opinions to support an argument. In the example, the writer presents both sides of the argument and supports it with examples and personal observations.
- **Errors in Reasoning:** Have students evaluate the argument. Ask: *Does the argument make sense? Is it reasonable and clearly supported with evidence?* Then ask students to look for overgeneralizations and other errors in reasoning in the argument.

Additional Questions

1. Why is the statement "Everyone loves Spirit Week" an overgeneralization? (**The statement is too broad and does not take into consideration the teachers and students who may not "love" Spirit Week.**)
2. What action is the writer calling for? (**to consider the plea and save Spirit Week**)

Avoiding Errors in Reasoning

Mistakes in reasoning can weaken an argument and show that the writer has not thought carefully about the points he or she wants to make. Here are some examples.

- **Overgeneralizations** are statements that are too broad to prove. *(Everyone likes to eat hot dogs. Everybody should have picnics in the summer.)* Using words such as *some, many, few, almost,* and *sometimes* can avoid an overgeneralization. Remind students that although they may agree with some overgeneralizations, agreeing with the statement does not make it true.
- **Circular reasoning** is an attempt to prove a statement by simply repeating it in different words. *(Our basketball team should win the title because they deserve to be number one.)*
- **Either/or statements** suggest that only two alternatives are available when there are many. *(Either we build a new community swimming pool, or no one will learn to swim.)*

Social Studies

Introducing the Concept

Briefly discuss challenges students face in social studies class—learning names, dates, and new terms as well as understanding complex series of interrelated events. Explain that a social studies textbook is designed to make key facts easy to find and understand.

Teaching Tips for the Social Studies Page

A **Lesson Title:** Mention that if students do not understand a word in the title, such as *Renaissance,* they should look for its definition in the text or in the glossary.

B **Lesson Subheads:** If students read the title and any subheads first, they will have a good idea of what the lesson covers—an effective prereading strategy.

C **Vocabulary Terms:** Tell students that after reading, they should be able to define these boldfaced, italicized, or underlined terms in their own words. Remind them to look for words that signal a definition or restatement, such as *this means, in other words, which is, or, also called,* and *such as.*

D **Maps and Map Titles:** Explain that maps work together with the text to make a concept clearer. Direct students to read the map's title carefully; if they do not, they will not understand what the map shows.

E **Pictures and Captions:** Warn students that captions often include details that are not in the main text—in this case, information on the source of Florence's wealth.

F **Organizational Techniques:** Point out that the second and third paragraphs of the sample page make comparisons and contrasts.

Additional Questions

1. Name some similarities and differences of Italian city-states. (similarities: all independent, all founded in the 1100s; differences: size, form of government)

2. If you don't understand the meaning of a term like *feudal* or *aristocrats* or *guilds* that appears in the lesson but is not defined, what should you do? (check the glossary, check a dictionary, or ask your teacher)

Additional Tips for Reading in Social Studies

• **Read and review objectives:** Many textbooks include objectives or goals for each lesson. Students can check their understanding by making sure they can answer what the goal or objective asks of them.

• **Make predictions:** Based on the lesson title and subheads, have students jot down one or two predictions about the lesson. After reading, ask them to look at their predictions again to see if they were right.

• **Find relationships to prior reading:** Encourage students to think about how the material relates to subjects they have covered before. For instance, how was the period after the Renaissance similar to or different from the period before it?

• **Overcome lack of prior knowledge:** Students will have no prior knowledge of many historical events. Suggest that students create word webs, charts, and other graphic organizers as they read. Knowing how facts are related makes them easier to remember.

• **Connect to students' lives when possible:** In some cases, students may be able to relate material they read to their own experiences. For example, students could compare and contrast children's daily lives in twelfth-century Europe with their lives.

Science

Introducing the Concept

Many textbooks pose special reading challenges for students. Science textbooks, for example, use highly specialized vocabulary and difficult, unfamiliar concepts. They also rely heavily on diagrams and illustrations. Let students know that these strategies will help them develop the special skills required for reading a science page.

Teaching Tips for the Science Page

A **Title and Subheadings:** When they see a lesson title or heading for the first time, encourage students to stop and think about what they expect to learn in the lesson.

B **Boldface and Italic Words:** Remind students that the boldface words on this page are vocabulary words. Encourage students to note definitions as they read.

C **Signal Words:** Science books often explain concepts by breaking them down into parts. Remind students that the signal words *first, second,* and *third* in the third, fourth, and fifth paragraphs can help them quickly recognize the different parts when reviewing or taking notes on the lesson.

D **Figure References:** Explain to students that in some cases, figure references point them to diagrams or illustrations that are critical to their understanding of the text. For this reason, they should be sure to look at the figure in the margin as soon as the reference comes up, rather than wait until the end of the paragraph or the end of the page.

E **Diagrams or Pictures with Captions:** Ask students to reread the caption under Figure 17-1 and visualize the difference between a centimeter-long nerve and a meter-long nerve.

Additional Tips for Reading in Science

• **Watch for cues in the text about connecting the science concept to everyday experiences.** Students may have little or no prior knowledge of the subject matter in a science lesson. However, many science lessons begin with a paragraph or two relating some everyday experience to the science concept. (For example, it might compare the spray from a punctured soda can to the eruption of a volcano.) As they read about new concepts, students should carefully consider the relationship between the concept and these and other everyday experiences.

• **Don't assume knowledge of familiar vocabulary terms; be sure to read definitions carefully.** Some science terms are familiar, everyday words that have a more specific meaning in science. (For example, the word *heat* is generally used to describe a feeling of warmth or hotness. In science, however, *heat* refers to a form of energy associated with the motion of atoms or molecules.) When they encounter familiar words among science vocabulary terms, readers should take care to read each term's definition, and not assume that they already know it.

• **Be alert to surprising information, or information that contradicts prior knowledge.** Readers may find that what they read in a science lesson contradicts what they think they know about the concept. (For example, the fact that falling objects accelerate at the same rate, no matter what their weight, is often surprising to people.) Readers should be alert to startling information or corrections of their prior knowledge, and be ready to consciously revise their understanding of the material.

Mathematics

Introducing the Concept

Textbooks, especially texts for subjects like math and science, pose special problems for readers. In addition to scanning the titles and headings, students must deal with very specific vocabulary and symbols. Acknowledge that reading a math page takes some special skills. Tell students that using these strategies will help.

Teaching Tips for the Math Page

A **Title and Headings:** Note that on this page, the first heading is labeled "Goal 1: Using Tables." Point out to students that because the lesson title is "Tables and Graphs," they may predict that Goal 2 will be "Using Graphs."

B **Explanations:** Mention that an explanation may also be a straightforward statement of why a concept is important and what the reader will be expected to do. Add that some explanations include diagrams or other visuals.

C **Goals or Objectives:** Suggest to students that they rewrite the lesson goals as questions. For example, "What are the relationships within a data set?" Creating these questions will help them understand the point of the lesson.

D **Vocabulary Words:** Tell students to underscore or note definitions as they read. On this page, *data* is defined and a vocabulary tip in the margin helps to extend the definition. Point out that some common words, such as *product base* and *power*, have special meanings in math.

E **Special Features:** Special boxes, notes, or highlighted text and other devices may signal extra materials. These features are designed to make the material easier to understand and remember.

F **Worked Out Solutions to Problems:** Make sure students understand each part of the example and know why the answer works. The example is their key to solving other problems like it.

Additional Questions

1. What is the pattern for the data in Example 1? **(The perimeters increase by 2.)**
2. What does the study tip tell you to do? **(add a fourth row to the table)**

Additional Tips for Reading in Mathematics

- **Watch for special reading situations:** Reading in math is not always left to right. For example, fractions are read from top to bottom.
- **Use a reading guide:** When reading a table that has many columns of information, a reader should use a ruler to help guide eyes across the page or down a column.
- **Watch for special words and symbols:** Every word and symbol must be read very carefully to avoid reading *hundred* as *hundredth* or *1.0* as *one-tenth*, for example.

Reading an Application

Introducing the Concept

People generally think of applications as something to fill out rather than something to read. But an application must be read carefully in order to be filled out correctly. Remind students that many applications have numerous features in common, and a few strategies can help them read the applications accurately.

Teaching Tips for the Application

A **Sections:** Encourage students to always scan something before reading it. This will give them a general idea of the application as a whole, and will help them put the different sections in context once they begin to read carefully.

B **For Office Use Only:** Point out to students that many applications have such a section for the people receiving the completed application. It frequently appears at the bottom of the application; students should take care to notice this label and avoid writing in these sections.

C **Difficult Words or Abbreviations:** Tell students that when they encounter words or abbreviations they don't understand, they should look them up or ask the person administering the application.

D **Other Materials:** Remind students that while it's very easy to overlook requests for supplementary materials, the application will not be considered complete without those materials.

More Practice with Applications

Here is another form that students might read and fill out. Reproduce it for your students and ask them the following questions.

```
SCOTT'S SKATE RENTAL      Today's Date _____

Name _____    phone _____

Address _____

Have you rented skates from us before?  Y/N  (cirlce one)

     (circle one)              (circle one)
     Male/Female         Figure skates/Speed skates        Skate size_____

                              (circle one)
Length of rental period     1 day     2 days     1 week

I agree to return the skates in good condition to Scott's Skate Rental by _____
                                                                          DATE
I am responsible for the loss of or any damages to the ice skates.

SIGNATURE _____
```

1. What is the purpose of this form? **(to sign up for skate rental)**

2. What different kinds of ice skates are available? **(figure skates or speed skates)**

3. Circle the agreement to be signed on this application. **(Students should circle the sentences beginning with "I agree" and ending with "ice skates.")**

4. What responsibility does the person renting the skates have? **(She or he is responsible for turning the skates in on time and paying for any loss or damages to the skates.)**

Reading a Public Notice

Introducing the Concept

Explain that it's important for students to read public notices so they are aware of events in their community. The following tips will help students tell which public notices apply to them.

Teaching Tips for the Public Notice

A **Title:** Point out that the title of the sample notice, a page from a local arts and entertainment guide, gives readers the main idea of the notice.

B **Relevance:** When reading a notice, students should think about whether the notice applies to them or to someone they know. Students can then filter out irrelevant notices and closely examine relevant ones.

C **Instructions:** Encourage students to look for instructions or requests in notices. The sample notice lists some instructions in italic type to make them stand out.

D **Logo or Credit:** The credit in the sample not only tells readers who created the notice but also gives them a place where they can go to get more information.

E **Details:** Since space on a notice is limited, many notices give sources where readers can find out more. This notice refers readers to another page in the guide for detailed information. It also gives a street address, two telephone numbers, and a Web site address.

F **Special Features:** This notice gives a telephone number that Spanish-speaking residents can call. Tell students that other notices may include information in other languages, Braille sections for the visually impaired, or references to TDD (Telephone Device for the Deaf) numbers.

Additional Questions

1. Where can you find more information about where the soccer team meets? **(page 14 of the same publication; calling the phone numbers or visiting the Web page might also give readers the information)**

2. What are participants required to bring to jazz band class? **(a musical instrument)**

3. Why do you think the notice includes information in English and Spanish? **(to make it easier for Spanish-speaking people to find out about the classes and participate in them; to reach a wider audience)**

Other Types of Public Notices

Other public notices that students should watch for include:
- **health and safety information,** such as road signs;
- **rules for public areas** such as parks, pools, libraries, beaches, and community centers;
- **announcements** of community events, meetings, and elections; and
- **instructions from the federal, state, or local government** describing how to register to vote, obtain a driver's license, or participate in a census.

Explain that some of these notices will use symbols or incomplete sentences, but students can examine them using many of the same techniques they used on the sample notice.

Reading a Web Page

Introducing the Concept

To make sure students understand the Web sites they read, they can use the tips in the *InterActive Reader*™ lesson as well as reading strategies they already know.

Teaching Tips for the Web Page

A **Web Address:** Explain that the abbreviations in a Web address can give clues about the site. For example, http://www.lookquick.com is probably a commercial site—it contains the abbreviation *.com.* The Public Broadcasting Service site, http://www.pbs.org, contains the abbreviation *.org,* which usually indicates a nonprofit company. Other abbreviations include *.edu* (educational) and *.gov* (government).

B **Title:** Point out that the LookQuick page has the title at the top, while the asteroids page has the title at the bottom. Both pages use large type to draw the reader's eye to the title.

C **Menu Bars:** Direct students' attention to the special menu bar at the bottom of the asteroids page. Explain that this menu bar gives options related to asteroids. The standard menu bar at the top of the Web browser lets users move back and forward through a site and print pages.

D **Links:** Links let users jump from page to page on one site or to a different site altogether. Remind students that links are not always checked for accuracy and timeliness by the person posting the link.

E **Interactive Areas:** Caution students not to give their home address or phone number or send pictures of themselves through the Web unless they check with a parent or teacher first.

Glossary of Web-Related Terms

bookmark: a saved link to a Web page. If you bookmark a site, you can call it up again without having to type in the Web address. A bookmark list is sometimes called a hotlist or a favorites list.

browser: a computer program that lets you look at and interact with material on the World Wide Web. Some commonly used browsers are Netscape Navigator and Internet Explorer.

chat room: an online service that lets users communicate "in real time"—immediately— rather than using the delayed communication of e-mail or electronic bulletin boards.

download: to copy a file from another computer. Text files, video clips, audio clips, and images can all be downloaded.

flame: an insulting or verbally abusive e-mail or posting.

http: Hypertext Transfer Protocol, the computer rules for exchanging information on the Web. Web addresses include the http coding, a colon, and two slashes (http://).

netiquette: etiquette on the Internet. One rule of netiquette is that users should be as polite in their e-mails as they would be in a letter or face to face.

search engine: a program that reviews millions of Web pages for keywords entered by a user.

spam: unsolicited or bulk e-mail. Such mailings often offer products for sale or ask users to visit the sender's Web site.

URL: a Uniform Resource Locator, or Web address, such as http://www.mcdougallittell.com.

Reading Technical Directions

Introducing the Concept

Reading technical directions can present some challenges because of difficult vocabulary and complex instructions. However, once students recognize that most technical directions can be broken down into easily recognizable parts, reading directions will become easier.

Teaching Tips for the Technical Directions

A **Read Directions:** Encourage students to read the directions from beginning to end at least once. Tell students that this is one of the most important steps in reading technical directions because it will provide an overall picture of what they must do.

B **Letters or Numbers:** Most directions provide letters or numbers to show the order in which the steps occur. If no numbers or letters are given, encourage student to insert the numbers themselves.

C **Visuals:** Remind students that a visual can simplify a step or locate specific parts of a product. For example, the visual of the remote control shows where specific buttons are located.

D **Action Verbs:** Tell students to underline or circle specific words that call for an action. Underlining an action verb can help a reader become more aware of the directions in each step.

E **Warnings or Notes:** Advise students not to skip warnings or notes because they often refer the reader to another page for more information, or they may tell the reader to take certain precautions before attempting a step.

Additional Practice Using Technical Directions

If students require additional practice, duplicate the directions below and ask students the questions that follow.

Operating Your Heater

1. Place the heater on a firm, level surface, about 1 meter (3 feet) away from the wall. DO NOT place the heater on any unsteady surface such as bedding or deep carpet.

2. Make sure the knob is on the Off position and plug the heater into a 120V, three-pronged outlet.

3. To operate the switch, push down the Selector knob while turning it clockwise to the desired position (See Fig. 1). Once the switch is turned on, the red power light will illuminate.

Note This child-resistant switch will prevent the heater from being turned on accidentally.

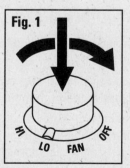

Fig. 1

1. Where should you not place the heater? (**bedding or deep carpet**)

2. What kind of outlet is required? (**120V, three-pronged outlet**)

3. According to the directions, would a child be able to turn on the heater accidentally? (**no**)

Product Information: Medicine Labels

Introducing the Concept

Labels appear on all over-the-counter medicines. You might tell students that learning how to read these labels will help them select the appropriate medicine for the condition they want to treat.

Teaching Tips for the Medicine Label

A **List of Conditions:** Make sure students understand that *indications* refers to the conditions or illnesses for which the medicine may be suitable. Encourage students to read this section carefully before purchasing any medicine.

B **Directions:** Remind students that they should always read the directions before taking any medicine. Point out that taking more than the recommended dose of a medicine may result in toxicity, a condition caused by chemical poisoning.

C **Warnings:** Tell students that they must also read any warnings before taking medicine. Inform them, too, that many pain-relieving medicines also include an alcohol warning. This warning states that users who drink more than three alcoholic drinks or more a day should consult a physician on when and how to take the pain relievers.

D **Reminder:** Point out that this sentence tells users what to do if children accidentally swallow the medicine. Tell students that this reminder appears on all OTC medicines— even those sold with child-proof caps.

Additional Questions

1. For how many days can this medicine safely be taken for pain? **(10 days)**
2. For how many days can this medicine safely be taken for fever? **(3 days)**
3. What should pregnant women or nursing mothers do before taking this product? **(seek the advice of a health professional)**

Other Types of Product Information

Students encounter many different types of product information in their daily life. For example:

• **Labels on food products** provide consumers with nutritional information. This information lists the amount of fat, carbohydrates, and other nutrients in a single serving of a particular food.

• **Clothing labels** provide cleaning instructions for the item. Failure to read and follow these instructions carefully can result in discolored, shrunken clothing.

• **Warranties** on appliances and electronic goods explain the consumer's rights and responsibilities if the product is not satisfactory.

Reading a Bus Schedule

Introducing the Concept

Students may have difficulty reading a bus schedule. The lists of headings and columns of numbers can be confusing. Tell students that using these strategies will help.

Teaching Tips for the Bus Schedule

A **Title:** Remind students to make sure that they are reading the correct schedule. Tell students to check the title carefully. Confusion can easily arise if someone looks at the schedule of Bus Route 332, for example, instead of Bus Route 333.

B **Date or Day Labels:** Tell students that many buses have several different operating schedules. Buses may publish schedules for weekday mornings, weekday afternoons, and weekday evenings. Many buses also have separate schedules for weekends and holidays. In addition, you may want to remind students that *A.M.* indicates morning hours, while *P.M.* refers to afternoon and evening hours.

C **Place Labels:** Point out that the place names, or stations, on this schedule are important points of reference. When reading the schedule, students should first determine and locate their starting point: the station from which they will be departing. Then they should find their destination or arrival point: the station they want to reach. Suggest that students circle and label their departure and arrival points.

D **Expressions of Time:** Before they consult a bus schedule, students should know their approximate departure time. They should then find their departure time under the correct station heading and use their finger or a ruler to trace along the row and find their arrival time under the appropriate station label. Again, students may want to circle or draw lines connecting the two times.

Additional Questions

1. What time would you arrive at Grand & Delaware if you caught the 11:28 A.M. bus from the Chestnut St. Mall? **(11:47)**

2. At what time can you catch the first bus leaving Lawrence Station? **(4:57 A.M.)** At what time does the last morning bus leave Memorial Hospital? **(12:09 P.M.)**

3. What stations are east of Grand & Lincoln? **(Memorial Hospital, Grand & Delaware, Three Rivers Station)**

Other Types of Schedules

Students encounter many different kinds of schedules in their daily lives. For example:
• train schedules and schedules for other modes of transportation
• class schedules for schools, parks, and sports centers
• rehearsal and practice schedules for extracurricular activities
• TV scheduling and movie listings

Vocabulary
Mini-Lessons

1 Explain to students that sometimes they can figure out the meaning of an unfamiliar word or term by thinking about the context, or the surrounding words of the sentence or passage.

2 Write the following paragraph on the board and read it aloud:

> **Maria suffered from *insomnia* last night. For hours, she tossed and turned and stared into the darkness. The next morning, she was so tired that she couldn't concentrate on her schoolwork.**

3 Then model how to use context to figure out the meaning of *insomnia:*

MODEL

I'm not sure what insomnia *means. I can look for context clues in the sentence this word is in and in the surrounding sentences. The phrases "she tossed and turned," "stared into the darkness," and "she was so tired" help me figure out that* insomnia *means "a state of sleeplessness."*

4 Now write the following paragraph on the board and read it aloud. Have a volunteer underline the context clues that could be used to help determine the meaning of the word *defiant.*

> **The protesters refused to leave when the police arrived. They linked arms and formed a chain. Then they sat down in the middle of the street. They were really quite *defiant.***

Point out to students that in the example above, a type of clue known as **details from general context** helped them figure out the meaning of *defiant.* Encourage students to use this strategy throughout the year, along with other common types of context clues:

Definition and Restatement

His son went to **culinary,** or cooking, school.

(The phrase following *culinary* helps define the word as meaning "having to do with cooking.")

Example

The book lists the world's worst **natural disasters,** including earthquakes, floods, and hurricanes.

(Earthquakes, floods, and hurricanes are examples of natural disasters.)

Comparison and Contrast

I feel **languid** today; however, usually I'm full of energy.

(The word *however* helps you understand that "full of energy" is the opposite of *languid.* Therefore, *languid* must mean "weary or tired.")

Here's How

See the next three pages for useful lessons on context clues that you can duplicate for students.

Context Clues (Example)

A good way to make sense of an unfamiliar word is to look at the **context**: the other words in the sentence and other sentences in the paragraph that might give clues to the meaning of the word. There are a number of ways you can use context clues to help you determine a word's meaning.

Sometimes a sentence will provide an **example** that will help you understand the meaning of the word. Examples are often signaled by words or phrases such as

like	for instance	this	such as	especially
these	for example	other	includes	

Here's How   Using Examples in Context to Figure Out an Unfamiliar Word

Try to *embellish* your short story; for example, describe the house by the river in more detail and have the heroine explain why she wants to paint it purple.

1. Identify the unfamiliar word.

(I'm not sure what the word *embellish* means.)

2. Read to see if there is a word that signals that an example may follow.

(I see the phrase *for example.* That phrase could point to an example.)

3. Find the example or examples.

(The phrases *describe the house by the river in more detail* and *have the heroine explain why she wants to paint it purple* follow the phrase *for example.* These must be examples of how the writer can *embellish* the story.)

4. Ask yourself how the example or examples relate to the unfamiliar word.

(Both examples are details that will make the story better.)

5. Use this information to figure out what the word means.

(Since both examples are details that the writer should add to the story to make it better, *embellish* must mean "to add details to something to make it better.")

6. Now, look up the unfamiliar word in the dictionary and jot the word and definition down in your personal word list.

embellish *v.* To make beautiful, to decorate; to add ornamental or fictitious details to

Context Clues (Comparison or Contrast)

A good way to make sense of an unfamiliar word is to look at the **context**: the other words in the sentence and other sentences in the paragraph that might give clues to the meaning of the word. There are a number of ways you can use context clues to help you determine a word's meaning.

Sometimes a sentence will provide a **comparison** or a **contrast** that will help you understand the meaning of the word. Certain words or phrases signal comparison or contrast.

Some Comparison Signals		Some Contrast Signals	
like	similar to	but	although
as	also	unlike	however
related	resembling	rather than	on the other hand

Here's How Using Comparison or Contrast to Figure Out an Unfamiliar Word

Unlike his friend Bud, who is stiff and clumsy on the basketball court, my brother is as *agile* as a dancer.

1. Identify the unfamiliar word.

   (I'm not sure what the word *agile* means.)

2. Read to see if there is a word or phrase that signals that a comparison or a contrast may follow.

   (I see the words *unlike* and *as*. *Unlike* could signal a contrast, and *as* could signal a comparison.)

3. Identify the comparison or contrast.

   (The sentence says that Bud is clumsy, unlike the brother who is agile and compared to a dancer.)

4. Use this information to figure out what the unfamiliar word means.

   (A dancer is usually graceful. Because the brother is compared to a dancer rather than to clumsy Bud, I think that *agile* means "graceful.")

5. Find the word in the dictionary and record it in your personal word list.

   agile *adj.* Characterized by quickness, lightness, and ease of movement

6. A sentence may contain only comparison or only contrast as a context clue. You can still use the strategy above to find the meaning.

Context Clues (Restatement)

A good way to make sense of an unfamiliar word is to look at the **context**: the other words in the sentence and other sentences in the paragraph that might give clues to the meaning of the word. There are a number of ways you can use context clues to help you determine a word's meaning.

Sometimes a writer will **restate** the meaning of a difficult word within a sentence, defining it for you. Restatements or definitions are often signaled by words or phrases such as

or	which is	that is
also called	also known as	in other words

Here's How) **Using Restatement in Context to Figure Out an Unfamiliar Word**

Anna decided to plant a *deciduous* tree; that is, a tree that loses its leaves in winter.

1. Identify the unfamiliar word.

(I'm not sure what the word *deciduous* means.)

2. Read to see if there is a word that signals that a restatement may follow.

(I see the phrase *that is.* What follows may include a restatement or definition.)

3. Find the restated information.

(The words *that is* point to *a tree that loses its leaves in winter.*)

4. Use this information to figure out what the unfamiliar word means.

(Because the sentence tells me that a deciduous tree loses its leaves in winter, I think that *deciduous* must mean "losing leaves in winter.")

5. Now, look up the unfamiliar word in the dictionary and jot the word and definition down in your personal word list.

deciduous *adj.* Falling off or shed at a specific season or stage of growth, as *deciduous leaves,* or *deciduous antlers*

1 Explain to students that sometimes they can figure out the meaning of an unfamiliar word by thinking about the meaning of the word parts it contains.

2 Write the word *irresistible* on the board and read it aloud. Model how to use the base word and affixes to figure out the meaning of the word.

You could say: I'm not sure what irresistible *means. I can try breaking the word into parts. I see the prefix* ir-, *which means "not," and which I have seen in other words, such as* irregular *and* irresponsible. *I see the base word* resist, *which means "to hold off, withstand, or refuse to give in to something." I also see the suffix* -ible, *which means "capable of, able, inclined to, or worthy." By combining the meanings of these word parts, I can figure out that* irresistible *must mean something like "not capable of being held off." When I look in the dictionary to see if I am right, I find that the definition is "too strong to resist; having an overpowering appeal."*

3 Explain to students that they can also break down compound words, which are made up of two words put together. Tell students that they can sometimes tell the meaning of a compound word by looking at the meaning of each word part. This strategy may be particularly useful for students learning English.

4 Write the word *seaport* on the board and read it aloud. Model how to break it into parts and figure out the meaning.

You could say: I've never seen the word seaport *before. I can try to figure out its meaning by breaking it into two words,* sea *and* port. *I know that a sea is a body of water, and a port is a place where boats can dock. I think a seaport must be a place that is on a body of water and where boats can dock.*

5 Share with students the following lists of commonly used prefixes, suffixes, and compound words.

Prefixes	Suffixes	Compound Words
anti- (against)	-ology (study of)	sunshine
cent- (hundred)	-ful (full of, resembling)	junkyard
tele- (distant)	-less (without)	snowsuit
tri- (three)	-er (person who does)	overcoat
un- (not)	-ment (action or process)	streetcar
mega- (large)	-ous (full of, resembling)	marketplace
ante- (before)	-ily (in the manner of, like)	spaceship
epi- (outside)	-ism (idea or theory)	skyscraper
poly- (many)	-ness (condition, quality, state)	snowboard

6 As the year progresses, you may wish to review this strategy. The following list provides additional words for you and your students to model.

Have volunteers draw vertical lines between the word parts, and ask them to explain how to use those parts to figure out the meaning of each word.

antisocial	resentful	telescope	laptop	unwilling	amusement
megaton	landlocked	heroism	musicology	wasteful	centimeter
overpower	refinement	tricycle	uneasily	newcomer	

Here's How

See the next three pages for useful lessons on working with prefixes, suffixes, and compound words. You can duplicate these lessons for students.

Word Parts (Prefixes)

A **prefix** is a word part attached to the beginning of a base word or root. The meaning of a prefix combines with the meaning of the base word or root. For example, the prefix *in-* often means "not," as in *indirect,* which means "not direct."

Here's How **Using Prefixes to Determine Word Meaning**

1. When you encounter an unfamiliar word, try to determine whether the word contains a prefix.

> **misinform**

(*Mis-* may be a prefix. The rest of the word is *inform,* which can stand on its own, so I think *mis-* is a prefix.)

---

2. Try to think of other words containing the same prefix. Think about what these words mean.

> **misbehave, misplace, misdeed, misjudge, mispronounce**

(I know that *misbehave* means to behave badly, and the meanings of the other words also involve something going wrong, so mis- must mean "bad" or "wrong.")

---

3. Look at the way the word was used in the sentence. On the basis of the context and on the meaning of the prefix, make an educated guess about the word's meaning.

(*Inform* means "to give information," and *mis-* means "wrong," so I think *misinform* may mean "giving wrong information.")

---

4. Look up the word's definition in the dictionary and compare it with your guess.

> **misinform** *v.* to provide with incorrect information

(*Misinform* means giving wrong information; my guess was correct.)

Word Parts (Suffixes)

A **suffix** is a word part attached to the end of a base word or root. Most suffixes determine a word's part of speech. Familiarity with common suffixes can help you determine the meaning of some unfamiliar words.

Here's How   Using Suffixes to Determine Meaning

1. When you encounter an unfamiliar word, try to determine whether the word contains a suffix.

   blissful

   (I think –*ful* must be suffix added to the word bliss. I also recognize –*ful* as a suffix because I've seen it in other words.)

2. Try to think of other words containing the same suffix. Think about what these words mean.

   careful, fearful, harmful, meaningful

   (I know that *careful* means "full of caution; paying attention to danger." The other words all have the idea of being full of something, so –*ful* probably means "full of."

3. Look at how the word was used in the sentence. On the basis of its context and the meaning of the suffix, make an educated guess about the word's meaning.

   (I know that *bliss* means "happiness; joy," so *blissful* must mean "full of happiness."

4. Look up the word's definition in a dictionary and compare it with your guess. If the word isn't listed on its own, you may need to look for it within the entry for its base word.

   blissful *adj.* Joyful; extremely happy

   (*Blissful* means "being full of joy;" my guess was correct.)

Word Parts (Compound Words)

A **compound word** is a word made up of two words put together. The meanings of the two word parts combine to form a new meaning. Sometimes the meaning of a compound word is obvious when you look at the meaning of each word part. For example, the word *birthday* is made up of the words *birth* and *day*. It simply means the day a person was born. Other times, the meaning is not as clear, but it is usually still related to the meaning of the two word parts.

Here's How   Understanding Compound Words

1. When you see an unfamiliar compound word, look first for its two word parts.

   chalkboard

   (The word parts of *chalkboard* are *chalk* and *board*.)

2. Look at the meanings of the two parts and think of how they might be related.

   (*Chalkboard* probably has something to do with both *chalk* and *board*. I know that a *board* is a flat piece of wood, and I know that *chalk* is something to write with. I think a *chalkboard* must be a flat surface that you can write on with chalk, but I don't think it's made of wood.)

3. Look up the word's definition in the dictionary. Compare it with your guess.

   chalkboard *n.* A smooth, hard panel designed for writing on with chalk; also called *blackboard* or *greenboard*.

   (My guess was correct.)

4. Some compound words have a meaning that doesn't make obvious sense. When you encounter such a word, break it into its word parts and see what sense you can make of it.

   pitfall

   (The word parts of *pitfall* are *pit* and *fall*. Does it have something to do with falling, or maybe with autumn?)

5. Look up the word's definition in the dictionary and compare it with your thoughts.

   pitfall *n.* An unexpected hazard or hidden danger: *the pitfalls of failing to plan ahead.*

   (Although *pitfall* doesn't literally mean "a pit that someone or something might fall into," it does mean "a danger that is difficult or impossible to predict." If a person fell into a pit, that would definitely be dangerous. So there is at least a loose connection between a *pitfall* and a hazardous situation.)

1 Explain to students that sometimes they can figure out the meaning of an unfamiliar word if they recognize its root from other, familiar words. You may want to explain that a **root** is a word part that contains the most important element of that word's meaning. A root must be combined with other word parts, such as prefixes or suffixes, to form a word.

2 Write the word *enumerate* on the board and read it aloud. Model how to use the root to help determine the word's meaning.

You could say: I've never seen the word enumerate *before. I think the root is* numer-; *I've seen that root in other words, such as* numerous *and* numeral. *I know that* numerous *means "many" and* numeral *means "number," so I bet* enumerate *has something to do with numbering or counting things. When I look up* enumerate *in the dictionary to confirm my guess, I see that it means "to count one by one; to determine the number of; to list."*

3 Now write the following chart on the board:

Root	Meaning
alt-	high *or* tall
bio-	life
cardi-	heart
fig-	form *or* shape
later-	side
migr-	move *or* travel
phon-	sound
tract-	drag
vor-	eat

4 Have volunteers use the information in the chart as they try to define the words below. Make sure they explain the process they used to figure out the meaning of each word.

altitude   attraction biography   biology   cardiogram   configure   disfigure
emigration   lateral   migrant   migratory   phonics   traction   voracious

5 As the year progresses, you may wish to review this strategy. The following chart provides you with additional words, roots, and meanings.

Root	Meaning	Examples
astr-	star	astral, astronaut
aud-	hear	audible, audience, audition
circum-	around *or* about	circumference, circumnavigate
dent-	tooth	indent, dentures
fract-, frag-	break	fracture, fragile
hydr-	water	hydrant, dehydrate
log-	word, speech, *or* idea	dialogue, epilogue
spec-	see *or* examine	inspect, spectator
vol-	desire *or* wish	volition, volunteer

Here's How

See the next page for useful lessons on using word roots to determine meaning. You can duplicate these lessons for students.

Word Parts (Roots)

Many English words, especially long ones, can be broken into smaller parts. A **root** is the core of a word, or the part that contains the most important element of the word's meaning.

Many words in English have their roots in other languages, particularly Greek and Latin. Knowing the meaning of Greek and Latin roots can help you to understand unfamiliar words.

Here's How Using Word Roots to Determine Meaning

1. When you encounter an unfamiliar word, first look for any prefixes or suffixes and remove them to try to isolate the root.

> **autograph**

(The word starts with *auto-*, which is a prefix meaning "self." After *auto-* is removed, what remains is graph. This part of the word must contain the root.)

2. Try to think of other words containing the same root. Think about what these words mean.

> **telegraph, photograph, paragraph, mimeograph**

(These words all have to do with something written or recorded.)

3. Look at the way the word was used in the sentence. On the basis of its context and its parts, make an educated guess about what the word means.

(I think that *autograph* might refer to something written. Since *auto-* means "self," maybe the word refers to something you write yourself.)

4. Look up the word's definition in a dictionary, and compare it with your guess.

> **autograph** *n.* A person's own signature or handwriting.

(*Autograph* means your own signature or handwriting. My guess was close.)

1 Tell students that an idiom is a phrase whose meaning is different from the meanings of its individual words put together. Explain to students that they can sometimes figure out the meaning of an unfamiliar idiom by thinking about its context, or the surrounding words of the sentence or passage.

2 Write the following sentences on the board and read them aloud:

"It's after midnight, and I'm really tired," Alison said. "I think it's time to *hit the hay.*"

3 Then model how to use context to figure out the meaning of *hit the hay.*

MODEL
I've never seen the phrase hit the hay *before, and I'm not sure what it means. To find out, I can look for context clues in the rest of the passage. Alison mentioned that it was after midnight and that she was tired. When it's late and I'm sleepy, I usually go to sleep. If I substitute* go to sleep *for* hit the hay, *it makes sense in the passage. Therefore, I think that* to hit the hay *means "to go to sleep."*

4 The following boldface sentences contain commonly used idioms. Write these sentences on the chalkboard (but not the translations given in parentheses). Ask students to read the sentences and use context clues to figure out the meaning of the idioms.

Gwen has the talent show *on her mind;* she thinks about almost nothing else. (Gwen thinks about the talent show a great deal.)

My sister showed us her engagement ring and announced that her boyfriend had *popped the question.* (The boyfriend asked her to marry him.)

Alan isn't quite finished with his science project—he still *has some loose ends to tie up.* (Alan has some small tasks to complete.)

My new catcher's mitt *cost me an arm and a leg.* I had to save my allowance for six weeks to buy it. (The mitt was expensive.)

We are leaving at five o'clock *sharp,* so you can't be even a minute late. (We are leaving exactly at five.)

Jackie and Tia had an argument, but after a while they were able to *iron out* their differences and be friends again. (They came to an agreement.)

5 As the year progresses, you may wish to review this strategy. The following list provides you with more idioms to share with your students.

Idiom	Meaning
get the lead out	*hurry up, move faster*
putting the cart before the horse	*reversing the correct or proper order of things*
at the drop of a hat	*immediately, right away*
blow a fuse	*become angry*
top banana	*the leader or most important person*
the works	*everything available*
scratched the surface	*just begun, not treated in a detailed fashion*

Here's How
See the next page for a useful lesson on understanding idioms. You can duplicate this lesson for students.

Understanding Idioms

An **idiom** is a set phrase whose meaning is different from the literal meaning of its individual words. For example, the idiom *to get someone's goat* has nothing to do with goats; it simply means "to tease, anger, or annoy someone."

Most idioms are so common in everyday speech that people use them without thinking about them. However, unfamiliar idioms can be very confusing. If you didn't know that *she got her feet wet* really means "she started a new project" or "she began learning something new," you might wonder what wet feet have to do with anything!

When you see an unfamiliar idiom, you can sometimes find clues in the idiom's context, or surrounding words and paragraphs.

Here's How **Understanding Idioms**

"Erica and Sylvie have so much in common, and they are both such friendly people," said Rachel. "Even before they became best friends, I knew they would *hit it off!*"

1. Identify the unfamiliar idiom.

(I'm not sure what *hit it off* means. Does it mean "to hit something"?)

2. Look for context clues, such as a restatement or explanation.

(I see that Rachel's first sentence is *"Erica and Sylvie have so much in common, and they are both such friendly people."* It seems that Rachel is explaining why Sylvie and Erica "hit it off.")

3. Use this information to figure out what the idiom means.

(Rachel is saying that Erica and Sylvie are similar, that they are both friendly, and that they are now best friends. If they are so much alike, they probably get along well together. I think *to hit it off* means "to like each other" or "to get along well.")

4. Some idioms appear in regular dictionaries under the definition of the phrase's main word. Look up this idiom in a regular dictionary or in a dictionary of idioms, under *hit.*

hit *v.* —*idioms. Informal.* **Hit it off.** To get along well with each other.

5. If you can't find the idiom in a dictionary, ask a teacher, a fellow student, or another adult what it means.

1 Explain to students that many words have more than one meaning. They can figure out which meaning of a word is being used in a sentence or passage by looking for clues in the surrounding context.

2 Write the following sentence on the board and read it aloud:

> **Rosa's *conviction* about the importance of helping others led her to volunteer at the shelter.**

3 Then model how to use context to figure out which meaning of the word *conviction* is being used:

MODEL
I'm not sure which meaning of conviction *is being used in this sentence.* Conviction *can mean "a guilty verdict," and it can also mean "strong belief." I can look for context clues in the sentence. The phrases "the importance of helping others" and "led her to volunteer at the shelter" help me figure out that, in this sentence,* conviction *means "strong belief."*

4 Now write the following sentence on the board and read it aloud. Have a volunteer underline the context clues that could be used to help determine which meaning of the word *stranger* is intended.

> **Although we didn't know the man, the *stranger* seemed eager to talk to us.**

5 If students are not familiar with a word or its multiple meanings, encourage them to look up the word in a dictionary. Sometimes dictionaries provide sample contexts to show the different meanings of a word. Tell students to compare the sample contexts and figure out the one that best fits the sentence. As the year progresses, you may wish to review these strategies.

The following chart provides you with additional words and some of their multiple meanings. Have students create sentences that demonstrate their understanding of the words' multiple meanings.

Word	Meanings	Word	Meanings
point	1. sharp end 2. significant idea 3. indicate something	tip	1. small amount of money 2. helpful hint 3. raise (one's hat) in greeting
sharp	1. pointed 2. clearly visible 3. mentally quick	strike	1. hit 2. refuse to work 3. a pitched ball that is swung at
dash	1. punctuation mark 2. run or rush 3. small amount of an ingredient	monitor	1. computer screen 2. keep close watch over 3. student who assists a teacher
wave	1. signal with the hand 2. crest in a body of water 3. curly hair	season	1. one of four periods of the year 2. add herbs and spices to food 3. become skilled through experience

Here's How

See the next page for a useful lesson on words with multiple meanings that you can duplicate for students.

Using Words with Multiple Meanings

Because language constantly changes to meet the needs of those who use it, many words in English have more than one meaning. These multiple meanings may lead to confusion, causing readers to misinterpret a writer's message.

Here's How **Selecting the Appropriate Meaning of a Word**

1. When you are not sure which definition of a word applies in a particular sentence, look for clues in the surrounding context.

> I looked everywhere for my little brother, but he had disappeared without a *trace.*

(I know that *trace* is a verb that is used to describe the act of drawing, but in this sentence the word seems to be used as a noun. Maybe *trace* can be a different part of speech and have another meaning.)

2. If the meaning you know does not make sense in the context of the sentence and you don't have enough clues to help you figure out the meaning, look up the word in a dictionary. Look for the definition that makes sense in the sentence.

(I see that there are several meanings for the word *trace,* including "to sketch," "evidence of someone's presence," and "a very small amount of something.")

3. Decide which dictionary definition works best in the sentence you are examining.

(In this sentence, *trace* refers to the lack of evidence of the little brother's presence, so in this case, *trace* probably is a noun meaning "evidence of someone's existence or presence.")

Teaching Decoding Strategies

Teaching Word Study Skills

By middle school, your students should have had years of instruction in systematic, explicit phonics and decoding skills. Good readers have well developed decoding skills which enable them to quickly and automatically identify printed words so that attention can be focused on the more challenging task of understanding.

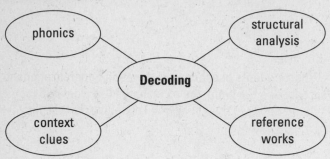

Phonics

Phonics is a system of teaching the basic sound-letter relationships in the English language. Phonics lays the foundation for young readers understanding the relationship between spoken and written words. Instruction is usually coupled with decodable text so students can apply skills to manageable reading and develop automaticity—the ability to recognize words in text automatically and effortlessly.

In the primary grades, phonics receives the main emphasis as a decoding strategy. The chart shows when phonics instruction usually occurs.

Phonics	Grade where taught
consonants (initial, medial, final)	through first half grade 1
consonant digraphs (/th/ *th*, etc.)	through grade 1
consonant clusters (*st, bl, br,* etc.)	through early grade 2
short vowels	first half grade 1
long vowels	through grade 1
r-controlled vowels (*er, ir, ar,* etc.)	through grade 2
diphthongs (*oi, oy,* etc.)	through grade 2
variant vowels (*ough, au, aw,* etc.)	through grade 2

As a result of phonics instruction, many young students can decode the vast majority of phonetically regular words they read. In the intermediate grades and beyond, the problem becomes how to decode irregular and multisyllabic words which appear increasingly in reading materials.

Structural Analysis

Structural analysis is a strategy used to figure out the meanings of multisyllabic words. When students encounter an unfamiliar multisyllabic word, they are taught to remove any prefixes, remove any suffixes, and look at the bases, roots or combining forms. Once they figure out the meanings of the parts of the word, they put the word back together again and check their understanding of the word within the context of the sentence and paragraph. You can help your students use structural analysis by teaching the procedure outlined below.

Example Sentence and Procedure

When Fred opened the old refrigerator the *malodorous* aroma convinced him to give the refrigerator a good cleaning.

1. If there is a prefix, take it off. (*-mal*)

2. If there is a suffix, take it off. (*-ous*)

3. Look at the base or root that is left, *odor*

4. Say to yourself, what do I know about the word odor? You might know it means *smell.*

5. Consider the meaning of the prefix, which you might recognize if you speak Spanish, because it is identical to the word for "bad" in Spanish. If you don't speak Spanish, think of other words that start with *-mal,* like *malformed, malnutrition, malpractice,* or *malcontent.* which would lead you to guess that *-mal* means "bad."

6. Consider the meaning of the suffix *-ous* which you might recognize from other words like *studious* and as a suffix that turns a noun into an adjective.

7. Put the meanings of the parts together, *bad + smell* in an adjective form.

8. Check your understanding in the context of the sentence, "When Fred opened the old refrigerator the bad smelling aroma convinced him to give the refrigerator a good cleaning." It fits!

9. If the sentence still does not make sense, look the word up in the dictionary.

You can help students recognize prefixes by making sure they know the four most common prefixes: *un-, re-, in-,* and *dis-,* which account for about 65% of all words with prefixes.

For additional suggestions on teaching structural analysis skills, see *The Language of Literature.*

Syllable patterns Instruction and practice in understanding the basic syllable patterns helps students break words into smaller parts and then use phonics skills to pronounce the word. The following pages contain lessons in understanding the **syllabication generalizations** that will support students' word attack skills. Although there are exceptions, we will use the word **rule** to help students remember them easily.

Rule 1: When there are two consonants between two vowels, divide between the two consonants, unless they are a blend or a digraph.

Rule 2: When there are three consonants between two vowels, divide between the blend or the digraph and the other consonant.

Rule 3: When there are two consonants between two vowels, divide between the two consonants between vowels unless they are a blend or a digraph. The first syllable is a closed syllable, and the vowel sound is short.

Rule 4: Do not split common vowel clusters, such as vowel digraphs, r-controlled vowels, and vowel diphthongs.

Rule 5: When you see a VCV pattern in the middle of a word, divide the word before or after the consonant. If you divide after the consonant, the first vowel sound is short. If you divide before the consonant, the vowel sound is long.

Rule 6: Always divide compound words between the individual words.

Rule 7: When a word includes an affix, divide between the base word and the affix (prefix or suffix).

When students use these syllabication generalizations to pronounce the word, they can match the word with a word already in their speaking vocabulary or look for meaningful word parts.

Quick Diagnostic Test

Use the list below to determine how well your students read multisyllabic words. The lists are organized by syllabication rule. If your students are unable to read some or all of these words, teaching them high-utility syllabication rules may help improve their decoding skills. Use the lessons on the following pages to assist you.

(Rules 1, 3)	(Rule 5)
picture	model
happen	robot
feather	crazy
follow	never
usher	final

(Rule 2)	(Rule 6)
angler	whirlwind
merchant	grasshopper
tumbler	grapevine
children	wastebasket
purchase	earring

(Rule 4)	(Rule 7)
party	readjustment
poison	rebound
feature	childish
royal	unavoidable
chowder	unselfish

Syllabication

LESSON 1: Consonant Blends and Digraphs in Multisyllabic Words

This lesson will help students chunk, or syllabicate, multisyllabic words that contain consonant blends and digraphs. Your students most likely recognize blends and digraphs when they see them in print; however, they may have problems decoding multisyllabic words if they attempt to syllabicate between the two letters in the blend or digraph. If you think your students would benefit from a review of blends and digraphs, begin with Parts 1 and 2. If not, you may go directly to Parts 3 and 4.

Part 1: Quick Review of Consonant Blends

Following are common consonant blends with examples of each. The two letters in each blend represent two sounds.

br	break, brand	sl	slick, slam
cr	crane, crack	-ld	field, hold
dr	drive, drip	-lk	milk
fr	free	-lp	help
gr	green	-lt	melt
pr	press	sc	scare
tr	true	sk	ski, risk
bl	blue	sm	smart
cl	clue, close	sn	snare, snack
fl	flame, flute	sp	spell, clasp
gl	glue, glide	st	state, twist
pl	please, plan	sw	switch, sway

DIRECT INSTRUCTION

To help your students focus on consonant blends, write the following sentences on the board.

> 1. <u>Brown</u> bears <u>slide</u> on the <u>frost</u>.
> 2. The <u>grand</u> <u>prize</u> was a <u>silk</u> <u>scarf</u>.
> 3. <u>Flutes</u> <u>fly</u> in <u>blue</u> <u>skies</u>.
> 4. <u>Sly</u> <u>smelt</u> <u>swim</u> in <u>swift</u> surf.

Ask a student to read aloud the first sentence. Call attention to the words *brown, slide,* and *frost.*

You could say: What two letters do you see at the beginning of *brown (br),* at the beginning of *slide (sl),* at the beginning and end of *frost (fr,-st)?* These are called consonant blends. The consonant blends are made up of two consonant letters and stand for two sounds. You will always say both sounds when you sound out a word.

Follow the same procedure with the remaining sentences.

Answers: #2: grand (*gr*), prize (*pr*), silk (*lk*), scarf (*sc*); #3: Flutes (*fl*), fly (*fl*), blue (*bl*), skies (*sk*); #4: Sly (*sl*), smelt (*sm, -lt*), swim (*sw*), swift (*sw*)

Part 2: Quick Review of Consonant Digraphs

Following are consonant digraphs and examples of each. The two letters in each digraph represent one sound.

ch cheat, check, touch
sh shine, fish, push
th (voiced) that, the, this
th (voiceless) think, teeth, thumb, thank
wh (wh blend) where, whoops, when, white, wheel

DIRECT INSTRUCTION

Write these sentences on the chalkboard.

> 1. How <u>much</u> <u>fish</u> does a <u>whale</u> eat?
> 2. <u>She</u> will <u>think</u> <u>the</u> <u>thing</u> is <u>cheap</u>.
> 3. <u>When</u> will you <u>change</u> and <u>wash</u> <u>the</u> <u>sheets</u>?
> 4. Do <u>white</u> hens have <u>teeth</u>?

Ask a student to read aloud the first sentence.

You could say: What two letters do you see at the end of *much (-ch),* at the end of *fish (-sh),* at the beginning of *whale (wh)?* The consonant digraphs are made up of two consonant letters but represent only one sound. You will say only one sound when you sound out a word.

Follow the same procedure with the remaining sentences.

Answers: #2: She (*sh*), think (*th*), the (*th*), thing (*th*), cheap (*ch*); #3: When (*wh*), change (*ch*), wash (-*sh*), the (*the*), sheets (*sh*); #4: white (*wh*), teeth (*th*)

Part 3: Syllabication Strategy: Consonant Blends and Digraphs

In the following lesson, students will use their knowledge of consonant blends and digraphs to syllabicate words. You may find it helpful to review the most basic syllabication rule: *Each syllable has one and only one vowel sound.*

DIRECT INSTRUCTION

Write Rule 1 and the example words on the chalkboard. Remind students that V stands for vowel and C stands for consonant. Ask a student to give examples of vowel and consonant letters.

> **Rule 1: VCCV**
> **When there are two consonants between two vowels, divide between the two consonants, unless they are a blend or a digraph.**
>
> **picture happen abrupt feather**

Have a student read Rule 1. Ask a student to explain the rule in his or her own words and then to read the first word. You could then say to students:

You could say: **Find the VCCV pattern in the word *picture* (ictu). Do you see a blend or digraph? (no) Where would you divide this word according to Rule 1? (between the c and the t) Look at each syllable. Pronounce the word. Do you recognize the word?**

Repeat the process with the remaining words.

Answers: hap/pen; a/brupt, feath/er

Write Rule 2 and the example words on the chalkboard.

> **Rule 2: VCCCV**
> **When there are three consonants between two vowels, divide between the blend or the digraph and the other consonant.**
>
> **angler merchant tumbler children**

Have a student read Rule 2. Ask a student to explain the rule in his or her own words and then to read the first word. You could then say to students:

You could say: **Find the VCCCV pattern in the word *angler* (angle). Do you see a blend or digraph? (yes) Where would you divide this word according to Rule 2? (between the *n* and the *gl*) Look at each syllable. Pronounce the word. Do you recognize the word?**

Repeat the process with the remaining words.

Answers: (mer/chant), (tum/bler), (chil/dren)

Part 4: Strategy Practice

Write the following words on the board. Have students divide the words according to the two rules, identify the rule, and pronounce the word.

Practice applying Rule 1

	Answers		Answers
scatter	scat/ter	whether	wheth/er
garden	gar/den	zipper	zip/per
crafty	craft/y	fashion	fash/ion
scarlet	scar/let	forget	for/get
traffic	traf/fic	respect	re/spect

Practice applying Rule 2

	Answers		Answers
hungry	hun/gry	toddler	tod/dler
concrete	con/crete	purchase	pur/chase
hundred	hun/dred	address	ad/dress
worship	wor/ship	supply	sup/ply
handsome	hand/some	employ	em/ploy

Cumulative practice

	Answers		Answers
written	writ/ten	nothing	noth/ing
constant	con/stant	lather	lath/er
secret	se/cret	sandal	san/dal
surplus	sur/plus	merchant	mer/chant
kindling	kin/dling	silver	sil/ver

LESSON 2: Short Vowels in Multisyllabic Words

When your students have trouble figuring out unfamiliar words in print, they are most likely having problems decoding the letters that stand for the vowel sound(s) in the word. Usually this is because the relationship between vowel sounds and the letters that represent them isn't as predictable as the relationship between consonant sounds and the letters that represent them.

This lesson will help your students syllabicate words that contain short vowels. If you think your students would benefit from a review of short vowels, you may begin with Part 1. If not, you may skip directly to Parts 2 and 3.

Part 1: Quick Review of Short Vowels

Of the vowel sounds in English, the short vowels have the most predictable relationship between the sounds and the letters that represent them.

DIRECT INSTRUCTION

To help students focus on short vowels, write the list below on the board.

at	end	in	on	up
bat	bend	fin	odd	cup
and	vest	lick	mop	duck
fad	tell	drip	trot	lump

Have a student read the first column of words.

You could say: **What vowel sound do you hear in each of these words? (/a/ or short a) What letter represents that sound in each of these words? (the letter *a*)**

Follow the same procedure with the remaining lists.

Answers: column 2: /e/ or short e; column 3: /i/ or short i; column 4: /o/ or short o; column 5: /u/ or short u

Part 2: Syllabication Strategy: Short Vowels

Use the following syllabication strategy to help your students figure out some of the vowel sounds in multisyllabic words. You will note that Rule 3 expands upon Rule 1 introduced in Lesson 1.

DIRECT INSTRUCTION

Write Rule 3 and the example words on the board. Remind students that V stands for vowel and C stands for consonant.

> **Rule 3: VCCV**
> **When there are two consonants between two vowels, divide between the consonants, unless they are a blend or a digraph. The first syllable is a closed syllable, and the vowel sound is short.**
>
> butter   lather   follow   usher
> summer   traffic   tender   invent

Have a student read Rule 3 and explain the rule in his or her own words.

Have a student read the first word.

You could say: **Find the VCCV pattern in the first word. (*utte*) Do you see a blend or a digraph? (no) Where would you divide this word according to Rule 3? (between the two *t*'s) What vowel sound do you hear in the first syllable? (short) Look at each syllable and pronounce the word. Do you recognize the word?**
Repeat this process with the remaining words.

Answers: but/ter, lath/er, fol/low, ush/er, sum/mer, traf/fic, ten/der, in/vent

Part 3: Strategy Practice

Write the following on the board. Have students divide the words according to the rule and pronounce the word.

	Answers		Answers
under	un/der	billow	bil/low
bother	both/er	enter	en/ter
bottom	bot/tom	number	num/ber
rather	rath/er	object	ob/ject
practice	prac/tice	dipper	dip/per
snapper	snap/per	silver	sil/ver
after	af/ter	grammar	gram/mar
cashew	cash/ew	sudden	sud/den
pulpit	pul/pit	vintage	vin/tage
pencil	pen/cil	member	mem/ber

LESSON 3: Vowel Clusters in Multisyllabic Words

This lesson will show students how to chunk, or syllabicate, multisyllabic words that contain vowel clusters: long vowel digraphs, r-controlled vowels, and vowel diphthongs. If your students aren't aware of vowel clusters, they might syllabicate between the two vowels in the cluster. In that case, they will syllabicate incorrectly and mispronounce the word when they attempt to sound it out. If you think your students would benefit from a review of vowel clusters, begin with Parts 1–3. If not, skip to Parts 4 and 5.

Part 1: Quick Review of Long Vowel Digraphs

In words with vowel digraphs, two vowel letters are represented by one vowel sound.

DIRECT INSTRUCTION

Write the list below on the board.

cream	play	boat
beast	gray	coal
bean	paint	goat
green	aim	row
peel	stain	slow

Have a student read the first column of words.

You could say: **What vowel sound do you hear in each of these words? (long e) What letters stand for the long e sound in *beast*? (*ea*) What letters stand for the long e sound in *green*? (*ee*) These are called vowel digraphs. Vowel digraphs are made up of two vowel letters that stand for one sound.**

Follow the same procedure with the remaining lists.

Answers: column 2: long a, *ay* in *gray, ai* in *paint;* column 3: long o, *oa* in *boat, ow* in *slow*

Part 2: Quick Review of R-controlled Vowels

In words with r-controlled vowels, the vowel sound is influenced by the *r* that follows it.

DIRECT INSTRUCTION

Write the list below on the board.

fern	car	born
dirt	star	cord
fur	arm	sort
her	yarn	more
birth	farm	horn

Have a student read the first column of words.

You could say: **These words all have the "er" sound. What letters stand for the "er" sound in *fur*? (ur) in *her*? (er) in *birth*? (ir) These are called r-controlled vowels. The r-controlled vowels are made up of a vowel and the letter *r.* In words with r-controlled vowels, the vowel sound is influenced by the *r* that follows it.**

Follow the same procedure with the remaining columns.

Answers: column 2: all words have the "ar" sound, letters are *ar;* column 3: all words have the or sound, letters are *or.*

Part 3: Quick Review of Vowel Diphthongs

DIRECT INSTRUCTION

To help students focus on vowel diphthongs write this list on the board.

oil	ouch
boil	cloud
boy	how
spoil	scout
toy	towel

Have a student read the first column of words.

You could say: **These words all have the oi sound. What letters stand for the oi sound in *boil*? (oi) in *boy*? (oy) These are called vowel diphthongs. Vowel diphthongs are made up of two vowel letters that stand for two vowel sounds.**

Follow the same procedure with the remaining column.

Answers: column 2: all words have the "ow" sound, letters are *ou* or *ow.*

Part 4: Syllabication Strategy: Vowel Clusters

Use the following syllabication strategy to help your students syllabicate words that contain vowel clusters.

DIRECT INSTRUCTION

Write Rule 4 and the example words on the board.

> **Rule 4:**
> Do not split common vowel clusters, such as long vowel digraphs, r-controlled vowels, and vowel diphthongs.
>
> **party   poison   feature   royal   chowder   garden**

Have a student read Rule 4. Have a student explain the rule in his or her own words.

Have a student read the first word.

You could say: Do you see a vowel cluster in this word? (yes) If you do, what is the cluster? (*ar*) Where would you avoid dividing this word according to Rule 4? (between the *a* and *r*) Where do you think you should divide the word? (after the cluster, between the *r* and *t*) Look at each syllable and pronounce the word. Do you recognize the word?

Repeat this process with the remaining words. In the case of *poison, feature,* and *royal,* students will be asked to syllabicate words for which they haven't learned all of the syllabication rules. Encourage them to try out what they know and attempt a pronunciation based on what they've learned so far.

Answers:

poison: (*oi*) avoid dividing between cluster; divide after the cluster

royal: (*oy*) avoid dividing between cluster; divide after the cluster

feature: (*ea*) avoid dividing between cluster; divide after the cluster

chowder: (*ow*) avoid dividing between cluster; divide after the cluster

garden: (*ar*) avoid dividing between cluster; divide after the cluster

Part 5: Strategy Practice

Write the following on the board. Have students divide the words according to the rules they know and pronounce the word.

	Answers		Answers
carton	car/ton	peanut	pea/nut
powder	pow/der	council	coun/cil
circus	cir/cus	purpose	pur/pose
mountain	moun/tain	moisture	mois/ture
maintain	main/tain	voyage	voy/age
fertile	fer/tile	mayor	may/or
darling	dar/ling	freedom	free/dom
coward	cow/ard	tailor	tai/lor
hornet	hor/net	eager	ea/ger
barter	bar/ter	order	or/der

LESSON 4: Short and Long Vowels in Multisyllabic Words

This lesson will help your students develop flexibility in applying syllabication strategies as they attempt to decode multisyllabic words.

Part 1: Quick Review

If you have skipped over Lessons 1–3, you may want to preview this lesson to be sure your students are prepared for a more complicated syllabication strategy.

Part 2: Syllabication Strategy: Is the vowel sound long or short?

Use the following syllabication strategy to help your students decide whether a vowel letter stands for a long or short vowel sound.

DIRECT INSTRUCTION

Write Rule 5 and the example words on the board. Remind students that V stands for vowel and C stands for consonant.

> **Rule 5: VCV**
>
> **When you see a VCV pattern in the middle of a word, divide the word either before or after the consonant. If you divide the word after the consonant, the first vowel sound will be short. If you divide the word before the consonant, the first vowel sound will be long.**
>
> **model   robot   crazy   never**

Have a student read Rule 5 and explain the rule in his or her own words.

Ask a student to read the first word.

You could say: **Find the VCV pattern in the first word. (*ode*) Where should you first divide the word? (after the *d,* the first consonant) What happens to the vowel sound in the first syllable? (The vowel sound is short) Say the word. Do you recognize it? (yes) When the consonant is part of the first syllable, the first syllable is called "closed."**

Ask a student to read the second word.

You could say: **Find the VCV pattern in the second word. (*obo*) Where should you first divide the word? (after the *b,* the first consonant) What happens to the vowel sound in the first syllable? (The vowel sound is short) Say the word. Do you recognize it? (no)**

Try the second part of the rule. Where should you divide the word? (before the consonant) What happens to the vowel sound in the first syllable? (The vowel sound is long) Say the word. Do you recognize it? (yes) When the consonant is part of the second syllable, the first syllable is called "open."

Repeat this process with the remaining words.

Answers: crazy: (*azy*) Divide after the *z,* the first consonant; vowel is short; no, do not recognize the word. Divide before the *z;* the vowel is long; yes, recognize the word.

never: (*eve*) Divide after the *v;* vowel sound is short; yes, recognize the word.

Part 3: Strategy Practice

Write the following words on the board. Have students divide the words and pronounce the words.

	Answers		Answers
legal	le/gal	final	fi/nal
gravel	grav/el	prefix	pre/fix
basic	ba/sic	level	lev/el
driven	driv/en	moment	mo/ment
minus	mi/nus	paper	pa/per
panic	pan/ic	soda	so/da
spider	spi/der	devil	dev/il
honor	hon/or	tiny	ti/ny
seven	sev/en		

LESSON 5: Compound Words

When students encounter multisyllabic words, they often don't try the obvious; i.e., to look for words or word parts they already know within the longer word. Lessons 5 and 6 will help students develop these skills.

Part 1: Syllabication Strategy: Compound Words

Use the following syllabication strategy to help your students determine where to divide a compound word.

DIRECT INSTRUCTION

Write Rule 6 and the example words on the board.

> **Rule 6:**
>
> **Divide compound words between the individual words.**
>
> grapevine   lifeguard   whirlwind
> butterfly   grasshopper

Have a student read Rule 6. Ask a student to explain the rule in his or her own words.

You could say: **When you see a multisyllabic word, stop and see if it is made up of one or more words that you already know.**

Have a student read the first word.

You could say: **How many words do you see in the first word? (two) Where should you divide the word? (between *grape* and *vine*)**

Repeat the process with the remaining words in the first row.

Answers: (life/guard), (whirl/wind)

Have a student read the first word in the second row.

You could say: **How many words do you see in the word? (two) Where should you divide the word? (between *butter* and *fly*) Where else should you divide the word? (between the two *t*'s) How do you know? (Rule 1 says to divide two consonants between vowels.)**

Repeat the process with the remaining words. (grass/hop/per)

Part 2: Strategy Practice

Write the following words on the board. Have students divide the words, identify the rule(s) they use, and pronounce the word.

	Answers		Answers
shipwreck	ship/wreck	buttermilk	but/ter/milk
postcard	post/card	notebook	note/book
screwdriver	screw/dri/ver	volleyball	vol/ley/ball
oatmeal	oat/meal	washcloth	wash/cloth
windmill	wind/mill	wastebasket	waste/bas/ket
dragonfly	dra/gon/fly	peppermint	pep/per/mint
pancake	pan/cake	hardware	hard/ware
earthquake	earth/quake	handlebar	han/dle/bar
pigtail	pig/tail	earring	ear/ring
wristwatch	wrist/ watch	weekend	week/end

LESSON 6: Affixes

This lesson will give students help in dividing multisyllabic words that contain one or more affixes. These are the kinds of words that give students the most problems because they tend to be long and can look overwhelming. If you think your students would benefit from practice with identifying prefixes and suffixes, start with Parts 1 and 2. If not, go directly to Parts 3 and 4.

Part 1: Quick Review of Prefixes

Recognizing prefixes in multisyllabic words can help your students chunk words into manageable parts. You may use the following list of common prefixes and their meanings to expand upon the lesson described below.

auto-	self	by-	near, aside
mis-	bad	under-	below
pre-	before	un-	not
re-	again	de-	from, down
with-	back, away	dis-	opposite
bi-	two	uni-	one
on-	on	be-	make
tri-	three		

DIRECT INSTRUCTION

Write the following prefixes and their meanings on the board.

auto-	self	bi-	two	un-	not

You could say: **The word part on the left side of each pair is called a prefix. Prefixes can be added to root words or base words to change the meaning of the word. Think of a word that begins with this prefix.**

Write the word on the board.

Follow the same procedure with the remaining prefixes. If you wish, include additional prefixes. Save the words and use them for syllabication practice later.

Possible answers: *auto-* (autobiography); *bi-* (bicycle, bifold,); *un-* (unhappy, unlikely)

Part 2: Quick Review of Suffixes

Recognizing suffixes in multisyllabic words can help your students chunk words into manageable parts. You may use the following list of common suffixes and their meanings to expand upon the lesson described below.

-ness	state or quality of	-less	without
-like	resembling	-ship	state or quality of
-ish	relating to	-ful	full of
-ways	manner	-er	one who
-ly	like, or resembling	-ous	full of
-ion	state or quality of	-ment	action or process

DIRECT INSTRUCTION

Write the following suffixes and their meanings on the board.

-ness	state or quality of	-ly	resembling
-ful	full of		

You could say: **The word part on the left side of each pair is called a suffix. When suffixes are added to root words or base words, they often change the part of speech of the root or base word. Think of a word that ends with this suffix.**

Write the word on the board.

Follow the same procedure with the remaining suffixes. If you wish, include additional suffixes. Save the words and use them for syllabication practice later.

Possible answers: *-ness* (happiness, sadness); *-ly* (quickly, lively); *-ful* (thankful, eventful)

Part 3: Syllabication Strategy: Affixes

Use the following syllabication strategy to help your students determine where to divide words that contain affixes.

DIRECT INSTRUCTION

Write Rule 7 and the examples on the board.

Rule 7:

When a word includes an affix, divide between the base word and the affix (prefix or suffix).

rebound	restless	unavoidable
preschool	childish	readjustment
disprove	joyous	unselfish

Ask a student to read Rule 7 and to explain the rule in his or her own words.

Have a student read the first word in column 1.

You could say: **What prefix do you see in *rebound*? *(re)* Where should you divide *rebound* according to Rule 7? *(re/bound)*** Continue with the remaining words in column 1. In each case, have students apply the rule, divide the word, pronounce the word, and then see if they recognize it.

Answers: pre/school; dis/prove

Have a student read the first word in column 2.

What suffix do you see in *restless*? *(less)* Where should you divide *restless*? *(rest/less)* Continue with the remaining words in column 2. In each case, have students apply the rule, divide the word, pronounce the word, and then see if they recognize it.

Answers: child/ish; joy/ous

Have a student read the first word in column 3.

What affixes do you see in this word? *(un, able)* Where should you divide the word? *(un/avoid/able)* Continue with the remaining words in column 3. In each case, have students apply the rule, divide the word, pronounce it, and then see if they recognize it. Note: In *avoid*, *a* is also considered a prefix, and *able* is considered a suffix. You can further divide the word as follows: un/a/void/a/ble.

Answers: re/adjust/ment and re/ad/just/ment; un/self/ish

If you wish to extend this lesson, have students analyze each word to see if they should apply additional syllabication rules.

Part 4: Strategy Practice

Write the following words on the board. Have students divide the words, identify the rule(s) they use, and pronounce the words.

Answers

uniform	uni/form (or u/ni/form)
fairly	fair/ly
beautiful	beau/ti/ful
unlikely	un/like/ly
recall	re/call
misfit	mis/fit
rigorous	rigor/ous (or rig/or/ous)
hopelessness	hope/less/ness
childlike	child/like
unwind	un/wind
selfish	self/ish
opinion	opin/ion (or o/pin/ion)
hardship	hard/ship
sticker	stick/er
sideways	side/ways
department	de/part/ment
disbelieve	dis/believe (or dis/be/lieve)
withstand	with/stand
become	be/come
refreshment	re/fresh/ment

Comprehension Mini-Lessons
with Graphic Organizers

1 For students who have trouble grasping the main idea of a paragraph or passage, discuss these points.

- The main idea is the most important idea in a paragraph or passage.
- The writer may state the main idea in a sentence. This sentence can appear at the beginning, middle, or end of a paragraph or passage.
- Sometimes the main idea is not stated; it is implied. The reader must then figure it out by thinking about the details and stating the main idea in his or her own words.

2 Duplicate the following paragraph. A master is provided on page 124. Have students follow along as you read it aloud, using it to model **stated main idea.**

> **Kids are collecting more than stamps and stickers these days. Some collect coins and bills from around the world. Others collect miniature houses and mansions. An eighth-grade girl in Detroit, Michigan, collects spiders.**

You could say: Writers often put the main idea in the first sentence so that readers will know what to expect. Kids are collecting more than stamps and baseball cards these days *seems like the main idea. The second and third sentences tell me the kinds of items kids collect. The last sentence states a specific case where a girl collects spiders. Each sentence provides a detail that supports the first sentence. It is, therefore, logical to conclude that the first sentence is the main idea.*

3 Duplicate the following paragraph. A master is provided on page 124. Have students follow along as you read it aloud, using it to model **implied main idea.**

> **Have you ever heard the saying, "One man's trash is another man's fortune"? There are a number of stories from people who have found valuable antiques at auction sales, rummage sales, or Salvation Army resale shops. Next time you think about throwing or giving something away, perhaps you should determine its value.**

You could say: Let's look at the first sentence for the main idea. It gives me a quote to think about. The second and third sentences give additional details about valuable objects. In this case the writer chose not to state the main idea. I'll have to figure it out by looking at all the details and seeing how they relate. Each sentence gives a detail about valuable objects mistaken for trash. Therefore, the implied main idea is that some objects may be worth more than we think.

4 Duplicate the following paragraphs and read them aloud. A master is provided on page 125.

> **If you have ever looked up at the sky and thought you saw something strange— perhaps something that looked like a flying saucer—you're not alone. Every year hundreds of people report seeing strange objects, or objects known as UFOs (Unidentified Flying Objects). However, most of these UFOs turn out to be something ordinary, such as meteors, military aircraft, or weather balloons. In some cases, people even make up stories and create fake photos for publicity.**
>
> **Most scientists do not believe that the planet Earth has been visited by alien beings. In fact, space exploration supports the belief that no other planet in our solar system has the technology that could send flying objects to Earth. In addition, the distance between our planet and the nearest star would make it extremely difficult for alien beings to visit Earth.**

5 Duplicate and distribute the Main Idea Web on the next page. Have students work in pairs to fill in the web with main ideas and details from both paragraphs. Correct responses are shown in the Answer Key on page 182.

6 Make additional copies of the Main Idea Web and have them available for students to use when necessary throughout the year.

Name   **Date**

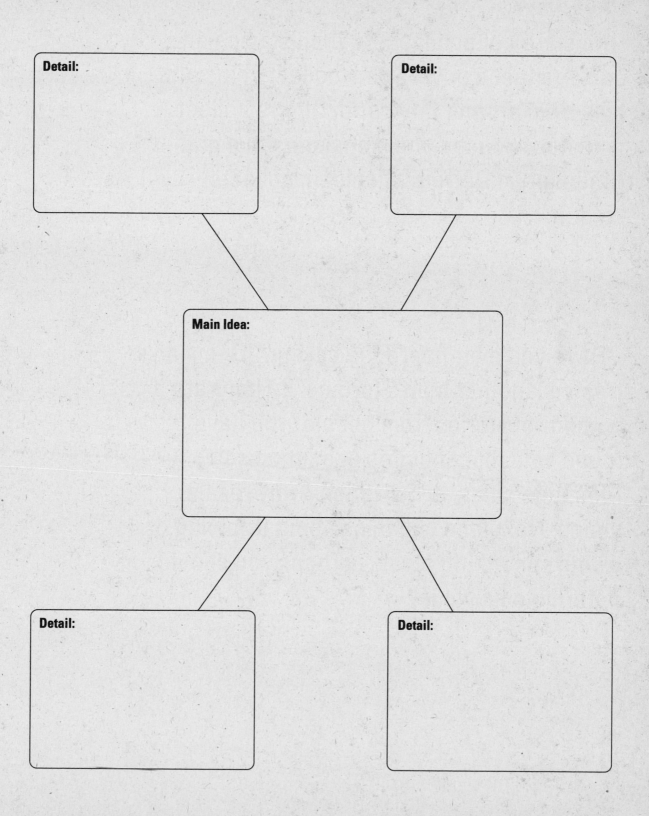

Detail:

Detail:

Main Idea:

Detail:

Detail:

Main Idea

Kids are collecting more than stamps and stickers these days. Some collect coins and bills from around the world. Others collect miniature houses and mansions. An eighth-grade girl in Detroit, Michigan, collects spiders.

Have you ever heard the saying, "One man's trash is another man's fortune"? There are a number of stories from people who have found valuable antiques at auction sales, rummage sales, or Salvation Army resale shops. Next time you think about throwing or giving something away, perhaps you should determine its value.

Main Idea

If you have ever looked up at the sky and thought you saw something strange—perhaps something that looked like a flying saucer—you're not alone. Every year hundreds of people report seeing strange objects, or objects known as UFOs (Unidentified Flying Objects). However, most of these UFOs turn out to be something ordinary, such as meteors, military aircraft, or weather balloons. In some cases, people even make up stories and create fake photos for publicity.

Most scientists do not believe that the planet Earth has been visited by alien beings. In fact, space exploration supports the belief that no other planet in our solar system has the technology that could send flying objects to Earth. In addition, the distance between our planet and the nearest star would make it extremely difficult for alien beings to visit Earth.

1 Ask students if they have ever told someone a story with events that weren't in the exact order in which they occurred in life. If details were out of order, the listener might ask questions to clarify the sequence. Explain that it is important to keep track of the sequence of events in order to understand the meaning of the story or how the plot moves forward, especially since the writer isn't available to answer questions. The following points will be useful to students who need more help.

- Sequence is the order in which events happen. Sequence refers to the chronological order in a story or piece of nonfiction. It may also refer to steps in a process or in following directions.

- Writers sometimes use words such as *first, next, after, before, then,* and *later* to connect ideas and indicate the order in which events occur.

- Words, phrases, or dates that tell when something is happening can also help readers figure out the sequence of events.

- A paragraph or story may begin telling about an event that happens in the present. Other sentences may tell about events that happened in the past leading up to the present.

- When events are not clearly laid out, it may help the reader to visualize in his or her mind how the events happened.

2 Duplicate the following paragraph. A master is provided on page 128. Have students follow along as you read it aloud, using it to model **sequence.**

> Auditions for *Fame* were held Saturday from 10:00 A.M. to 2:00 P.M. in the auditorium. Julie woke up early that morning to finish reading the play. At 9:30 A.M. her mother drove her to school for the audition. As she walked into the auditorium, she grew nervous, but once she saw her friends, she relaxed a bit. During auditions, Julie read a few scenes and did a monologue. At the end of auditions, Mrs. Martinez announced that callbacks would be posted outside her door on Monday.

You could say: The first sentence gives me information about auditions for the play Fame. *Chances are that the first sentence is not the first event in the sequence. The second sentence tells me that Julie woke up early. The third sentence tells me Julie's mother drove her to school at 9:30 A.M. The rest of the sentences tell me about Julie's day at the auditions. So if I were to list the order of events, I would say that Julie woke up early Saturday morning to finish reading the play; then her mother drove her to school; next she met some friends; and finally she auditioned.*

3 Duplicate the following paragraph. A master copy is provided on page 128. Have students follow along as you read it aloud.

> Last weekend my history class visited Washington, D.C. On Saturday morning we visited the White House. After the White House, we visited the Lincoln Memorial. The statue of Abraham Lincoln is 19 feet high and faces the Reflecting Pool, another attraction in D.C. Following our visit to the Lincoln Memorial, we walked over to the Vietnam Veterans Memorial. More than 58,000 names of American soldiers who died in the war are carved into this memorial. Finally our day ended at the Tidal Basin, where we rented paddleboats for a ride on the water.

4 Duplicate and distribute the Sequence Flow Chart on the next page. Work with students to fill in the first event. Then have them complete the chart. Tell students to highlight any words or phrases that helped them determine the order of events. Ask volunteers to share how they mapped out the events of the paragraph. Possible responses are shown in the Answer Key on page 182.

5 Make additional copies of the chart on page 127 and have it available for students to use throughout the year.

Name   **Date**

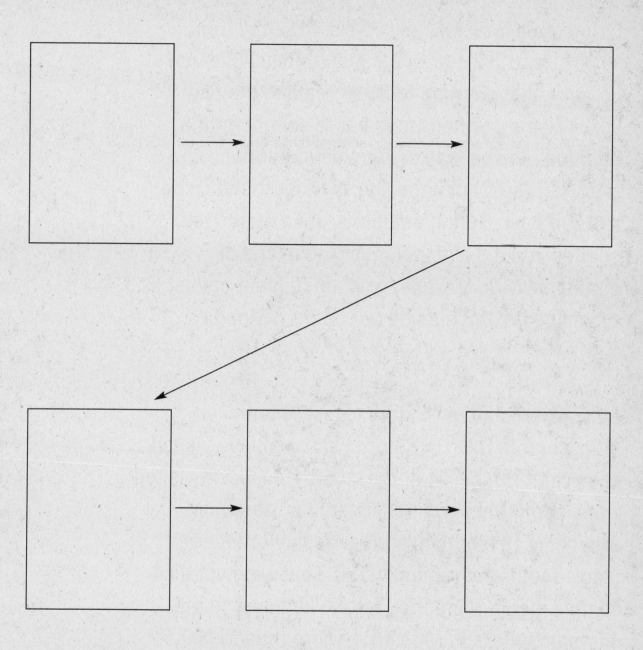

Sequence

Auditions for *Fame* were held Saturday from 10:00 A.M. to 2:00 P.M. in the auditorium. Julie woke up early that morning to finish reading the play. At 9:30 A.M. her mother drove her to school for the audition. As she walked into the auditorium, she grew nervous, but once she saw her friends, she relaxed a bit. During auditions, Julie read a few scenes and did a monologue. At the end of auditions, Mrs. Martinez announced that callbacks would be posted outside her door on Monday.

Last weekend my history class visited Washington, D.C. On Saturday morning we visited the White House. After the White House, we visited the Lincoln Memorial. The statue of Abraham Lincoln is 19 feet high and faces the Reflecting Pool, another attraction in D.C. Following our visit to the Lincoln Memorial, we walked over to the Vietnam Veterans Memorial. More than 58,000 names of American soldiers who died in the war are carved into this memorial. Finally our day ended at the Tidal Basin, where we rented paddleboats for a ride on the water.

Cause and Effect

1 Write the following sentence on the board and read it aloud.

> **Jada fell off her bike because the neighbor's dog ran right in front of her.**

Ask students which event caused the other event to happen *(The dog running in front of Jada caused her to fall off her bike).* Discuss the following points.

- A **cause** is an action or event that makes something else happen.
- An **effect** is what happens because of a certain action or event.

Explain that cause-effect relationships may contain one or more of these characteristics.

- Writers use clue words or phrases *(because, since,* and *as a result)* to indicate causes and effects. However, clue words alone do not automatically indicate a cause-effect relationship. One event must make another event happen.
- A single cause can result in more than one effect *(The dog running in front of Jada caused her to fall off her bike and skin her knee).* Also, several causes can lead to a single effect *(Because I studied hard and got enough sleep, I got an A on the test).*
- Sometimes a series of events are linked in a cause-and-effect chain in which one event causes another, which in turn causes another, and so on *(Because I studied hard and got enough sleep, I got an A on the test. Because I got an A, my mom bought me an all-day pass to the amusement park).*

Warn students to watch out for events that happen in sequence. Just because one event follows another doesn't mean the first event caused the second one. For example, read the following sentence. *After the football game ended, the sun came out.* The football game's end did not cause the sun to come out.

2 Duplicate the following paragraph. A master is provided on page 133. Ask students to follow along as you read it aloud, using it to model **cause and effect.**

> **Last summer there was very little rain. Because of the dry conditions, there were more forest fires than usual. People's lawns and gardens were brown and sun-baked. Water supplies were very low, and many cities and towns put limits on how much water people could use.**

You could say: The first sentence tells what happened. The second sentence has a signal word, because, *that may indicate a cause-effect relationship. In sentences three and four, it is logical to say that the dry weather also caused the dried-out lawns and gardens and reduced the water supplies. One cause can result in more than one effect.*

Now look at the last sentence. It is an example of a cause-and-effect chain in which the first event (the lack of rain) *caused another event* (reduced water supplies), *which in turn caused another event* (cities and towns limited water use).

3 Write on the board these signal words: *because, so, since, as a result, for this reason.* Duplicate the following paragraph. A master is provided on page 133. Have students follow as you read it aloud.

> **Last year, I started volunteering at the local animal shelter. As a result, I have learned a great deal about animals. I am also in much better shape than I was because I walk dogs so often. I have often thought about becoming a veterinarian or animal trainer. For this reason, I chose to interview a veterinarian for my Career Day project.**

4 Duplicate and distribute the Cause-and-Effect Chart on the next page. Work with students to fill in the first cause-and-effect relationship. Possible responses are shown in the Answer Key on page 182.

5 Make copies of the additional Cause-and-Effect Charts on pages 131–132 and have them available for students to use at appropriate times throughout the year.

Cause	→	Effect(s)

Name   **Date**

Single Cause with Multiple Effects

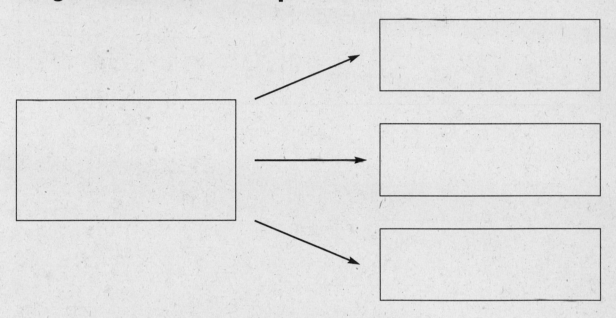

Multiple Causes with Single Effect

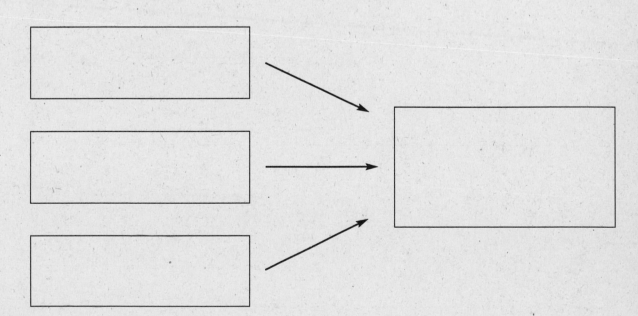

Name   **Date**

Cause-and-Effect Chain

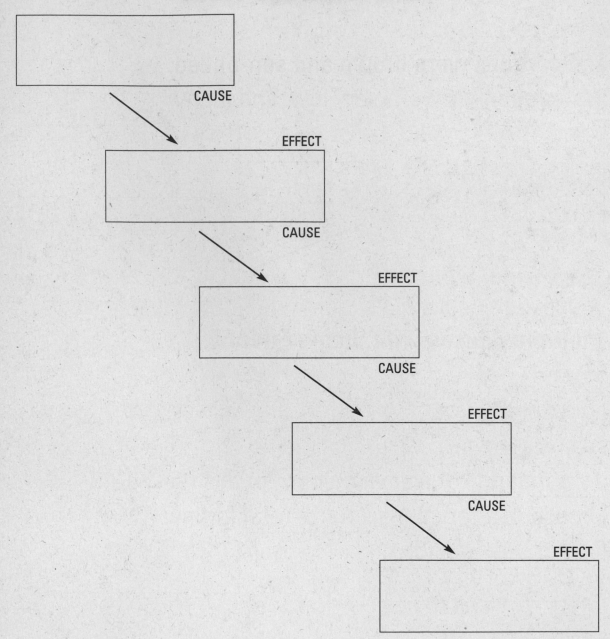

Cause and Effect

Last summer there was very little rain. Because of the dry conditions, there were more forest fires than usual. People's lawns and gardens were brown and sun-baked. Water supplies were very low, and many cities and towns put limits on how much water people could use.

Last year, I started volunteering at the local animal shelter. As a result, I have learned a great deal about animals. I am also in much better shape than I was because I walk dogs so often. I have often thought about becoming a veterinarian or animal trainer. For this reason, I chose to interview a veterinarian for my Career Day project.

Comparison and Contrast

1 The following points will be helpful to students who have trouble understanding the terms compare and contrast.

- **Comparing** means to think about the ways in which two or more people or two or more things are alike. *(Cats and chipmunks sleep an average of 15 hours a day.)* Writers sometimes use words such as *both, same, alike, like, also, similarly,* and *too* to make comparisons. *(Both cats and chipmunks sleep an average of 15 hours a day.)*

- **Contrasting** means to think about ways in which two or more people or two or more things are different. *(Girls usually stop growing between the ages of 17 and 18. Boys usually stop growing between the ages of 19 and 20.)* Writers sometimes use words or phrases such as *unlike, but, although, instead, yet, even though, however,* and *on the other hand* to contrast two or more things. *(Girls usually stop growing between the ages of 17 and 18, unlike boys, who stop growing between the ages of 19 and 20.)*

- Sometimes there are no signal words. Readers must figure out what the writer is comparing and contrasting from the details given.

2 Duplicate the following paragraph. A master is provided on page 136. Have students follow along as you read it aloud, using it to model **compare and contrast.**

> **Although moths and butterflies belong to the same insect group, there are many differences between them. Most butterflies fly during the daytime, while moths fly at dusk or at night. Most butterflies have knobs at the end of their antennae; moths do not. Most butterflies have slender, hairless bodies in contrast to the plump, furry bodies of moths.**

You could say: The first sentence tells me that two insects, moths and butterflies, are being compared. The second sentence contains the word while, *which signals a way in which moths and butterflies are different. The third sentence gives me an additional fact about butterflies and moths without using a signal word. The last sentence contains the phrase* in contrast to, *which signals an additional difference between butterflies and moths. Therefore, moths and butterflies are alike in that they both belong to the same insect group. The difference is in their sleeping habits and their physical features, or the way they look.*

3 For reference, write on the board the signal words and phrases listed in the second bulleted item. Then duplicate the following paragraph and read it aloud. A master is provided on page 136.

> **Growing up in America during the 1890s was much different from growing up today. Children as young as 10 years old held full-time jobs in order to help their families. Many of these children worked 14 hours a day for as little as 27 cents. Today, however, children are not allowed to hold part-time jobs until they are at least 14 years old. Federal laws also restrict the number of hours teenagers work. While some teenagers today work out of necessity to help their families, most do so to earn spending money or to save for college.**

4 Duplicate and distribute the Venn Diagram on the next page. Have students fill in the diagram, using information in the paragraph to compare the differences between growing up today versus growing up in the 1890s.

5 Have volunteers share the information in their diagrams by first describing the two subjects that are being compared and then describing their differences. Possible responses are shown in the Answer Key on page 183.

6 Make additional copies of the diagram on page 135 and have it available for students to use at appropriate times during the year.

Name   **Date**

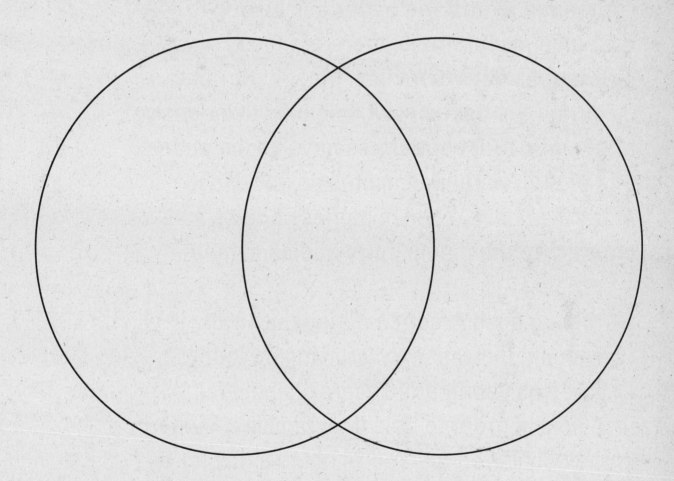

Comparison and Contrast

Although moths and butterflies belong to the same insect group, there are many differences between them. Most butterflies fly during the daytime, while moths fly at dusk or at night. Most butterflies have knobs at the end of their antennae; moths do not. Most butterflies have slender, hairless bodies in contrast to the plump, furry bodies of moths.

Growing up in America during the 1890s was much different from growing up today. Children as young as 10 years old held full-time jobs in order to help their families. Many of these children worked 14 hours a day for as little as 27 cents. Today, however, children are not allowed to hold part-time jobs until they are at least 14 years old. Federal laws also restrict the number of hours teenagers work. While some teenagers today work out of necessity to help their families, most do so to earn spending money or to save for college.

1 Present students with the following situation:

Fewer and fewer customers have been going to your local movie theater. Today, you notice that the box office is boarded up and the movie posters have been taken down. What inference can you make? (Students will most likely say that the theater has gone out of business.) For students who need more help making inferences, discuss the following points.

- It is not possible for writers to include every detail about what is happening in a work of literature.

- Often writers purposely choose to hint at details rather than state them; this can add meaning and suspense for the reader.

- Inferences are logical guesses based on clues in the text and on the reader's own knowledge and common sense.

- To make inferences, readers must: look for details that the writer provides about character, setting, and events; think about what they already know about a topic; and connect the story to their own personal experiences.

2 Duplicate the following paragraph. A master is provided on page 139. Ask students to follow along as you read it aloud, using it to model the skill **making inferences.**

> **Kirsten sat on the sidelines, cheering wildly whenever her team had the ball or scored a basket. Every time one of her teammates sat down for a rest, Kirsten leaned forward and watched her coach with eager, shining eyes. However, each time the coach sent another player onto the court, and Kirsten slumped back down on the bench.**

You could say: The first sentence tells me that Kirsten is watching a basketball game. She supports her team because she cheers wildly whenever they have the ball. The second sentence tells me that Kirsten is a player on the basketball team; it refers to the other players as "her teammates." From the description of her body language—leaning forward and eagerly watching the coach—I can also infer that she wants to play. In the third sentence, I learn that the coach keeps sending in other players. A slumping posture often suggests that someone is depressed. So I can infer that Kirsten is disappointed and depressed that she's not allowed to play.

3 Duplicate the following passage. A master is provided on page 139. Have students follow along as you read it aloud.

> **With only a minute left to play, the score was tied. Kirsten and the other players sat with their hands tightly clasped and their eyes fixed on the court. As one of Kirsten's teammates ran down the floor, she slipped and fell. The coach ran to the girl and helped her walk, limping, off the court. When he got back to the bench, the coach motioned to Kirsten to enter the game. She jumped up and ran onto the court. Her heart pounded so hard that she thought the others must hear it. With only seconds remaining, the ball was passed to Kirsten. She dribbled it down the court, aimed, and shot. With a swoosh, the ball fell through the basket. Just then the buzzer sounded. Kirsten's teammates swarmed around her, thumping her on the back. She looked at them all with a happy, dazed smile.**

4 Duplicate and distribute the Inferences Chart on the next page. Work with students to fill in the first row. Then have them add to the chart any other inferences they make about the passage. Sample responses are shown in the Answer Key on page 183.

Inference Chart

Selection Information	+	My Opinion/ What I Know	=	My Inference/ My Judgment
	+		=	
	+		=	
	+		=	
	+		=	

Making Inferences

Kirsten sat on the sidelines, cheering wildly whenever her team had the ball or scored a basket. Every time one of her teammates sat down for a rest, Kirsten leaned forward and watched her coach with eager, shining eyes. However, each time the coach sent another player onto the court, and Kirsten slumped back down on the bench.

With only a minute left to play, the score was tied. Kirsten and the other players sat with their hands tightly clasped and their eyes fixed on the court. As one of Kirsten's teammates ran down the floor, she slipped and fell. The coach ran to the girl and helped her walk, limping, off the court. When he got back to the bench, the coach motioned to Kirsten to enter the game. She jumped up and ran onto the court. Her heart pounded so hard that she thought the others must hear it. With only seconds remaining, the ball was passed to Kirsten. She dribbled it down the court, aimed, and shot. With a swoosh, the ball fell through the basket. Just then the buzzer sounded. Kirsten's teammates swarmed around her, thumping her on the back. She looked at them all with a happy, dazed smile.

1 To introduce the concept of predicting, ask students to make a guess about what they will do after school based on what they already know. Use the following points to explain how the strategy applies to reading a story.

- When you **predict,** you try to figure out what will happen next, based upon what has already happened.

- To make a **prediction,** you must combine clues in a story plus your own knowledge and experience to make a reasonable guess.

- Good readers make and revise predictions about characters, setting, and plot as they read. Sometimes they don't even realize they're doing it.

- Sometimes you must first make a guess or inference about what is happening before you can predict what will happen next. *(Shana's stomach growled. She set her book aside and walked into the kitchen.)* You might infer that Shana is hungry. Since she is walking into the kitchen, you could then use the inference to predict that she is about to get something to eat.

2 Duplicate the following paragraph. A master is provided on page 142. Have students follow along as you read it aloud, using it to model the skill of **predicting.**

> **James put on his coat with the holes in the pockets and headed for the front door.**

You could say: The first sentence tells me that James has put on a coat. Since he is heading for the front door, I think that James is going somewhere. I'll read further to see if my prediction is right.

> **As he walked toward the bus stop, he fished the correct change out of his wallet and placed it in his coat pocket.**

You could say: The second sentence tells me that James is going to take a bus. He placed the money for the bus in his coat pocket. However, since the pockets have holes, I predict that the change will fall onto the ground.

> **James got to the bus stop just as the bus pulled up. He reached into his pocket and was shocked to find that it was empty. With a sinking feeling, he realized that he didn't have any more money.**

You could say: My predictions were right. Based on the fact that James has no more money, I can also predict that he won't be able to board the bus.

3 Duplicate the following passage. A master is provided on page 142. Instruct students to follow along as you read it aloud. Afterwards, students should be ready to infer what has happened and to predict what will happen next.

> **At the end of the school day, Carla went to her locker. She tossed all but one of the books in her backpack into her locker. Carla thought that she'd have just enough time to read the book and write the report that was due tomorrow.**
> **As Carla walked out of the school, she ran into Daria and Elena. "We're going to grab a pizza," said Daria. "Want to come?"**
> **Carla thought about the book in her pack. There'll be plenty of time, she told herself. "Sure," she said, joining her friends.**
> **The three friends lost track of the time as they sat chatting in the small restaurant. Suddenly the owner announced, "Closing time, ladies."**
> **The girls hurried out of the restaurant, and the owner locked the door behind them. When he turned out the lights, he didn't notice Carla's backpack under one of the tables.**

4 Duplicate and distribute the Predicting Chart on the next page. Have students work in pairs to complete the chart. Possible responses are shown in the Answer Key on page 183.

Name   **Date**

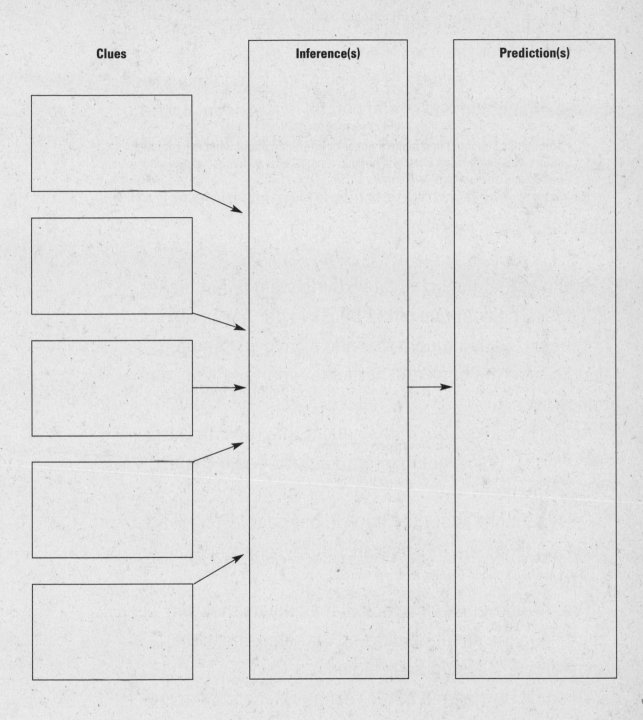

Clues

Inference(s)

Prediction(s)

Predicting

James put on his coat with the holes in the pockets and headed for the front door.

As he walked toward the bus stop, he fished the correct change out of his wallet and placed it in his coat pocket.

James got to the bus stop just as the bus pulled up. He reached into his pocket and was shocked to find that it was empty. With a sinking feeling, he realized that he didn't have any more money.

At the end of the school day, Carla went to her locker. She tossed all but one of the books in her backpack into her locker. Carla thought that she'd have just enough time to read the book and write the report that was due tomorrow.

As Carla walked out of the school, she ran into Daria and Elena. "We're going to grab a pizza," said Daria. "Want to come?"

Carla thought about the book in her pack. There'll be plenty of time, she told herself. "Sure," she said, joining her friends.

The three friends lost track of the time as they sat chatting in the small restaurant. Suddenly the owner announced, "Closing time, ladies."

The girls hurried out of the restaurant, and the owner locked the door behind them. When he turned out the lights, he didn't notice Carla's backpack under one of the tables.

1 Use examples from textbooks, newspapers, magazines, and pamphlets as you discuss the following points about distinguishing fact and opinion:

- A **fact** is a statement that can be proven or disproven through observation, experience, and research. A fact may include supporting evidence such as statistics or quotations from a recognized expert.

- An **opinion** is a statement that tells what a writer thinks, believes, or feels about a subject. It cannot be proven true or false.

- A writer may use words and phrases such as the following to signal an opinion: *according to, I think, in my opinion, perhaps, seem, ought to, should, bad, good, better, worse, excellent, terrible.* A writer may also use words that appeal to the reader's emotions.

- Sometimes a writer will use one or more facts to support an opinion.

- A single statement can contain both a fact and an opinion.

- A statement that you agree with is not necessarily a fact.

2 Duplicate the following paragraph. A master is provided on page 145. Have students follow along as you read it aloud, using it to model the skill of distinguishing between **fact and opinion.**

> **School cafeterias should serve foods with more nutritional value. Most cafeterias include such high cholesterol, fattening foods as frozen pizza, hamburgers, cheeseburgers, fries, and nachos. Students would benefit from healthy foods like vegetable soups, salads, pastas, and fresh fruits.**

You could say: Actually, I agree with the point the writer is making, but I need to determine if these statements are facts or opinions. First I look for numbers, statistics, or quotations from experts. If I don't find any, there's a good chance that the statements are the writer's opinion.

Next I look for words that might signal opinions. The first sentence contains the signal word should. *This statement can't be proven even if it appears to be true. The second sentence contains the word* most, *which tells me that the writer is admitting that there are exceptions; this sentence can probably be proven. The third sentence does not include any signal words, but I've read health journals that would agree with this statement. Therefore, the last sentence can also be proven.*

3 For reference, write on the board the signal words and phrases listed in the third bulleted item. Then duplicate the following paragraph and read it aloud. A master is provided on page 145.

> **Wildlife conservation is important to the survival of wild animals and plants. If we continue to build more homes, farms, and industries where wild animals nest and breed, many animals will die. In addition, pollution, such as pesticides and other chemicals, also damages wildlife habitats. Farmers should protect wild rabbits and quails by reducing the use of harmful pesticides and fertilizers. Other people should help by donating money to wildlife organizations.**

4 Duplicate and distribute the Two-Column Chart on the next page and ask students to use it to list the facts and opinions in the paragraph. Suggest that they highlight any signal words that helped them distinguish between the two types of statements.

5 Have volunteers share their completed charts, explaining why they listed each statement where they did. Correct responses are shown in the Answer Key on page 184.

6 Make additional copies of the chart on page 144 and have them available for students to use at appropriate times during the year.

Name

Date

Fact and Opinion

School cafeterias should serve foods with more nutritional value. Most cafeterias include such high cholesterol, fattening foods as frozen pizza, hamburgers, cheeseburgers, fries, and nachos. Students would benefit from healthy foods like vegetable soups, salads, pastas, and fresh fruits.

Wildlife conservation is important to the survival of wild animals and plants. If we continue to build more homes, farms, and industries where wild animals nest and breed, many animals will die. In addition, pollution, such as pesticides and other chemicals, also damages wildlife habitats. Farmers should protect wild rabbits and quails by reducing the use of harmful pesticides and fertilizers. Other people should help by donating money to wildlife organizations.

Narrative Elements

1 Duplicate the following passage and read it aloud. A master is provided on page 148.

> I have a five-year-old sister named Chloe who wants to be just like me. Sometimes this is fine with me, and sometimes it is a big problem. Let me explain.
>
> It was April, and I had been working on my science project for three weeks. I was using our garage as my laboratory. I had three hamsters in one cage and three in another. I was feeding one group extra fruits, nuts, and grains and the other group a regular diet. Then I watched them to see which group was more active.
>
> I knew something was wrong as I walked up the hill to our house. The garage door was open. I ran in and saw that the cages were open and the hamsters were gone. Did Chloe have something to do with this? Probably.
>
> I found Chloe in the kitchen. "Chloe," I asked, "where are the hamsters?"
>
> Chloe gave me a very serious look. "I have a *science project* to do, Alice," she explained. "I am a *scientist,* and Pepper is my assistant."
>
> Pepper? Our cat? Oh, no. "You know that Pepper is not supposed to go in the garage while the hamsters are there," I told Chloe. "She might think that they are her lunch."

Ask students when and where this story takes place *(in a garage one April)*. Have them tell whom the story is about *(Alice and her sister Chloe)*. Ask them what the story problem is *(The hamsters Alice is using in her science project are missing)*.

2 Discuss with students the following elements of a narrative:

- The **setting** is when and where a story takes place. It helps the reader visualize the story where it occurs. Also, a setting creates a context for the events that take place. For example, if you are reading a story that takes place in a desert, you would know that the characters are unlikely to face a flood.

- **Characters** are the people in a story. The main character is the person whom the story is mostly about. Stories are effective when the characters seem real or interesting, and the reader cares about what happens to them. Characters in a story can also be animals or imaginary creatures.

- The **plot** is the series of events that happen in a story. Most stories have a problem, or **conflict,** that the main character must try to resolve. The **resolution** is the solution to the problem. In general, plot is driven by conflict. In other words, the events in a story generally revolve around the conflict, and the events that occur either contribute to the problem or to the solution.

3 Continue the story by duplicating the following passage and reading it aloud. A master is provided on page 149.

> I tried to think of what to do. Should I keep questioning Chloe? Should I look for the cat and what was left of the hamsters? Just then, Dad walked into the kitchen.
>
> "We're scientists," Chloe told him.
>
> "Dad, the hamster cages are empty and I don't know where the cat is!" I said.
>
> "I noticed that Pepper was trying to get into the garage, so I took the hamsters out of their big cages and put them into smaller ones," Dad explained. "That way, I could keep an eye on them until you got home. They're in the living room now. Don't worry—I kept the two groups separate, so you will know which is which."
>
> "Thank goodness they're okay," I said. "I'm almost done with the project."
>
> "I can help you!" Chloe said.

4 Duplicate and distribute the Story Map on page 147. Work with students to fill in the setting and characters. Then have them complete the plot portion of the map. Possible responses are shown in the Answer Key on page 184.

5 Make additional copies of the Story Map and have them available at appropriate times.

Story Map

Setting	Characters

Plot

Problem:

Events:

1

2

3

4

Resolution:

Narrative Elements

I have a five-year-old sister named Chloe who wants to be just like me. Sometimes this is fine with me, and sometimes it is a big problem. Let me explain.

It was April, and I had been working on my science project for three weeks. I was using our garage as my laboratory. I had three hamsters in one cage and three in another. I was feeding one group extra fruits, nuts, and grains and the other group a regular diet. Then I watched them to see which group was more active.

I knew something was wrong as I walked up the hill to our house. The garage door was open. I ran in and saw that the cages were open and the hamsters were gone. Did Chloe have something to do with this? Probably.

I found Chloe in the kitchen. "Chloe," I asked, "where are the hamsters?"

Chloe gave me a very serious look. "I have a *science project* to do, Alice," she explained. "I am a *scientist,* and Pepper is my assistant."

Pepper? Our cat? Oh, no. "You know that Pepper is not supposed to go in the garage while the hamsters are there," I told Chloe. "She might think that they are her lunch."

Narrative Elements (continued)

I tried to think of what to do. Should I keep questioning Chloe? Should I look for the cat and what was left of the hamsters? Just then, Dad walked into the kitchen.

"We're scientists," Chloe told him.

"Dad, the hamster cages are empty and I don't know where the cat is!" I said.

"I noticed that Pepper was trying to get into the garage, so I took the hamsters out of their big cages and put them into smaller ones," Dad explained. "That way, I could keep an eye on them until you got home. They're in the living room now. Don't worry—I kept the two groups separate, so you will know which is which."

"Thank goodness they're okay," I said. "I'm almost done with the project."

"I can help you!" Chloe said.

Additional Graphic Organizers

On the following pages you will find additional graphic organizers that can be used in a number of different situations to help students comprehend and monitor what they read. Consult the chart below to decide how and when to use each graphic organizer.

Graphic Organizer	Purpose	When and How to Use
K-W-L Chart (page 153)	To help students comprehend a nonfiction selection	*Before Reading:* 1. Identify the topic for students. 2. Have students write what they already **know** about it in the *K* column. 3. Have them write what they **want** to find out in the *W* column. *During Reading:* 4. Have students record what they **learn** in the *L* column.
Q & A Notetaking Chart (page 154)	To help student memorize key facts in a nonfiction selection	*During Reading:* 1. Tell students that as they read they should turn each heading or main idea into a question and write it in column 1. *After Reading:* 2. Have students answer their questions without opening their books. 3. Have students reread the selection to find answers to any questions they could not answer.
Concept Web (page 155)	To guide students to think of related words or concepts	*Before Reading:* Have students form small groups. List key concepts or vocabulary words on the board. Ask students to discuss meanings, fill out a web for each concept or word by writing it in the center of the web, and then writing related terms in the ovals around the center.
Reflection Chart (page 156)	To help students stop and think about key points or events	*During Reading:* 1. Ask students to note important or interesting passages in the left column. 2. Have them record in the right column their thoughts about each passage noted.
Event Log (page 157)	To help students keep track of story events	*During Reading:* 1. Have students list each event as they read about it. *After Reading:* 2. Students should use the list to give an oral retelling or summary of the selection.

Graphic Organizer	Purpose	When and How to Use
Story Frames (page 158)	To help students summarize story events	*After Reading:* 1. Ask students to draw sketches of key events in the selection. 2. Have them use the sketches to retell the selection orally.
Plot Diagram (page 159)	To help students classify events as being part of the exposition, rising action, climax, or falling action	*After Reading:* 1. Review the terms *exposition, rising action, climax,* and *falling action* with students. 2. Encourage students to use the diagram to list the events that form each of these plot phases.
Character Profile Chart (page 160)	To help students identify character attributes	*During or After Reading:* Have students write the character's name at the center and then list qualities and behaviors that exemplify these qualities in the surrounding boxes.
New Word Diagram (page 161)	To help students understand new vocabulary they encounter	*During or After Reading:* 1. Have students write a new word in the box at the top of the diagram. 2. Encourage them to think of—or look in the dictionary for—synonyms and antonyms of the word and record them in the appropriate boxes. 3. Ask students to think of real people or characters they've read about who they associate with the concept of the word. They can then add the names to the diagram.
Reading Log (page 162)	To encourage students to keep track of what they read	*After Reading:* Have students record on this form each selection they read during the year. Review the form periodically with students.

K-W-L Chart

Name _____   **Date** _____

Topic: _____

K What I Know	W What I Want to Find Out	L What I Learn

Name   **Date**

Turn the Heading or Main Idea of Each Passage into a Question	Write a Detailed Answer Here
1.	
2.	
3.	
4.	
5.	
6.	
7.	

Name   **Date**

Name

Date

Quotation or Paraphrase from Text (include page number)	Thoughts About It

Name **Date**

Event 1
Event 2
Event 3
Event 4
Event 5
Event 6
Event 7
Event 8
Event 9
Event 10

Name

Date

Plot Diagram

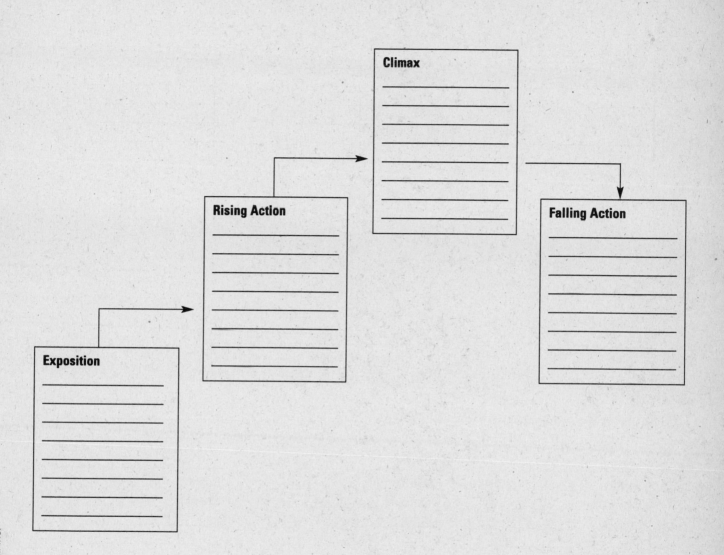

Character Profile Chart

Name ____________________ Date ____________________

Quality: ____________
Example: ____________

Quality: ____________
Example: ____________

Quality: ____________
Example: ____________

____
Character's Name

Quality: ____________
Example: ____________

Quality: ____________
Example: ____________

Quality: ____________
Example: ____________

Name   **Date**

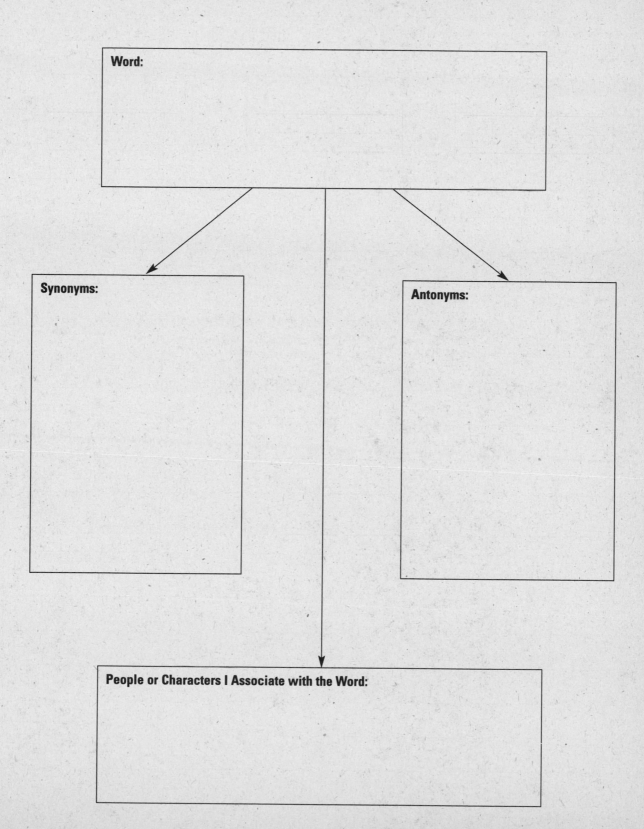

Word:

Synonyms:

Antonyms:

People or Characters I Associate with the Word:

Name   **Date**

Selection Title	Type of Literature	Date Finished	Reactions

Answer Key

Seventh Grade, page 2
Connect to Your Life, page 2
Possible response: I saw someone showing off all the new clothes she just bought.
Key to the Story, page 2
Possible responses: Everyone knows you don't speak French. People don't respect you for pretending to be something you're not.
Pause & Reflect, page 6
1. trying out for basketball
2. Responses will vary. Students may reply that Victor seems to be really attracted to Teresa, he seems friendly and outgoing, and most likely, he'll try to get to know her better.

Reread, page 7
Victor has let slip that he has Teresa on his mind. The girls in the class can tell that he has a crush on her.
Pause & Reflect, page 9
1. waits for her after homeroom; mentions her name in English class; looks for her after lunch
2. Students should underline: "Yeah, that's me." (line 93) Students should circle: "Hi, Teresa" or "How was your summer?" (lines 94–95)

Read Aloud, page 10
embarrassed
Pause & Reflect, page 12
1. praises him; smiles at him; asks him to help her study
2. Responses will vary. Possible response: Victor wants to learn enough French so that Teresa doesn't find out he can't speak it.
3. Possible response: I think Victor's lie is only going to get him into more trouble down the road.

Challenge, page 12
Teresa enjoys school and is serious about learning. Details: Teresa lingers to talk to the homeroom teacher about learning ballet (lines 80–85); Teresa asks Victor to study French with her (lines 230–234).

Active Reading SkillBuilder, page 13
Responses will vary depending on pupils' experiences. Possible response: (Common) We are both in seventh grade. (Different) I take studying very seriously. (Common) We both like to laugh with our friends. (Different) I don't have crushes.
Follow Up: Responses will vary, but students should list similarities and differences between a minor character and themselves.

Literary Analysis SkillBuilder, page 14
(Responses will vary. Possible responses are provided.)
Setting First day of school
Details wobbly table; waited in line for a half hour
Character's Feelings bored, a little excited
Setting Homeroom
Details students squirmed in chairs
Character's Feelings anxious
Setting Hall
Details Victor lingered, blushed, trudged
Character's Feelings embarrassed

Setting Cafeteria
Details girls giggling, Victor blushed
Character's Feelings self-conscious
Setting French class
Details room grew silent, river of nervous sweat, weak from failure, rosebushes of shame became bouquets of love
Character's Feelings humiliated, enthusiastic
Words to Know SkillBuilder, page 15
A. 1. portly
    2. bluff
    3. linger
    4. scowled
    5. elective
    6. trudge
    7. conviction
    8. quivered
    9. sheepishly
    10. ferocity
B. Accept responses that accurately use *bluff* as a sort of cliff or dune and *quiver* as a noun meaning a pack to hold arrows.

Thank You, M'am, page 16
Connect to Your Life, page 16
Responses will vary. Possible responses: political awareness, honesty, skepticism, keeping informed, taking part, helping out
Key to the Story, page 16
Responses will vary. Possible response: My sister; She taught me how to ride a bike.
Pause & Reflect, page 19
1. picks the boy up by his shirt front; asks him why he wanted to steal her purse; asks about his life at home
2. Responses will vary. Students may predict that Mrs. Jones will give the boy a stern lecture about the evils of stealing, possibly including a description of the punishments that await those who do so. She might also tell the boy that she will be on the lookout for him just in case he's thinking about trying to steal again.

Read Aloud, page 20
Responses will vary. Most students will say that they did not expect Mrs. Jones to offer to buy something for a boy who has just tried to snatch her purse. Some will find Mrs. Jones's statement less unusual, because Mrs. Jones must be an unusual person, since she has brought Roger into her home and offered to feed him.
Pause & Reflect, page 21
1. Responses will vary. Some students may feel Mrs. Jones is kind, generous, motherly, concerned, and caring. Others may feel that Mrs. Jones's openness toward Roger is naïve and that she may be getting into a dangerous situation.
2. Possible responses: Roger may not run because he has begun to feel some affection for Mrs. Jones, who has been kind, though stern with him. Roger may also be afraid of Mrs. Jones, who has overpowered him once already.

Pause & Reflect, page 22

1. Responses will vary. Possible response: She wants Roger to know that she has wanted things that she could not afford but has not stolen to get them.
2. Responses will vary according to how students feel about Roger. Some may think that Mrs. Jones has taught Roger a valuable lesson: that kindness and goodness can be an alternative to violence. Others may feel that the last line of the story, that Roger never saw Mrs. Jones again, indicates that he returns to his old ways.

Challenge Details show that Roger's attitude toward Mrs. Jones changes from simple fear to a mixture of fear, bewilderment, affection, and respect as the story develops.

Active Reading SkillBuilder, page 23

(Responses will vary. Possible responses are provided.)

2. Roger is afraid and sweats and struggles.
3. Mrs. Jones feeds and forgives Roger.
4. Roger doesn't try to escape.
5. Roger thanks Mrs. Jones.

Literary Analysis SkillBuilder, page 24

(Responses will vary. Possible responses are provided.)

- Mrs. Jones grabs Roger. External
- Mrs. Jones must decide what to do with Roger. Internal
- Roger needs to decide whether to run from the boarding house. Internal
- Roger needs to decide whether or not to continue stealing money. Internal

Words to Know SkillBuilder, page 25

A. 1. presentable   4. barren
    2. mistrust   5. suede
    3. frail
B. 1. mistrust   3. barren
    2. presentable   4. suede
C. Accept responses that accurately use at least **two** Words to Know.

Names/Nombres, page 26

Connect to Your Life, page 26

Answers will vary. Students may mention such things as trying out for a sport, giving a party, not being shy, introducing yourself to other students.

Key to the Essay, page 26

Responses will vary. Be sure that students fill in each part of the flow chart.

Pause & Reflect, page 29

1. angry
2. Responses will vary. Some students may agree that it is unimportant; others may feel that their names are an important part of their identity and that it is important that people pronounce them correctly.

Pause & Reflect, page 31

1. Mauricia had a harder time because her name was mispronounced in many ways; Ana's name was hardly ever mispronounced.

2. Students may star the following details: husband had insisted that the first daughter be named after his mother Mauran; combination of Mauran and her own mother's name, Felicia.

Pause & Reflect, page 32

1. Responses will vary. Possible response: Alvarez wanted to fit in. She was feeling embarrassed at being singled out as different.
2. Responses will vary. Possible response: I see a colorful place with lots of people talking and buying things. There are spicy foods and maybe some interesting music.

Mark It Up, page 33

Students may underline the following: noisy, foreign-looking, fat, dark mourning dresses, hair nets, droopy mustaches, baby-blue or salmon-colored suits, white shoes, fedora hats (lines 145–151); constantly speaking among themselves in florid-sounding phrases, rococo consonants, rich, rhyming vowels (lines 155–157).

Pause & Reflect, page 34

1. embarrassed
2. to express an opinion, inform

Challenge, page 34

Responses will vary. Possible responses: Some students may say that having two cultures and knowing two languages mark you as different from the dominant culture and open you up to prejudicial treatment; other students may say that having two cultures and knowing two languages enrich your experience and expand your understanding in a way that a person with a single language and culture can never know.

Active Reading SkillBuilder, page 35

(Responses will vary. Possible responses are provided.)

(Purpose) To inform or to explain how names of immigrants were changed by mispronunciation

(Supporting Text) Alvarez is pronounced Elbures, Alberase, and Alburest in the beginning of the essay.

Julia (Hoo-le-ah) was pronounced Jew-lee-ah, Judy, Judith, and Juliet.

The other mothers mispronounce Mauricia's name.

(Purpose) To explain or inform how an immigrant may feel in a new country and to express an opinion

(Supporting Text) Mother is embarrassed by Mauricia's name and gives it as Maureen.

Julia's initial desire to be known by her Dominican name fades, and she just wants to blend in with the other girls.

Julia does not like being singled out as a foreigner.

Julia was embarrassed when her extended family came to school events.

Literary Analysis SkillBuilder, page 36

(Responses will vary. Possible responses are provided.)

(Main issue) How people mispronounce ethnic names.

(Author's observations) People don't pay attention to how their actions might make immigrants feel different.

(Author's attitude) She has a sense of humor about her subject.

(What the author learned) She learned that sometimes it is interesting to be "different."

(What the author wants the reader to know/feel/do) She wants the reader to understand how it may feel to have someone mispronounce his or her name.

Follow Up: Dialogues should be based on information from the selection.

Words to Know SkillBuilder, page 37

A.
1. exotic
2. chaotic
3. convoluted
4. ethnicity
5. inevitably
6. ironically
7. initial
8. merge
9. specify
10. usher

B. Accept responses that accurately use at least **five** Words to Know.

Zebra, page 38

Connect to Your Life, page 38

Responses will vary. Students may suggest business ventures, stories, dance parties, vacation plans, and short stories.

Key to the Story, page 38

Responses will vary. Possible responses: Memorial Day; Martin Luther King, Jr. Day.

Pause & Reflect, page 41

1. stirring up dust as he runs
2. Running down Franklin Avenue, Zebra does not look where he is going when "a huge rushing shadow appeared in his line of vision and crashed into him." (page 41, lines 52–53) Students may correctly infer that the rushing shadow is a car.
3. "But they were not at all certain about his hand." (page 41, lines 63–64)

Pause & Reflect, page 44

1. has a small black dog with him
2. The man's left arm is missing. Students might be reminded that as he notices this, Zebra's hand is hurting.

Reread, page 45

Responses will vary. Some students will say yes, since the man's asking about Zebra's hand suggests he would not mind the question. Others will say no, because they feel it would be rude to ask such a personal question of a person they had just met.

Pause & Reflect, page 46

1. when vacation begins; whether students might like an art class
2. He visits the nurse because his hand is hurting and he hopes that she can do something to help him.

Pause & Reflect, page 48

1. Possible response: Zebra's story may indicate that he feels that his hand will never get better.
2. Possible response: Zebra's story is more personal. Kevin and Mark's stories are fantasies. Andrea's story about a woman scientist who heals trees is closest emotionally to Zebra's.

Pause & Reflect, page 50

1. Responses will vary. Details might include: the tiny hills that rise and fall on his face, glistening beads of sweat on his forehead, his fingers and palm smudged with black ink and encrusted with colors

2. Possible responses: I want to know what your name is, where you are from, what happened to your arm, why you want to teach an art class in my school.

Pause & Reflect, page 52

1. He draws a picture of a zebra.
2. Possible response: Zebra's imagination has taken over. He used to imagine himself as a zebra when he ran; now he imagines a zebra running where his name had been crossed out.

Pause & Reflect, page 55

1. He was wounded in the war in Vietnam.
2. She believes Zebra will use his imagination and be distracted from his injury.

Reread, page 55

Responses will vary.

Pause & Reflect, page 58

1. He was a helicopter pilot.
2. Responses will vary. Some students will say yes, because John Wilson seems like a friendly person and they may be curious to know what he means by seeing in a new way. Others may say no, because they feel John Wilson seems strange and perhaps threatening.
3. Possible response: to see with imagination

Reread, page 59

Possible response: Zebra is learning that to draw something, he needs to look not at what he wants to draw but the space around it.

Pause & Reflect, page 61

1. "without thinking he had been using his left hand, and the two curled fingers had straightened slightly to his needs." (lines 666–668)
2. It reminds him of John Wilson.

Read Aloud, 61

Possible response: They are now more considerate toward each other.

Pause & Reflect, page 62

1. Details: the zebra and the helicopter racing together and the landscape that looks like a face (lines 713–717); Zebra likes and admires John Wilson and knows that Wilson likes him and wants to help him.
2. Leon was an artist and a buddy who served with John Wilson in Vietnam. The inference is that he was killed in the war.

Pause & Reflect, page 65

1. Responses will vary. Most students will be moved by John Wilson's letter, which shows his feelings about Leon Kellner and Zebra as well.
2. Possible response: It shows respect. Zebra's imagination comes alive over what he feels strongly about.

Challenge, page 65

Zebra sees himself in a new way. Details: Students might compare and contrast the descriptions of Zebra when he is alone near the tall fence in the schoolyard and his hand hurts him (page 42, lines 91–95), the description of him when he sees the drawing John Wilson has made of him (page 51, lines 383–384), and the description of him at camp (page 63, lines 737–749).

Answer Key (continued)

While Zebra remains alone at the end of the story, he has found a friend in John Wilson, a person who saw his potential; and, while Zebra's hand is still not completely healed, he can use it to make drawings and sculptures.

Mark It Up, page 66
Students' sketches will vary but should depict something they care deeply about.

Active Reading SkillBuilder, page 67
(Responses will vary. Possible responses are provided.)
Character or event: Running
Details from story: "racing down Franklin Avenue, he had given himself that push and had begun to turn into an eagle."
My experiences: An eagle flies very high and swiftly.
What I can infer: Zebra is running very fast and not thinking about where he is.
Character or event: Accident
Details from story: "a huge rushing shadow appeared in his line of vision and crashed into him and plunged him into a darkness from which he emerged very, very, slowly"
My experiences: Large, fast-moving objects on city streets are usually cars, trucks, or buses.
What I can infer: A vehicle struck Zebra.
Character or event: Zebra
Details from story: "Most times Zebra would stand alongside the basketball court or behind the wire screen at home plate and watch games."
My experiences: People usually watch from the bleachers or other areas.
What I can infer: Zebra tends to be a loner.
Character or event: Mrs. English
Details from story: "Mrs. English stood staring awhile at the letter. She turned away and touched her eyes."
My experiences: I touch my eyes to wipe away tears.
What I can infer: Mrs. English is going to cry.

Literary Analysis SkillBuilder, page 68
(Responses will vary. Possible responses are provided.)
Character: Zebra
Traits: loves running, imaginative, loner, observant, sad
Motives: has a lot of pain from his injured hand, curious, takes the art class, wants to make something special for Mr. Wilson
Character: John Wilson
Traits: collector of odds and ends, shy, kind, artistic
Motives: wants to teach art, looks for a gift in honor of his friend who died in Vietnam

Words to Know SkillBuilder, page 69
A. 1. exuberantly
2. wince
3. gaunt
4. disciplinarian
5. intricate

B. 1. encrusted
2. jauntily
3. menacing
4. poised
5. tensing

Eleanor Roosevelt, page 70
Connect to Your Life, page 70
Possible response: a world where no one is hungry and there is no prejudice or racism among people

Key to the Biography, page 70
Responses may include: struggled to end poverty, fought for racial justice, ambassador to the United Nations, helped write the Declaration of Human Rights

Pause & Reflect, page 73
1. outgoing, cheerful, playful
2. Possible responses: old, wealthy, famous

Pause & Reflect, page 75
1. She was cold and neglectful. She set up harsh rules. She was absent-minded.
2. be brave, get an education, help suffering people

Pause & Reflect, page 77
1. Responses will vary. Most students will indicate Roosevelt's ability to ask searching questions and think for herself.
2. Possible responses: Roosevelt was obedient, but she showed independence; she was wealthy, but she identified with those who were not.

Pause & Reflect, page 79
1. F: energetic, outgoing, carefree, athletic; E: serious, timid, shy, brooding
2. Too often Mammá made the decisions about such things as where they would live, how their home would be furnished, how the children would be disciplined. (lines 242–245)

Pause & Reflect, page 81
1. Possible response: She insisted that he not be treated as a sick person, but continue his life as a public servant.
2. Possible responses: Franklin's dependence on her may have brought out her own strength; the struggle with polio may have strengthened her convictions.

Pause & Reflect, page 82
1. Possible responses: active; informing Franklin about issues she thinks important and persuading him to her point of view
2. Possible response: She advocated causes that would make the lives of poor and disadvantaged people better.

Pause & Reflect, page 85
1. supported the DAR
2. 2, 1, 4, 3

Reread, page 87
Possible response: Eleanor Roosevelt worked with great energy and commitment to improve the lives of the disadvantaged and to seek social justice.

Pause & Reflect, page 88
1. Responses will vary. Many students will indicate Eleanor Roosevelt's United Nations ambassadorship.
2. Responses will vary.

Challenge, page 88
Responses will vary. Stevenson meant that Eleanor Roosevelt, rather than merely complaining about social injustices, worked to overcome them. Students may cite Roosevelt's work on behalf of the poor, against racism, and for human rights.

Mark It Up
Responses may include: ambassador to the United Nations, teacher, advocate for children, helped League of Women Voters, helped Women's Trade Union League, "president's conscience," soup-kitchen worker, fighter against racial prejudice

Active Reading SkillBuilder, page 89
(Responses will vary. Possible responses are provided.)

1892–1894 Eleanor misses her father dreadfully; she is sent to live in her grandmother's dreary house; sits alone and reads; alone and unhappy

1902 Grandmother brings Eleanor home; forces her to go to parties and dances; Eleanor is not comfortable; begins working with poor children

1905 Eleanor is still timid but very busy; has trouble with Franklin's mother; does not enjoy or fit in with Franklin's lifestyle; becomes silent and cold

1917 Eleanor becomes very involved in the war effort; works 15-16 hours a day

1921 Eleanor convinces Franklin to remain active in politics; she gets involved in politics; she works on behalf of women

1932 Depression; Eleanor works in soup kitchens; visits slums; urges president to create the National Youth Administration; lectures; writes column; fights prejudice

1941 Eleanor helps Red Cross; gives blood; sells war bonds; visits soldiers in hospitals

1945 Eleanor helps draft UN Declaration of Human Rights; travels around the world; advises presidents and kings

Literary Analysis SkillBuilder, page 90
(Responses will vary. Possible responses are provided.)

Signal Word: A few months later
Event: Her father died.
Reveals: She determined to lead a life that would have made him proud.
Signal Word: just before (she turned fifteen)
Event: Her grandmother decided to send her to boarding school in England.
Reveals: She started becoming her own person.
Signal Word: meanwhile
Event: She fell in love with FDR.
Reveals: Her marriage would cause her to become very public and influential.
Signal Word: during (the next nine years)
Event: They had five more children.
Reveals: She was dominated by her mother-in-law.
Signal Word: even after (retiring)
Event: She continued to travel, write a newspaper column, and appear on TV.
Reveals: She remained active.
Follow Up: Responses will vary. Students may think her sense of duty would have caused her to devote herself to her husband, or they may feel her sense of responsibility toward the world would have driven her to be active for social change.

Words to Know SkillBuilder, page 91

A. 1. B
2. E
3. A
4. C
5. D

B. 1. combatant
2. priority
3. prominent
4. brooding
5. migrant

The War of the Wall, page 92
Connect to Your Life, page 92
Students' responses and drawings will vary. Accept any response that names a place and lists and illustrates some of its special features.

Key to the Story, page 92
Responses will vary. Accept both famous and little-known people who have importance to the student as a role-model and/or hero.

Pause & Reflect, page 95
1. Jimmy Lyons's; he was a young man from the neighborhood who was killed in Vietnam.
2. Responses will vary. Most students will probably answer yes, noting the narrator's comment about pitching pennies and Lou's comment about the smell of bubble gum and kids' sweat.

Pause & Reflect, page 97
1. Possible response: The painter lady paints the wall white. Then she divides it into sections by taping pieces of string to it and marks the sections with blue chalk.
2. She ignores Lou when he speaks to her. When the Morris twins offer her the dinner their mother has prepared for her, the painter lady tells them to tell their mother that she has brought her own dinner along.

Pause & Reflect, page 99
1. angry and forceful
2. Responses will vary. Most students will feel that the painter lady's apparent lack of sensitivity to the concerns of the residents suggests that there will be some sort of conflict between the painter lady and them.

Pause & Reflect, page 101
1. They have a hard time getting people to notice their work.
2. They plan on getting even with the painter lady for taking over their wall by covering her painting with graffiti.

Reread, page 103
Responses will vary. Most students will probably say that the narrator and Lou are amazed and pleased to see themselves depicted on their wall. That the painter lady has included them indicates that she has not taken away "their" wall after all.

Pause & Reflect, page 104
1. heroes from African-American history; people in the neighborhood; flags of African nations
2. Responses will vary. Possible response: Because they had chiseled Jimmy Lyons's name into the wall when they learned he wasn't coming home from Vietnam; the inclusion of his name on the wall means that it is still a memorial to his sacrifice.

Challenge, page 104
Possible response: The reaction of both children and adults when they see the wall is not just surprise but also recognition. "[I]t looked like a block party" next to the wall (line 237); "half the neighborhood was gathered" there (238–239). Some of the onlookers have stopped what they are doing to see the wall. Many of Mama's customers have "napkins still at the throat" (253), and a man in the barbershop has "half his face shaved" (255). Mr. Eubanks proudly assesses the artist's work (257–258). The narrator says "It was something" (263–264) and recognizes

faces of neighbors and famous people (264, 278–279). "I could hardly believe my eyes," the narrator says (281–282). Side Pocket proudly lectures about liberation flags. Lou "gasped," and the narrator "couldn't breathe" when they saw Jimmy Lyons's name (305, 307–308).

Active Reading SkillBuilder, page 105
(Responses will vary. Possible responses are provided.)
Cause: The Morris twins try to give the painter dinner.
Effect: She doesn't want it and says she has brought her own.
Cause: The painter is picky about her food at the restaurant.
Effect: The narrator's mother is impatient with her.
Cause: The cousins learn about spray-painted subways in New York.
Effect: They decide to spray-paint the wall.
Cause: The mural is completed.
Effect: The neighborhood admires everything about it. The cousins admire it, too.

Literary Analysis SkillBuilder, page 106
(Responses will vary. Possible responses are provided.)
Conflict: The painter ignores Side Pocket and the others.
Between whom? Painter vs. Side Pocket.
Conflict: The narrator gets even angrier when she refuses the food.
Between whom? Narrator vs. Painter
Conflict: The narrator's mother gets impatient with the painter over her questions about food.
Between whom? Mama vs. Painter
Conflict: The mother feels she should have had more patience with the artist, but the narrator and Lou don't agree.
Between whom? Narrator and Lou vs. Mama
Climax: The narrator and Lou decide to spray graffiti on the wall.
They buy paint and go to the wall.
They are shocked and delighted by the mural.

Words to Know SkillBuilder, page 107
A.
1. liberation
2. inscription
3. scheme
4. beckon
5. liberation
6. drawl
7. scheme
8. inscription
9. scheme
10. to honor him

Rikki-tikki-tavi, page 108
Connect to Your Life, page 108
red-tailed hawks: jackrabbits, mice; *house cats:* mice; *bats:* flying insects

Pause & Reflect, p. 112
1. curious, friendly, playful, restless
2. Possible responses: He will bite Teddy; he will cause a lot of trouble; he will protect Teddy from snakes.

Mark It Up, page 113
Possible responses: hood; big black cobra; five feet long; lifted one-third of himself from the ground; balancing to and fro; wicked snake's eyes.

Pause & Reflect, page 115
1. is bitten by Rikki-tikki
2. Possible response: Rikki-tikki is young and inexperienced, so he misses his opportunity to kill the cobras.

Pause & Reflect, page 117
1. Students should circle lines 230–233. He bites him through the neck.
2. Answers will vary: Rikki-tikki may believe that he is going to have to fight the cobras, Nag and Nagaina.

Pause & Reflect, page 119
1. timid—C; impatient—R; bold—R; helpless—C; sneaky—C; fearless—R
2. Nag is nearby.

Mark It Up, page 121
Possible response: battered to and fro as a rat is shaken by a dog; body was cartweeled over the floor; dizzy, aching, shaken to pieces; hot wind knocked him senseless

Pause & Reflect, page 122
1. Possible responses: They think the humans will be easier to kill; Rikki-tikki is likely to fight back; they think that with the family gone, Rikki-tikki will leave of his own accord.
2. Possible response: He will go to Darzee to find out where the eggs are and then destroy them.

Read Aloud, page 123
heroic
Pause & Reflect, page 125
1. Possible response: She pretends to be wounded and lures Nagaina away from her eggs.
2. He breaks them open and kills the baby cobras that are about to emerge.
3. Possible response: Having followed Darzee's wife to near the house, Nagaina decides to put into action her plan to kill the family.

Pause & Reflect, page 128
1. distracts Nagaina with one of her eggs
2. Possible responses: Nagaina will escape from the garden with her egg; she will hide in her hole and plan another attack on Rikki-tikki another day; Rikki-tikki will kill her and destroy her egg.

Pause & Reflect, page 130
1. Possible responses: determination, bravery, foolishness.
2. Possible responses: Many students may say that Rikki-tikki is brave and loyal, that they admire him, that he's a hero.

Challenge, page 130
Nag and Nagaina would find Rikki-tikki-tavi an aggressor and an invader of their territory who threatens their lives and the lives of their offspring. Details that would change: Darzee and his wife might be described as traitors; Nag and Nagaina might be described as intelligent and protective of their family; Rikki-tikki's attack on the eggs might be described as murder.

Mark It Up, page 130
Students' drawings will vary, but should depict a scene from the story.

Active Reading SkillBuilder, page 131
(Students' predictions will vary. Answers below show what actually happens in the story.)
1. **What happens:** Nothing happens to Teddy, although his mother fears Rikki-tikki will bite him.
2. **Prediction:** they will fight; **What happens:** Rikki-tikki and Nag fight, but neither is harmed.

3. **Prediction:** they will fight; **What happens:** Rikki-tikki fights and kills Karait.
4. **Prediction:** he will try to kill the family; **What happens:** Rikki-tikki stalks and fights Nag. Teddy's father shoots Nag.
5. **Prediction:** this will help her get Nagaina's eggs; **What happens:** Nagaina leaves her eggs unprotected and chases Darzee's wife.
6. **Prediction:** there will be a fight and one of them will die; **What happens:** Rikki-tikki emerges from the hole unharmed and announces that Nagaina is dead.

Literary Analysis SkillBuilder, page 132
(Responses will vary. Possible responses are provided.)
- Darzee is a tailor bird. He has little common sense, and is fearful and cowardly. He says he is miserable, cries about the babies, and annoys Rikki with his singing.
- Darzee's wife is a tailor bird. She is smart and sensible. She plays a clever trick on Nagaina, pretending to be sorrowful.
- Chuchundra is a muskrat. He is a coward. He creeps around the wall, whimpers, and can't make up his mind.
- Nag is a cobra. He is heartless, vicious, and dangerous. He plans to kill the humans and probably would have done so had not Rikki prevented him.
- Nagaina is a cobra. Like her husband, she is a dangerous killer. She is also ruthless and vengeful. She blames Teddy's father for killing Nag and plans to take revenge on Teddy.

Words to Know SkillBuilder, page 133
A. 1. cower
   2. scuttle
B. 1. cower   4. scuttle
   2. revive   5. cunningly
   3. consolation
(Animal) weasel

A Retrieved Reformation, page 134
Connect to Your Life, page 134
Responses will vary. Possible Response: (Character) Adam Zebrin; (from) "Zebra"; (Cause of Change) Meeting an art teacher who has a disability; (change) Zebra feels less sorry for himself and more able to express himself and care about others. Realistic.
Key to the Story, page 134
Words related to reformation: reform, reformatory, reform school, form, formation, reform movement, reformed
Pause & Reflect, page 137
1. safe-cracking; breaking into safes
2. confident, well-connected
Reread, page 139
Jimmy is extremely skilled at his profession.
Pause & Reflect, page 140
1. He is the detective who caught Jimmy. He works only on important cases.
2. to rob the Elmore bank
3. He is a skillful worker.

Pause & Reflect, page 142
1. He has fallen in love.
2. buy new tools; rob a bank
Read Aloud, page 144
Jimmy's safe-cracking tools are in the suitcase.
Pause & Reflect, page 145
1. Possible response: He thinks Jimmy's marriage is part of a plan to rob the bank.
2. Responses will vary. Possible response: Jimmy will not want to reveal his past to Annabel and her family, but if he is truly reformed, he will use his safe-cracking skills to save Agatha.
Pause & Reflect, page 146
1. Possible response: He believes that revealing that he has been a safe-cracker will end his chances of marrying Annabel, so he wants the rose to remember her by when he leaves.
2. surrender to Ben Price
3. Responses will vary. Most students, will think that it is noble and redemptive for Jimmy to have sacrificed his own happiness to save Agatha.
Challenge, page 146
Students' suggestions should deal with how Jimmy explains himself and his past to Annabel and her family, and how they react.
Active Reading SkillBuilder, page 147
(Responses will vary. Possible responses are provided.)
Jimmy Valentine: Students will probably strongly admire him because he willingly sacrifices his future to save a child.
Ben Price: Students will probably strongly admire Ben Price because he responds to Jimmy's heroism by freeing him.
Annabel Adams: Some readers may like Annabel because she is sweet and loyal; others may dislike her dependence.
Agatha Adams: Most student responses will be neutral because her character is one-dimensional.
Mr. Adams: Most student responses will be neutral because his character is one-dimensional.
Literary Analysis SkillBuilder, page 148
(Responses will vary. Possible responses are provided.)
- Jimmy begins cracking safes again, and Ben Price investigates the crimes. Rising Action
- Jimmy arrives in Elmore, falls in love with Annabel, and reforms. Rising Action
- Ben Price tracks Jimmy to Elmore, and Agatha is trapped inside the vault. Rising Action
- Jimmy opens the vault and rescues Agatha. Climax
- Ben Price allows Jimmy to go free. Falling Action

Words to Know SkillBuilder, page 149
1. C   6. C
2. B   7. C
3. A   8. A
4. C   9. C
5. D   10. D

Answer Key (continued)

The Pasture, page 150
A Time to Talk, page 150
Connect to Your Life, page 150
Possible responses: get to know others better, working together is more fun, learn new things, get to share your feelings with others, accomplish more.
Pause & Reflect, page 152
1. clean the pasture spring; bring the calf home
2. Responses will vary. The speaker says that the chores won't take long; at the same time, he seems to want to make them last longer and share them because they are pleasant to him.
Pause & Reflect, page 153
1. talking to friends
2. Responses will vary. Some students will say yes, because the speaker seems inviting and friendly. Others will say no, because they wouldn't waste time talking to somebody who doesn't seem to have anything particular in mind to say.

Active Reading SkillBuilder, page 154
(Responses will vary. Possible responses are provided.)
"A Time to Talk"

When a friend calls to me from the road☉
And slows his horse to a meaning walk,☉
I don't stand still and look around⟵
On all the hills I haven't hoed,☉
And shout from where I am, "What is it?"☉
No, not as there is a time to talk.☉
I thrust my hoe in the mellow ground,☉
Blade-end up and five feet tall,☉
And plod:☉ I go up to the stone wall
For a friendly visit.

Literary Analysis SkillBuilder, page 155
(Responses will vary. Possible responses are provided.)
"The Pasture"
calf   d
young   e
tongue   e
too   c

"A Time to Talk"
road   a
walk   b
around   c
hoed   a
is it   d
talk   b
ground   c
tall   e
wall   e
visit   d

The Noble Experiment, page 157
Connect to Your Life, page 157
(Responses will vary. Be sure each row has one check mark.)
Pause & Reflect, page 159
1. He was unhappy about the racial discrimination he had suffered.
2. allow black and white fans to sit together
Pause & Reflect, page 160
1. R, B, R, B
2. determined, strong
Pause & Reflect, page 162
1. Possible response: He pretended that he was recruiting for a new Negro League.
2. Wendell Smith brought Robinson to a Red Sox tryout—2; Councilman Muchneck told the Red Sox to hire black players—1; Red Sox officials praised Robinson but didn't call—3; Smith told Rickey that Robinson was major-league material—4.
Pause & Reflect, page 164
1. Here we go again (line 172); another time-wasting experience (lines 172–173).
2. Responses will vary. Some students will say yes, Sukeforth may have expected Robinson to jump at what appeared to be a great opportunity; others will say no, Sukeforth was experienced enough to know that Robinson was likely to be skeptical of the offer.
Mark It Up, page 165
Possible responses: My heart began racing; I was thrilled, scared, and excited; I was incredulous; I was speechless.
Pause & Reflect, page 166
1. Rickey was honest, direct, and a little harsh.
2. challenging, brave
Mark It Up, page 167
Rickey was sincere; he had a passion for justice; he had a deep, quiet strength.
Pause & Reflect, page 168
1. gentleman
2. passion for justice
Pause & Reflect, page 170
1. Responses will vary. Some students might think that Robinson's greatest challenge would be keeping his temper in the face of insults and dirty tricks; others might think it would be playing well under such pressure.
2. Responses will vary. Some students will admire Robinson's determination; others will admire his ability to perform under intense pressure; others will think his ability to look back on the events of his own life with such objectivity is admirable.
Challenge, page 170
Students' answers will vary but should be supported by examples from the autobiography.

Active Reading SkillBuilder, page 171

(Responses will vary. Possible responses are provided.)

1. Coach Branch Rickey shared a room with an African-American player who was denied accommodations at a hotel. The man sobbed, and Rickey never forgot it.
2. After Rickey became boss of the Brooklyn Dodgers, he decided to hire an African-American player on the team. He knew that he had to do it in secret.
3. Robinson and two other players tried out with the Red Sox, but Robinson did not believe that the officials were sincere.
4. Dodger Scout Clyde Sukeforth approached Robinson and asked if the player would meet with Branch Rickey, who was considering hiring him for the Brown Dodgers.
5. Rickey explained that he wanted to hire Robinson for the regular team, but that he wanted a man of strong character. Could Robinson withstand all the abuse? After considering the offer, the player agreed to sign. It was still a secret.

Literary Analysis SkillBuilder, page 172

(Responses will vary. Possible responses are provided.)

2. Rickey had to hide his intentions to scout the best African-American baseball player without arousing racist opposition to his plan.
3. Rickey wanted to know if one of the three was the athlete he was looking for.
4. Rickey wanted to talk to Robinson to see if he had the personal qualities he would need.
5. Rickey wanted to know everything he could find out about the athlete on whom the success of the experiment would depend.
6. Rickey didn't want Robinson to have any illusions about the degree of opposition he would face.
7. Rickey wanted to test Robinson's reactions and self-control.
8. Rickey wanted Robinson to be the first African-American player to integrate the National League.

Words to Know SkillBuilder, page 173

1. B
2. D
3. A
4. C
5. C
6. A
7. D
8. C
9. A
10. A

Casey at the Bat, page 174

Connect to Your Life, page 174

Possible response: (athlete) Hakeem Olajawon (admire) his ability to have fun and be cheerful in the heat of competition (under pressure) He will usually smile and remain calm.

Key to the Poem, page 174

Students might mention things such as fear of failure, fear of letting down teammates, exhilaration, pleasure at being the center of attention, confidence, and eagerness to beat the opposing team.

Pause & Reflect, page 177

1. They score hits that get them on base.
2. Possible response: The crowd feels that Casey is its only hope. The crowd had all but given up. They were certain that Flynn or Blake would strike out. When both of these players scored hits that put them on base, the crowd goes wild as Casey steps up to bat, certain that he will score a hit.

Pause & Reflect, page 179

1. tears in his eyes
2. Responses will vary. Most students will feel that Casey is more arrogant and less responsible than the athlete they chose.

Mark It Up, page 180

Students' drawings will vary, but all should include a scene from the poem.

Pause & Reflect, page 181

1. Possible response: At the end of the game, the crowd feels discouraged, disillusioned, and extremely disappointed. What they never thought possible has happened—mighty Casey has struck out!
2. Responses will vary. Some students will feel yes, Casey did his best. Sometimes athletes lose even when they do their best. But most will probably feel that, no, Casey did not do his best. He let two good pitches go past him out of "haughty grandeur" and when he finally swung, he showed more anger than skill.

Challenge, page 181

Students are likely to find that the exaggerations heighten the comic effect of the poem. Students may also say that they aren't able to take Casey's playing seriously, realizing the exaggerations. They may mark: "it's likely they'd have killed him had Casey not raised his hand" (line 36); "one scornful look from Casey and the audience was awed" (line 42).

Active Reading SkillBuilder, page 182

(Responses will vary. Possible responses are provided.)

stanza 5; question: Will Casey get the hit?

stanza 11; question: Will Casey strike out?

stanza 13: How will the crowd treat Casey, now that he has struck out?

Literary Analysis SkillBuilder, page 183

With a smile of honest charity great Casey's visage shone;

He stilled the rising tumult, he made the game go on;

He signaled to the pitcher, and once more the spheroid flew;

But Casey still ignored it, and the umpire said, "Strike two."

"Fraud!" cried the maddened thousands, and the echo answered "Fraud!"

But one scornful look from Casey and the audience was awed;

They saw his face grow stern and cold, they saw his muscles strain,

And they knew that Casey wouldn't let the ball go by

again.

The sneer is gone from Casey's lips, his teeth are

clenched in hate,

He pounds with cruel vengeance his bat upon the plate;

And now the pitcher holds the ball, and now he lets it go,

And now the air is shattered by the force of Casey's blow.

Oh, somewhere in this favored land the sun is shining

bright,

The band is playing somewhere, and somewhere hearts

are light;

And somewhere men are laughing, and somewhere

children shout,

But there is no joy in Mudville: Mighty Casey has struck

out.

Follow Up: Students' readings should reflect their markings.

Amigo Brothers, page 184

Connect to Your Life, page 184

Possible response: I would feel scared, because I know I might lose the friendship and the competition would be even harder than normal.

Key to the Story, page 184

Possible response: I would agree with him because the fact that we are friends is not part of the competition.

Pause & Reflect, page 187

1. They just want to have fun.
2. Possible responses: You should not let the fight get in the way of your friendship; find other things to talk about besides the fight; remember how long you've been friends; go to the movies or do something else together as soon as the fight is over.

Read Aloud, page 189

Possible response: The two boys are close enough to be family. They care enough about each other that they want their friendship to continue just as it was before the fight. They are not embarrassed to show affection.

Pause & Reflect, page 190

1. to fight as if they had never met before
2. Possible responses: Yes, because they are both determined to win the championship. No, because the fight might end their friendship.

Pause & Reflect, page 192

1. He'll win in the first round.
2. Responses will vary. Possible response: Watching *The Champion* helps Felix to "psyche himself up" for the fight.

Watching the movie gives Felix an image of a champion who fights with all of his strength to win the match. It also gives him an image of Tony as "the challenger," the opponent he has to beat to be the champion.

Pause & Reflect, page 194

1. a private talk between Felix and Antonio right before the fight
2. Responses will vary. Students might answer that they would feel proud and excited that two neighborhood boys were competing for such a famous championship. The match has brought lots of famous fighters into the neighborhood, and everyone has been involved in the preparation. Some who have known Felix and Antonio might be concerned that the fight might threaten their friendship.

Pause & Reflect, page 195

1. Responses will vary. Possible responses: Antonio: Felix has been training really hard, so I'll have to do my best to beat him. Felix: There's no way Antonio is going to be easy on me.
2. Antonio is not thinking about their friendship.

Pause & Reflect, page 198

1. Possible responses: "Antonio knew the dynamite that was stored in his amigo brother's fist" (lines 325–326); "Antonio slipped away from Felix, crashing two lefts to his head" (lines 329–330); "Felix bobbed and weaved, bobbed and weaved, occasionally punching his two gloves together" (lines 359–360); "Felix had [him] entangled into a rip-roaring, punching toe-to-toe slugfest" (lines 379–380); "Rights to the body. Lefts to the head. Neither fighter was giving an inch" (lines 382–383).
2. Possible responses: Yes, because they are really fighting hard and it seems like somebody is going to get hurt. No, because they both know that to win you have to fight really hard and they respect that in each other.

Pause & Reflect, page 200

1. Possible response: Because the match is over and it is time to be friends again. Felix and Antonio are serious fighters, but they are also close friends. They leave before the winner is announced because they want to be friends, not opponents.
2. Responses will vary. Students may have been drawn to one character over another and so would choose either boy as winner. The author portrays both as possible winners. Given how they leave the ring together, it could be said that the friendship between Felix and Antonio is the real winner.

Challenge, page 200

Most students will answer that the boys handled the tension very well. Students may be impressed by the boys' decision not to be around each other in the final days before the fight, days when tension would be at its highest. In a way, their decision is to be "two heavy strangers that want the same thing" (lines 103–104). Some students may be skeptical about Felix's prediction that, when the fight is over, they can "get it together again like nothing ever happened" (lines 125–126). Students might be reminded that the boys embrace as amigo brothers after they make this promise and they return to that embrace when they leave the ring.

Mark It Up, page 200
Details should include the two boys as the author described them. Antonio as lean and lanky with straight hair; Felix as short and husky with curly hair, leaving the ring, arm in arm. Students could also draw the crowd and announcer in the background.

Active Reading SkillBuilder, page 201
(Responses will vary. Possible responses are provided.)
Students may update their predictions in response to story details.
Prediction 1: They will fight hard.
Detail 2: Both lie awake thinking about how not to hurt the other.
Prediction 2: They will not fight hard.
Detail 3: They agree to separate and meet as strangers.
Prediction 3: They will fight hard.
Question: Will they remain friends after the fight?
Detail 1: They had each already won several medals.
Prediction 1: They will remain friends.
Detail 2: They decide to spend time apart before the fight.
Prediction 2: They will no longer be friends.

Literary Analysis SkillBuilder, page 202
(Responses will vary. Possible responses are provided.)
What I'm Curious About:
Who will win?
Will they still be friends?
Will anyone be badly hurt?
What Adds to the Suspense?
The boys both dream of being champion.
The boys each experience internal conflicts.
The fight is moved to a larger space.
There is no first round knockout.
They are evenly matched.
The details of the fight: no one is emerging as the winner.
Follow Up: We are left in suspense as to the winner. Maybe the author is trying to say that who wins is less important than the relationship between Antonio and Felix.

Words to Know SkillBuilder, page 203
A. 1. improvise   6. pensively
   2. barrage   7. game
   3. evading   8. bedlam
   4. dispel   9. feint
   5. perpetual   10. unbridled
B. Accept responses that accurately use **five** Words to Know.

The Monsters Are Due on Maple Street, page 204
Connect to Your Life, page 204
How I React to Danger: Responses will vary. Students may say that they would hide, lock the door, call the police, or shout for help.
How Groups React: Responses will vary. Students may say that groups prepare defenses, protect each other, and help each other.
Key to the Drama, page 204
Possible responses: prejudice: racism, hate, fear, ignorance; suspicion: fear, doubt, threat, deceit

Mark It Up, page 207
"Various people leave their porches or stop what they are doing to stare at the sky" (lines 36–38).
Pause & Reflect, page 208
  1. Responses will vary. Some students will find Maple Street appealing because it is so peaceful; others will find it boring and stifling.
  2. Responses will vary. Some students may predict that monsters from outer space will invade Maple Street.
Reread, page 209
Responses will vary. Possible response: The monsters have interrupted the power in some way.
Pause & Reflect, page 210
  1. A fire rages out of control.
  2. Possible response: The residents of Maple Street are anxious and frightened by the mysterious events.
Pause & Reflect, page 214
  1. Possible response: They are afraid and unable to explain the strange occurrences; therefore, they will accept any explanation, no matter how fanciful.
  2. Responses will vary. Most students will find Tommy's explanation illogical, alarmist, and paranoid.
Pause & Reflect, page 218
  1. He works on his own car.
  2. Responses will vary. Students who think the neighbors have good reason to be suspicious may cite their own fear of people who in some way are different from themselves; students who think the neighbors do not have reason for being suspicious may mention that all "reasons" given are circumstantial and superficial.
Read Aloud, page 222
Students will respond yes or no according to their personal experience and perspective.
Reread, page 223
Charlie shoots and kills Pete Van Horn.
Pause & Reflect, page 224
  1. Possible response. The people on Maple Street assume that they understand each other's motives, but in fact don't seem to know one another very well. They don't show any loyalty to one another; instead, they suspect whomever the mob leaders accuse. Students should circle evidence that supports their response.
  2. Responses will vary. Some students may think that the police will be called and Charlie will be arrested; others may think that the neighbors will come to their senses; still others may think that more guns will be found and there will be more killing.
Reread, page 225
Les Goodman has become the accuser, and Charlie has become the accused.
Pause & Reflect, page 227
  1. 2, 4, 1, 3
  2. The people have gone from friendly neighbors to frightened participants in a mob, ready to turn on each other.
  3. Responses will vary. To entertain and to express an opinion are the most likely responses.

Pause & Reflect, page 228
1. "They pick the most dangerous enemy they can find . . . and it's themselves" (lines 638–640).
2. Possible response: The attitudes, prejudices, and thoughts of humans can be used as weapons.

Challenge, page 228
The narrator introduces the setting and situation of the drama, comments on it, and then, at the end, states the theme. Students may mark lines 29–31 and 651–660.

Active Reading SkillBuilder, page 229
(Responses will vary. Possible responses are provided.)
Details: Object roars across sky; things stop working.
Purpose: to entertain.
Details: Tommy insists that aliens have landed.
Purpose: to entertain.
Details: Aliens discuss the behavior of the Maple Street neighbors.
Purpose: to express; to entertain.
Details: Narrator discusses prejudices.
Purpose: to express; to persuade.

Literary Analysis SkillBuilder, page 230
(Responses will vary. Possible responses are provided.)
Camera Directions: Moves over to a shot of two small boys buying ice cream.
Visual Impression: Everyday scene is interrupted by startling noise and light. The viewer sees the shock and surprise on the boys' faces.
Camera Directions: Camera takes us across the porches again.
Visual Impression: The camera shows different people trying to turn on lights, operate machinery, use telephones. The viewer discovers, along with the characters, that something is wrong.
Follow Up: Students' discussions should reveal an understanding of the details of the drama. The play opens with a shot of the night sky, and the return to the shot of the night sky at the end of the play indicates that the action has come full circle. At the end, however, viewers understand the significance of the perspective.

Words to Know SkillBuilder, page 231
A.
1. True	6. False
2. False	7. True
3. True	8. True
4. True	9. True
5. False	10. False

B. Accept responses that accurately use at least **four** Words to Know.

Dark They Were, and Golden-Eyed, page 232
Connect to Your Life, page 232
Responses will vary. Be sure that students complete each sentence.

Key to the Story, page 232
Responses will vary. Students might suggest words such as *discover, conquer, settle, exploit, explore, assimilate, hardship, trade,* and *barter.*

Pause & Reflect, page 235
1. threatened, frightened, worried
2. Some students may say that they would stay on Mars because the trip is so long; others would go back to Earth because the Martian landscape is frightening.

Pause & Reflect, page 236
1. Possible responses: The Bitterings are afraid of the unknown, of being alone, of Martians, of ghosts, of losing themselves and becoming other people.
2. to escape a war
3. Possible responses: agree, because the Earth people are isolated and Mars seems frightening; disagree, because nothing and nobody is actually threatening them.

Pause & Reflect, page 237
1. It cuts off communication with Earth and the possibility of return.
2. Though Bittering is *frightened,* he tries to be *brave* in front of his family.

Reread, page 239
They named Martian places after rich Earth people.

Pause & Reflect, page 240
1. lines 151–153: "In spite of this, the Earthmen had felt a silent guilt at putting new names to these ancient hills and valleys."
2. He is afraid they have changed.

Pause & Reflect, page 241
1. They are changing in color, shape, smell, and in other ways.
2. Eating the vegetables will cause the Bitterings to change—H; the vegetables may be poisonous—H; the vegetables look much as they always have—C; the house looks different—H; the house has not changed—C.

Read Aloud, page 242
Harry is amazed that Sam's eyes have changed from gray to yellow.

Pause & Reflect, page 243
1. Bittering: We must make every effort to return to Earth; Others: We would rather stay on Mars where life is peaceful and pleasant.
2. He is shocked that his eyes are changing color.
3. Possible responses: yes, because he is determined; no, because it is a difficult task, nobody will help him, and he is changing too.

Read Aloud, 244
Harry is becoming a Martian.

Pause & Reflect, page 245
1. She is dark and golden-eyed.
2. She does not want to return to Earth, and she wants Harry to stop worrying about that and start enjoying life on Mars.

Read Aloud, page 246
The children are becoming Martians.

Reread, page 247
because he is the only one who wants to return to Earth

Pause & Reflect, page 248
1. He is changing into a Martian.
2. Responses will vary. Some students will say yes, because Harry's desire to return to Earth has been very strong throughout the story; others will say no, because Harry is slowly but surely becoming a Martian.

Mark It Up, page 250

They no longer want the things they brought with them from Earth.

Pause & Reflect, page 251

1. He is beginning to like living on Mars, and the villa is pleasant.
2. Leaving the cottage means saying goodbye to all his material connections with Earth. Some students may say that it means the end of his life as a human.

Pause & Reflect, page 252

1. Possible response. The Martian summers are scorching hot and windy. Everything is eerily quiet.
2. He has forgotten that he is from Earth; he is getting younger looking.

Pause & Reflect, page 254

1. Harry and his family have become Martians.
2. Possible response: They will eventually become Martians, just as the Bitterings have.

Challenge, page 254

Students will notice that the Martian wind is almost always strong and challenging. It often makes the characters feel alone or alienated. Later in the story it is more inviting—"the soft wind in the air" (line 644)—but still seems somewhat eerie.

Active Reading SkillBuilder, page 255

(Responses will vary. Possible responses are provided.)

Setting

"The wind blew as if to flake away their identities."

"They saw the old cities, lost in their meadows, lying like children's delicate bones among the blowing lakes of grass."

"warm hearth, potted blood-geraniums"

"A river of wind submerged the house."

"the cinnamon dusts and wine airs, to be baked like gingerbread shapes in Martian summers"

"The boards, all warped out of shape."

"little white chess cities"

"Blue marble halls, large murals"

"Summer moved like flame upon the meadows."

"painted houses flaked and peeled"

"Rubber tires . . . hung suspended like stopped clock pendulums in the blazing air."

Characters

"children with their yellow hair hollered"

"I feel like a salt crystal . . . in a mountain stream, being washed away."

"Sweat poured from his face and his hands and his body; he was drenched in the hotness of his fear."

"He put out his sun-browned hand."

"little, very dim flecks of new gold captured in the blue of his eyes"

"felt his bones, shifted, shaped, melted like gold"

"Dark she was, and golden-eyed, burnt almost black by the sun . . . the children metallic in their beds"

Events

"Its lid gave a bulging pop."

"The web gone, the rockets lying in jigsaw heaps of molten girder and unsnaked wire"

"The days were full of metal sound."

"The town filled with a silent, heavy dust from their passage."

"rocket frame began to rust"

"they walked silently down a path of clear-running water"

"a rocket fell out of the sky"

"It lay steaming in the valley. Men leaped out of it shouting . . ."

Literary Analysis SkillBuilder, page 256

(Responses will vary. Possible responses may include some of the following events.)

- The Bitterings settle in the human colony. They wonder what happened to the Martians.
- Humans rename the landmarks.
- David notices movement in the mountains where the old Martian villas are.
- War on Earth destroys rockets.
- Harry notices changes in plants, an animal, and people.
- Harry begins to build his own rocket.
- His son Dan wishes to be called by a Martian name; his wife Cora's eyes have turned golden.
- Harry, his family, and the other humans abandon the settlement and move to the mountains.
- In the autumn, Harry and Cora reject the idea of moving back to the valley. They have become Martians.
- A new group of colonists arrives from Earth.
- They plan to establish colonies and rename landmarks.

Words to Know SkillBuilder, page 257

A.		B.	
1.	A	1.	flimsy
2.	C	2.	recede
3.	D	3.	dwindle
4.	B	4.	amiss
5.	E	5.	forlorn

C. Accept responses that accurately use at least **four** Words to Know.

The Highwayman, page 258

Connect to Your Life, page 258

Responses will vary. Accept any response that describes giving up something of value for a loved one.

Key to the Poem, page 258

Responses will vary. Possible responses: what he stole, what he did with the money.

Pause & Reflect, page 261

1. The repetition of the word suggests the beat of the horse's hooves as it gallops down a road.
2. A gold compass.

Pause & Reflect, page 265

1. They are in love.
2. He will return to see her.

Pause & Reflect, page 267

1. From Tim the ostler, who spied on the highwayman and Bess and heard the highwayman promise that he would return.
2. Bess escapes.
3. Possible responses: I felt the redcoats were *rude, obnoxious, creepy, threatening, mean to Bess.*

Read Aloud, page 269

Possible response: scared that the redcoats will harm the highwayman and upset and angry that she can't do anything to help him

Answer Key (continued)

Pause & Reflect, page 271
1. She sacrifices her life by causing the musket to fire and warn him.
2. Responses will vary. Some will say the highwayman will be warned by the musket shot and escape. Others may say that he will be worried about Bess and try to save her.

Pause & Reflect, page 273
1. shoot him down
2. Responses will vary. Possible responses: the highwayman riding across the moor, the eyes of Tim the ostler, Bess tied up and looking out at the road, the highwayman riding back "with the white road smoking behind him"

Challenge, page 273
Possible responses: The poem would be more sad. Without the last two stanzas, the last image of the poem would be that of the highwayman lying dead on the road. In the last two stanzas, the highwayman and Bess are reunited forever. The last two stanzas place the events of the poem squarely in the realm of romantic myth and legend.

Active Reading SkillBuilder, page 274
(Responses will vary. Possible responses are provided.)
lines 4–6 and in every following stanza/repetition
lines 7–12 admiring description of highwayman/tone
line 18 red knot and dark hair/imagery
line 30 though hell should bar the way/word choice
line 32 like a brand/simile
lines 46–47 hell at one dark window/word choice
line 57 hours crawled by like years/simile
line 67 Tlot-tlot/onomatopoeia
line 65+ tension growing/mood

Literary Analysis SkillBuilder, page 275
(Responses will vary. Possible responses are provided.)
Tim the ostler is hidden, waiting, face = "white and peaked," eyes = "hollows of madness," hair = "like moldy hay"
The highwayman tells the landlord's daughter he'll return by moonlight. repetition of "by moonlight," hair = "black cascade of perfume"
A redcoat troop arrives. "marching—Marching—marching"
They set a trap for the highwayman, using the landlord's daughter. gagged and bound, "death at every window"
She works until she can touch the gun. her struggle: she twisted, writhed, stretched and strained
The highwayman returns. "riding—riding—riding"
The landlord's daughter kills herself and warns highwayman. "shattered her breast"
He runs, but returns when he learns she is dead. "face grew grey," red spurs and coat (make you think of blood)
The redcoats kill him.
It is said he still comes, and she is there. repetition of opening of poem

from Exploring the *Titanic*, page 276
Connect to Your Life, page 276
Possible responses: the San Francisco earthquake; the explosion of the *Hindenburg*; the flood of the Mississippi River, the summer of fire in 1988. Details will vary.

Key to the Informative Article, page 276
Responses will vary. Accept charts with reasonable responses.

Pause & Reflect, page 279
1. help immigrants
2. Lines 8–12: "In his [Morgan Robertson's] story, the *Titan*, a passenger ship . . . , sails from England headed for New York." With many rich and famous passengers on board, the *Titan* hits an iceberg in the North Atlantic and sinks.

Pause & Reflect, page 280
1. Responses will vary. Students might mention the rudder as big as an elm tree; propellers as big as a windmill; 882 feet long, almost the length of four city blocks; high as an eleven-story building; four funnels, each big enough to drive two trains through; three anchors weighing 31 tons.
2. Possible responses: senior captain; natural leader; popular with crew members and passengers; 35 years' experience; excellent safety record; final tribute

Pause & Reflect, page 282
1. Responses will vary. Students might mention the Verandah, Palm Court, squash court, swimming pool, Turkish bath, gymnasium, or Grand Staircase.
2. Possible responses: These are people that readers may know something about; knowing more about the passengers makes the events seem more vivid.
3. Responses will vary. Some students may say that the author includes names of rich and influential people to show the popularity of the *Titanic*. Others may say that the names give the story of the *Titanic* more authenticity.

Mark It Up, page 283
Students may circle the following: "the bottom layer consisted of the lowly manual workers; the next layer was the third class passengers; after that came the second class"; "then finally there was the icing on the cake in first class"

Pause & Reflect, page 284
1. immigrants —3; teachers, professionals, merchants —2; manual workers —4; wealthy aristocrats —1
2. Lines 186–187: Did it mean the *Titanic* might be too big a ship to handle safely?

Reread, page 286
Icebergs are difficult to spot on clear, calm, moonless nights when there is no wind to kick up surf around them.

Pause & Reflect, page 287
1. seven times
2. had radio problems

Reread, page 289
The ship could stay afloat even if the first four compartments were flooded, but water was pouring into the first five compartments and would inevitably flood the others.

Pause & Reflect, page 290
1. calmed Ruth's mother
2. so the reader continues to identify with all the passengers aboard; to show the different ways each group reacts to the disaster

Pause & Reflect, page 293
1. The passengers panicked.
2. A second lifeboat nearly falls on the lifeboat Ruth is in.

Reread, page 295

Responses will vary. Students may mention that they would feel sorrow for their friends and relatives who perished or might be struggling in the icy water; they might also say they would feel relieved to have survived; they might mention wondering about whether they would be rescued or not; they might feel anxiety about how long they might have to stay in the lifeboat and if their ordeal was over yet.

Pause & Reflect, page 296

1. Possible response: The captain recognized that there was nothing more the crew could do to help the passengers.
2. Responses will vary. Some students will be impressed by the civility of the passengers and crew; others will focus on the lack of preparation of the shipping company and crew.

Challenge, page 295

Possible responses: Why didn't the captain take the iceberg warnings more seriously? Why wasn't the *Titanic* equipped with enough lifeboats? How did survivors cope with their loss? How was the news of the sinking of the "unsinkable" *Titanic* met by the public? by the shipbuilding industry? Where exactly did the *Titanic* go down? When did the rescue operations end? What measures were taken to ensure that such a disaster did not occur again?

Mark It Up, page 296

Responses will vary. Accept charts with the third category (What I Learned) filled in. Possible responses: Many iceberg warnings were issued before the crash. The band played to the very end. Survivors heard continuous cries of drowning people.

Active Reading SkillBuilder, page 297

(Responses will vary. Possible responses are provided.)

Fact

- On May 21, 1911, the hull of the Titanic was launched.
- The ship was 882 feet long.
- Captain Edward J. Smith was given command.
- First-class rooms had carpets, wooden wall panels, and marble sinks.
- The whistles were the biggest that had ever been made.
- The captain ordered the lookouts to keep a sharp watch for ice.
- The ship had received seven warnings of icebergs the day it sank.
- Just after midnight the captain ordered the lifeboats uncovered.
- The radio men waited until they heard water gurgling before they abandoned their post.

Opinion

- Everything about the ship was on a nightmare scale.
- The richness and size were astounding.
- The captain was a natural leader and popular.
- The dining room was beautiful.
- The last night was the kind of night that made one feel glad to be alive.
- There was more confusion in the third-class decks.

Literary Analysis SkillBuilder, page 298

(Responses will vary. Possible responses are provided.)

New

- The ship had mechanically operated watertight compartments.
- Passengers liked to send wireless messages to their friends.
- The scale of the ship was huge.
- Passengers enjoyed the latest exercise equipment.
- People had use of the SOS distress signal.

Old

- Manual laborers stayed in the lowest level of the ship.
- First-class passengers had their own promenade deck.
- Workers had to work long shifts.
- There were barriers between first and third class.
- Women and children got saved first.

Words to Know SkillBuilder, page 299

A.
1. feverishly
2. dazzled
3. indefinitely
4. eerie
5. novelty

Quality of the *Titanic:* safety.

B.
1. B
2. D
3. E
4. A
5. C

from **Long Walk to Freedom,** page 300

Connect to Your Life, page 300

Responses will vary. Possible related words: responsibility, growth, opportunity, uncertainty, equality, fairness, competition, rights, stress

Pause & Reflect, page 303

1. Possible response: Although apartheid was established to subordinate black Africans to whites, it actually produced men who became strong through their resistance to apartheid.
2. conquers the fear he or she feels
3. the opposite of hate; people can learn it; a sign of humanity

Pause & Reflect, page 305

1. his family
2. Mandela put his duty to his *people* above his duty to his *family*.
3. Possible response: None of my people is free unless all are free.

Pause & Reflect, page 306

1. Possible responses: They were also imprisoned by their prejudices and narrow-mindedness; they are not truly free if they are taking away someone else's freedom.
2. Responses will vary.

Challenge, page 306

Possible response: "learn to hate" in lines 36 and 37; "my commitment" in lines 54 and 57; "obligations" in lines 58–60 (also "to his"); "Free" repeated four times in lines 84–85; "freedom of my people" in lines 109 and 110; "the chains on" repeated four times in lines 120–122; This memoir has some of the characteristics of a speech, one of which is repetition, which is useful for forcefully driving home a point and provoking an emotional response.

Active Reading SkillBuilder, page 307

(Responses will vary. Possible responses are provided.)

Main Idea

Mandela believes that if people can be taught to hate, they can also be taught to love.

Supporting Details

He knows that deep in every human heart is mercy and generosity.

No one is born hating others.

Love comes more naturally than hate.

He could always see humanity in the prison guards.

Literary Analysis SkillBuilder, page 308

(Responses will vary. Possible responses are provided.)

Experiences in Mandela's Life

As a child, Mandela likes to swim and roast mealies under the stars.

He lives as a young man in Johannesburg.

Mandela joins the African National Congress.

Mandela experiences hardships in prison.

He walks out of prison.

What He Learned from Them

Looking back, he realizes that he was truly born free.

He sees that his people are not free to live full lives.

He sees that people pay a high price to fight for what they believe in.

He is not willing to enjoy advantages others can't share.

He learns that even in the guards he can still see a "glimmer of humanity."

He sees that neither oppressor nor oppressed is free.

He learns that real freedom is not just being free oneself, but respecting and enhancing the freedom of others as well.

Follow Up: He started with a small picture of personal freedom and ended with a global view. He realized that all people, whatever their color, need to be free.

Words to Know SkillBuilder, page 309

A.
1. incomprehensible
2. indivisible
3. resiliency
4. transitory
5. curtail

B. Accept interviews that accurately use all **five** Words to Know.

from Anthony Burns, page 310

Connect to Your Life, page 310

Responses will vary. Be sure students list three individual examples.

Key to the Biography, page 310

Possible responses: What had his life as a slave been like? How did he escape? Did he escape alone? What risks did he face by escaping? Where did he go when he got out of the South? Did he travel on the Underground Railway? How was he treated in the North?

Pause & Reflect, page 314

1. He begins to plan his escape.
2. Possible responses: He is so scared that he can barely speak. He feels trapped like an animal. He feels sick to his stomach.

Pause & Reflect, page 316

1. his mother
2. Responses will vary. Possible responses: He feels weighted down by the chains around his wrists and the loneliness in his heart. He feels hot and cold with fear, knowing that Colonel Suttle wants to return him to slavery.

Pause & Reflect, page 316

1. They did not want local groups opposed to slavery to find out because these groups would try to prevent Burns from being taken back to the South. They feared the abolitionists might use legal means or force.
2. Fugitive Slave Act

Pause & Reflect, page 318

1. A, A, S, S, A
2. Possible response: Possible questions include: What will happen to Anthony Burns? How will Theodore Parker and Coffin Pitts try to save Anthony Burns?

Pause & Reflect, page 319

1. Responses will vary. I am angry because the Fugitive Slave Act permits escaped slaves from other states to be captured in Massachusetts and transported back into bondage.
2. Charles Mayo Ellis, Richard Henry Dana

Pause & Reflect, page 320

1. Anthony is frightened and in despair. Details: does not reply, looks through space, sadness and fear, appears to be in a trance, unmindful of his situation (lines 245–248)
2. They looked at him with suspicion.

Pause & Reflect, page 322

1. sometimes put aside his beliefs to keep his law clients
2. Responses will vary. Many students will find Dana's shipping to California as a common sailor as the most impressive detail about him. Others will find his defense of fugitive slaves most impressive.

Mark It Up, page 323

small scar on his cheek; hideously deformed; Dana assumed at once that Burns had been awfully mistreated by his owner

Pause & Reflect, page 324

1. Dana wants to defend Burns before the court.
2. afraid and confused

Pause & Reflect, page 326

1. Burns should be called up to the bench.
2. Responses will vary. Possible response: Burns is feeling loneliness, scared, and hungry.

Pause & Reflect, page 328

1. Possible response: First—Anthony Burns appears in court before Commissioner Loring; Second—Coffin Pitts alerts Reverend Theodore Parker, who in turn alerts the Boston Vigilance Committee; Third—Reverend Leonard Grimes talks to Anthony Burns and tries to give him hope; Last—Richard Henry Dana wants to represent Anthony before Commissioner Loring.
2. Predictions will vary. Most students will believe that Burns will finally allow Dana to defend him, and they may feel that Dana will win his freedom. Other students will believe that Burns is right, that he will be sent back to Virginia.

Read Aloud, page 329

Anthony is sure that he will be returned to his owner and that if he tries to defend himself in court his treatment will be harsher.

Pause & Reflect, page 330

1. Colonel Suttle
2. to identify Anthony Burns as the fugitive slave mentioned in the affidavit

Pause & Reflect, page 333

1. time to decide whether he wants a defense
2. If he "played dumb" he could avoid giving information to his opponents.

Pause & Reflect, page 335

1. as a victory for slavery
2. Parker wanted people to know because he wanted those who would support Burns's cause to be at the courthouse to prevent Burns from being taken back to the South. Students may circle the following: "man was stolen" (line 707); "Shall Boston steal another man?" (line 714); "no free citizen of Massachusetts is dragged into slavery" (lines 721–722).

Pause & Reflect, page 336

1. They changed their minds and set Anthony free.
2. Possible response: I felt sorry that Anthony Burns had to go through such an ordeal and hoped that he would win his freedom.

Challenge, page 336

Possible response: Because Burns's case became highly publicized and because his return to slavery seemed cruel and unjust, Burns became a symbol for abolitionism and the anti-slavery cause. Students may circle lines 701–714 to support this view.

Active Reading SkillBuilder, page 337

(Responses will vary. Possible responses are provided.)

Question: Will Anthony Burns allow one of the abolitionist lawyers to represent him and try to free him?

Evaluate: Ellis seems to offer good reasons for disqualifying Loring as judge in this case.

Connect: I can sense that Ellis is outraged and angry. I would feel the same way if I were in his place.

Visualize: I visualize Dana as slumped in his chair and dejected looking

Predict: The abolitionist lawyers will find some way of helping Burns.

Literary Analysis SkillBuilder, page 338

(Responses will vary. Possible responses are provided.)

Main Character: Anthony is aware of things going on around him, but he can't focus and he feels lightheaded. This helps me empathize with Anthony and connect with his situation.

Other Characters: Richard Dana persists in following Anthony's case until Anthony agrees to let him be his lawyer. This helps me to see how devoted Dana is to the cause and that Anthony might be gaining some hope.

Plot: The plot is basically told in the first two paragraphs. This helps me understand the context for the story and how the story fits in history. It prepares me for the events to come.

Conflict: The abolitionists versus the Fugitive Slave Law. The information about this group and this law helps me to understand the conflict in the U.S. during this time. It helps me to appreciate Anthony's story.

Dialogue: Anthony responds twice that it is no use, that Mars Charles knows him and that his fate might be worse if he resists. This dialogue, written in Anthony's dialect, helps me understand Anthony's fears and feelings of hopelessness.

Words to Know SkillBuilder, page 339

A.
1. contradict
2. throbbing
3. peer
4. petty
5. alleged

B.
1. E
2. C
3. J
4. H
5. D
6. A
7. I
8. F
9. G
10. B

End Unit Answer Key

Reading a Magazine Article, page 342
Mark It Up

1. Students should circle the photos of the baby lion and porcupine.
2. Students should underline "Now You're Speaking My Language." Students should circle "Say What?"
3. animal communications
4. The paragraph is separated from the rest of the text and is set in boldface type.
5. Students should underline *phonations*. Students should double underline *pheromones*.
6. Koko and Michael, two gorillas who use sign language to talk to their human trainers

Reading a Textbook, page 344
Mark It Up

1. scientific measurement; length
2. Students should underline the three sentences under "Lesson Objectives."
3. Students should circle the words under "New Terms."
4. meter
5. 1/1000
6. Students should circle the caption following "Figure 1–7." The numbers measure centimeters. The lines between each pair of numbers measure millimeters.

Reading Graphs and Charts, p. 346
Mark It Up

1. The line graph shows the average monthly temperatures for Juneau, Alaska.
2. Students should circle the point for the month of July.
3. Students should shade the month of July for the highest temperatures and the month of January for the lowest temperatures. The difference is 32°F.

Reading a Map, p. 347
Mark It Up

1. The purpose of the map is to show high temperatures and precipitation in various regions of the United States.
2. rain
3. See student map and make sure students underline Billings, Detroit, and Memphis.

4. Students should circle the northern tip of Maine, the area between Colorado and Nebraska, and the middle region of Oregon.

5. Students should mention that Kansas City is likely to have showers.

Reading a Diagram, p. 348
Mark It Up

1. A microscope is used to make tiny objects look larger. Students should draw a box around the text under the heading *COMPOUND MICROSCOPE* at letter A.

2. Students should circle and name the eyepiece, the low-power objective, and the high-power objective.

3. Students should draw an arrow pointing to the stage.

4. Students should put an asterisk next to the mirror and the diaphragm.

5. with the coarse adjustment, the fine adjustment, or the revolving nosepiece

6. The high-power objective gives a closer view.

Main Idea and Supporting Details, page 350
Mark It Up

1. Students should underline "In Columbus's time, doctors did not know how to treat many illnesses."

2. Students should circle the five sentences that follow the main idea sentence.

Problem and Solution, page 351
Mark It Up

1. Students should underline the sentence, "Why not open up the school gym and cafeteria for students after school?"

2. Students could circle any sentence in the second paragraph except for the proposed solution.

3. Possible answers: Yes, I think it's a good idea, because students like to play sports and would enjoy staying after school to do so; *or* No, I think it's a bad idea, because the last thing any kid wants to do at three o'clock is head back into the school.

Sequence, page 352
Mark It Up

1. Students should underline *the egg, the caterpillar, the pupa,* and *the adult.*

2. Students should circle *At first, about 10 days, When, In the second stage, As, during, Once, last, In the third stage, immediately, Then, After, Finally, As,* and *In a short time.*

3. (Answers will vary. Sample responses are provided.)

   1. **The egg** For about the first 10 days, the butterfly is a baby insect inside an egg.

   2. **The caterpillar** Next, the egg cracks open and a hungry caterpillar crawls out. The caterpillar sheds its skin several times.

   3. **Pupa** The pupa grows a hard shell called a chrysalis. Then it goes through the changes that will make it a butterfly.

   4. **Butterfly** Finally, the adult butterfly breaks from the chrysalis.

Cause and Effect, page 354
Mark It Up

1. Students should double underline the following: "they killed the biggest elephants"; "Not surprisingly, many of the largest elephants have vanished"; "Today, tusks are only about half the size they were a hundred years ago."

2. Students should circle *since, because, consequently,* and *led to.*

3. **Effect:** The African elephant was placed on the endangered species list.
   Cause: A law was passed in 1989 that put an end to international ivory trade.
   Effect: The number of African elephants began to increase.
   Cause: Some African countries objected to the law.
   Effect: The law was slightly loosened in 1997.

Comparison and Contrast, page 356
Mark It Up

1. Students should circle *both, both, the same, about the same, both, the same,* and *also.*

2. Students should underline *But, more, But, yet, but,* and *different.*

3. Possible answer: Mirror-image twins are identical twins who are mirror images of each other—for example, one is right-handed, and one is left-handed. Students should circle the third paragraph.

4. (Answers will vary. Sample responses are provided.)
   Annie: has more freckles, straighter toes
   Both: wear contact lenses; lost baby teeth at about same time; got only cavity in same tooth at same age; are best friends; fight over everything; agree that being a twin can be weird, fun, and cool
   Elizabeth: no asthma, fewer freckles, has a crooked toe

Argument, p. 358
Mark It Up

1. Students should circle the words *argue, warn, feel* (The word *feel* should be circled two times in addition to the first one done for students.)

2. Students should circle the phrase "Spirit Week encourages us to be better students."

3. If Spirit Week isn't canceled, teachers warn that the school will no longer be a good place to learn.

4. **Pros**
   Spirit Week is a way to show creativity.
   Spirit Week gives students a sense of pride.
   Spirit Week teaches students how to work in groups and how to plan and organize an event.
   Cons
   Students may forget to do their homework.
   A few students skip classes and some go to a different lunch period.
   Students spend extra time in the bathrooms.
   Some students goof around in class.

Social Studies, page 360
Mark It Up
1. Italy *or* northern Italy
2. Students should circle *Renaissance* and *republic.* They should underline *rebirth or revival, a renewed attention to ideas from classical Greek and Roman culture,* and *a government whose head of state is not a monarch.*
3. 1454; Students should put a star by the map title.
4. wool; Students should put a box around the caption.
5. Possible answer: Other European countries had strong central governments, but Italy had many small states instead.

Science, page 362
Mark It Up
1. the nervous system; Students should put a star next to the title.
2. Students should circle *Parts and Functions of the Nervous System* and *Neurons and Impulses.*
3. The central nervous system consists of the brain and spinal cord. The peripheral nervous system connects the brain and spinal cord with the rest of the body.
4. Students should underline the words *first, second,* and *third.*
5. Students should circle *Figure 17–1* at the top of the second paragraph.
6. Students should circle the spinal cord.

Mathematics, page 364
Mark It Up
1. table and graphs; the title
2. numbers or facts that describe something
3. Students should circle the first Student Help tip.
4. Students should underline *to be useful* or *so you can look for patterns and relationships.*
5. Students should underline "Make a table to organize the data" and "Then describe a pattern for the data."
6. Students should circle the text and chart under *Solution* in the middle of the page and the text under *Solution* at the bottom of the page.

Reading an Application, page 366
Mark It Up
1. section 1: camper information; section 2: session information; section 3: for office use only
2. Students should cross out section 3.
3. Students should put an asterisk next to *Emergency Contact, Health Information,* and "Can you swim?"
4. Students should underline *membership card* and *doctor's note.*
5. Answers will vary. Some students may circle *NA.*
6. C
7. Students should fill out the application completely and correctly, according to the instructions. They should leave the bottom section blank.

Reading a Public Notice, page 368
Mark It Up
1. upcoming activities at the Springfield Youth Center

2. Students should circle the sentence at the top of the page.
3. jazz band
4. Students should put a star next to the name and address of the youth center.
5. Students should put a box around the phone numbers and the Web address at the bottom of the page.
6. C

Reading a Web Page, page 370
Mark It Up
1. Students should put a star by http://www.lookquick.com/search/+asteroids+hit+Earth and by http://www.finditout.org/science/space/asteroid.html.
2. Students should circle the part of the site that reads "Could an asteroid hit Earth?"
3. Did an asteroid cause the dinosaurs to die out?
4. Bibliography
5. C

Reading Technical Directions, p. 372
Mark It Up
1. step 1: *press;* step 2: *select;* step 3: *press;* step 4: *use, select,* and *press;* step 5: *follow* and *select;* step 6: *press;* step 7: *press;* step 8: *repeat* and *use*
2. Students should box steps 4, 5, and 8.
3. The Enter button will return the screen to TV viewing.
4. Step 3
5. The On/Off timer will not work until the clock on the television has been set.
6. C

Product Information: Medicine Labels, page 374
Mark It Up
1. Students should circle "minor aches and pains associated with the common cold, headache, toothache, muscular aches, backache, for the minor pain of arthritis, for the pain of cramps, and for the reduction of fever."
2. 8
3. children under 12 years of age
4. consult a physician
5. Students should draw an arrow pointing to the warning that begins "Keep this and all medicines. . . ." A physician or poison control center should be contacted immediately.
6. A

Reading a Bus Schedule, page 375
Mark It Up
1. Grand Avenue; Students should circle the title "Bus Route 333: Grand Avenue."
2. weekday; Students should circle the label "Weekday Mornings—Eastbound."
3. Students should place an "X" by Memorial Hospital and Grand & Delaware.
4. 9:22 A.M.; Students should underline the appropriate time under Three Rivers Station.
5. D

Comprehension Mini-Lesson Answer Key

Main Idea and Details

Main Idea	Details
Paragraph 1: **If you have ever looked up at the sky and thought you saw something strange— perhaps something that looked like a flying saucer—you're not alone.**	• Every year hundreds of people report seeing strange objects, or objects known as UFOs (Unidentified Flying Objects). • However, most of these UFOs turn out to be something ordinary, such as meteors, military aircraft, or weather balloons. • In some cases, people even make up stories and create fake photos for publicity.
Paragraph 2: **Most scientists do not believe that the planet Earth has been visited by alien beings.**	• In fact, space exploration supports the belief that no other planet in our solar system has the technology that could send flying objects to Earth. • In addition, the distance between our planet and the nearest star would make it extremely difficult for alien beings to visit Earth.

Sequence

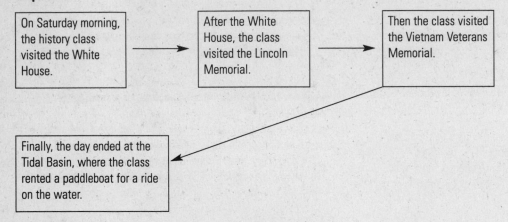

On Saturday morning, the history class visited the White House. → After the White House, the class visited the Lincoln Memorial. → Then the class visited the Vietnam Veterans Memorial.

Finally, the day ended at the Tidal Basin, where the class rented a paddleboat for a ride on the water.

Cause and Effect

Cause	→	Effect(s)
The narrator started volunteering at an animal shelter.	→	He or she has learned about animals. He or she walks dogs frequently. He or she is in better shape.
The narrator wants to work with animals in the future.	→	He or she interviewed a veterinarian for a school project.

Comparison and Contrast

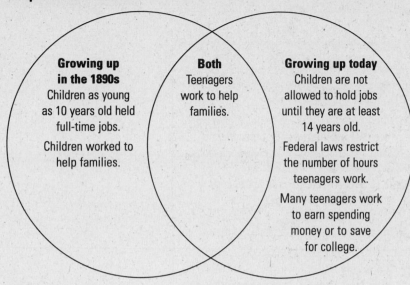

Growing up in the 1890s
Children as young as 10 years old held full-time jobs.

Children worked to help families.

Both
Teenagers work to help families.

Growing up today
Children are not allowed to hold jobs until they are at least 14 years old.

Federal laws restrict the number of hours teenagers work.

Many teenagers work to earn spending money or to save for college.

Making Inferences

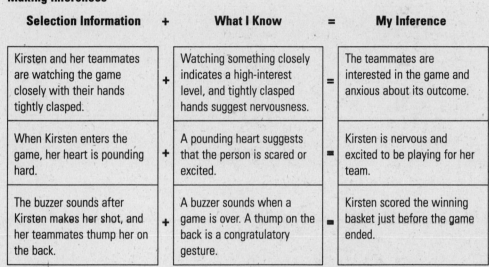

Selection Information	+	What I Know	=	My Inference
Kirsten and her teammates are watching the game closely with their hands tightly clasped.	+	Watching something closely indicates a high-interest level, and tightly clasped hands suggest nervousness.	=	The teammates are interested in the game and anxious about its outcome.
When Kirsten enters the game, her heart is pounding hard.	+	A pounding heart suggests that the person is scared or excited.	=	Kirsten is nervous and excited to be playing for her team.
The buzzer sounds after Kirsten makes her shot, and her teammates thump her on the back.	+	A buzzer sounds when a game is over. A thump on the back is a congratulatory gesture.	=	Kirsten scored the winning basket just before the game ended.

Predicting

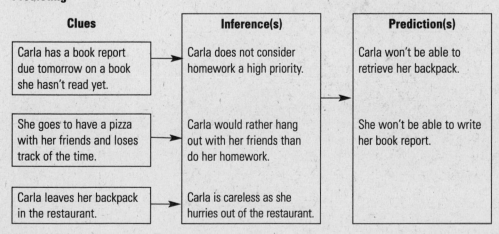

Clues	Inference(s)	Prediction(s)
Carla has a book report due tomorrow on a book she hasn't read yet.	Carla does not consider homework a high priority.	Carla won't be able to retrieve her backpack.
She goes to have a pizza with her friends and loses track of the time.	Carla would rather hang out with her friends than do her homework.	She won't be able to write her book report.
Carla leaves her backpack in the restaurant.	Carla is careless as she hurries out of the restaurant.	

Fact and Opinion

Fact	Opinion
• Wildlife conservation is important to the survival of animals and plants. • If we continue to build more homes, farms, and industries where wild animals nest and breed, many animals will die. • In addition, pollution such as pesticides and other chemicals also damages wildlife habitats.	• Farmers should protect wild rabbits and quails by reducing the use of harmful pesticides and fertilizers. • Other people should help by donating money to wildlife organizations that promote the protection and safety of animals and plants.

Narrative Elements

Setting in a garage one April	**Characters** Chloe, Alice, Dad (Some students may also mention Pepper the cat and the six hamsters.)

Plot

Problem: The hamsters Alice is using in her science project are missing, and her younger sister Chloe may know where they are.

Events:
1. Alice comes home to find the garage door open and the hamsters gone.
2. Chloe is pretending to do a science project, with Pepper the cat as her "assistant."
3. Alice questions Chloe and Dad about where the hamsters are.

Resolution: Dad tells Alice that he has moved the hamsters and that they are safe.